The Accidental Life

The Accidental Life

An Editor's Notes on Writing and Writers

Terry McDonell

 Alfred A. Knopf   New York   2016

www.aaknopf.com

Knopf, Borzoi Books, and the colophon are registered trademarks of Penguin Random House LLC.

Due to limitations of space, permissions to reprint previously published material can be found following Sources.

Library of Congress Cataloging-in-Publication Data
Names: McDonell, Terry, [date] author.
Title: The accidental life : an editor's notes on writing and writers / Terry McDonell.
Description: First edition. | New York : Alfred A. Knopf, 2016.
Identifiers: LCCN 2015046066 (print) | LCCN 2016008926 (ebook) |
ISBN 9781101946718 (hardcover : alk. paper) | ISBN 9781101946725 (ebook) |
ISBN 9780451494238 (open market)
Subjects: LCSH: McDonell, Terry, 1944– | McDonell, Terry, 1944– —Friends and associates. | Periodical editors—United States—Biography. | Journalism. | Authorship.
Classification: LCC PN4874.M48396 A3 2016 (print) | LCC PN4874.M48396 (ebook) |
DDC 070.5/1092—dc23
LC record available at http://lccn.loc.gov/2015046066

Jacket photograph by Joanie McDonell
Jacket design by Chip Kidd

Manufactured in the United States of America
First Edition

FOR STACEY
FOR NICK
FOR THOMAS
AND
FOR WILL

This is a book about writers and their work and working with them. Editing is what I wanted to write about. But it is also about friends, some of them now dead, so it is about that, too. What follows is not strictly chronological. It bounces around a little. So did I.

ROBERT TERRY MCDONELL: born U.S. Naval Air
Station, Norfolk, Virginia, August 1, 1944; freelance photographer, writer,
1969–72; reporter, Associated Press, 1972–73; reporter, *LA*, 1974–75;
associate editor, *San Francisco Magazine*, 1975–76; associate editor, *City*
magazine, 1976–77; senior editor, *Outside* magazine, 1977–78; managing
editor, *Outside* magazine, 1978–79; editor in chief, *Rocky Mountain
Magazine*, 1979–80; managing editor, *Rolling Stone*, 1981–83; assistant
managing editor, *Newsweek*, 1983–85; consulting editor, *Manhattan,
Inc.*, 1986–87; editor in chief, *Smart* magazine, 1987–89; editor in chief,
Esquire, 1990–93; editor in chief, publisher, *Sports Afield*, 1993–96;
editor, *Men's Journal*, 1996–99; editor in chief, *Us Weekly*, 1999–2002;
managing editor, *Sports Illustrated*, 2002–5; editor, Time Inc. Sports
Group, 2006–12; senior editorial adviser, Time Inc., 2012; freelance
writer, New York, 2012–.

Contents

I

II

III

IV

I

Go in fear of abstractions.

— EZRA POUND

My Editor

THERE IS NOTHING FINER than deciding to write.

And if, like me, you were a young writer in the 1970s, there was almost too much to write about. Norman Mailer actually complained about this. Vietnam had a lot to do with it because friends had been there, or had gone and weren't coming back. And there was The Movement, however you defined it, and the music and the drugs, and everyone drank and had sex with each other. No one wants to read any more about that, but there was a shocking inevitability to the way things were turning out.

Something else was always there too, just beneath the surface, no matter how uncomfortable or embarrassing it was to define. Writers talked about it, about writing and being writers. Ken Kesey said, "I'd rather be a lightning rod than a seismograph." That's the kind of writer we all wanted to be. What if writers *were* the story? What an idea.

Depending on how well you wrote and how often you changed jobs or assignments, other writers came in and out of your life. Some of them were already famous and others would be soon, but celebrity didn't matter because you knew something together—the private thrill that comes from writing a clear and unique sentence. The craft of it. James Salter liked to "rub words in his hand, to turn them around and feel them." Writing is exactly that, and there is no work like it because it is so complicated to know when you are done. Riffing about writing journalism, Renata Adler wrote, in her novel *Speedboat*, about giving "a piece of sugar to a raccoon, which in its odd fastidiousness would wash that sugar in a brook till there was nothing left."

Editors can help with that.

BEFORE I BECAME AN EDITOR, I had an intuition about what readers wanted: they wanted to read whatever I wanted to write. Sure they did. I just needed a little editing sometimes. Every editor I ever had, including the bad ones, was strict about a piece living or dying by its language—even if they couldn't write themselves, which of course they couldn't. That's why they were editors. Or so I thought until I met the editor who made me an editor.

His name was Bob Sherrill—*the Other* Bob Sherrill. He used *the Other* to distinguish himself from Robert Sherrill, the writer who had just published *The Saturday Night Special,* a book about handguns so smart that *the Other* Bob Sherrill said you just wanted to hold it up to your forehead. *The Other* Bob Sherrill was Robert Sherrill's editor for a while, and he was my editor, too.

At forty-one, he was known in the magazine world to be crazy and shrewd and kind all at once. He was said to be especially good with young writers, and was also known for outdressing them in his white high-top Chuck Taylors with the fluorescent red laces (untied), his baggy blue-and-white seersucker suits and his black T-shirts, a green-and-pink silk bandanna around his neck and a Black Watch beret over his shaggy strawberry blond hair. Plus his Ray-Bans, rain or shine. Bob was colorful.

He was also a bit surreal, a flipped-out literary ice-cream man, but handsome too, and women liked him, and I worked for him as a reporter at a start-up weekly called *LA* that we were saying was like, you know, "the *Village Voice,* but for Los Angeles." Bob never said that, though. He had come west on an "editorial whim" (his phrase) after some turbulent years in New York at *Esquire,* where he had been a sly packager and helped "midwife" (ditto) journalistic innovations from Dubious Achievements to that genre-cracking run of pieces that defined the New Journalism. Tom Wolfe, Gay Talese, Truman Capote, Mailer—every writer in the country knew the growing roll call and wanted to be on it. Bob had edited many of them and liked to talk about how they got their story ideas.

"From editors, of course," he would say, riding shotgun with a Mexican beer between his knees, motoring around Southern California with one or another of the young writers who worked for him. Bob had hired me thinking he was getting a solid wire service reporter, which I was not—although I had spent time in Beirut and Amman during the 1970 Jordanian civil war that became known as Black September and had been picked up by AP Newsfeatures in New York. What I was, was ambitious and that's what Bob said he liked about my story ideas—that, and that I had been reading *Esquire* since high school, was a little older than the other reporters, and had the best car.

Bob would never let you use *eventful* in a piece but this particular day was that for me, driving us both down the coast in my Fiat convertible to a party in Dana Point thrown by a former AP reporter named Pat McNulty, who had reinvented himself as the editor of *Surfer* magazine. I knew McNulty and the invitation had come through me. When I'd told Bob about it, I'd said there would be surfers for sure but also journalists, maybe a couple novelists, and also people in the new MFA program at U.C. Irvine, where McNulty was teaching. If there was a West Coast literary "scene" (a word Bob liked) to match up with Tom Wolfe's recent piece on surf culture, "The Pump House Gang," this would be it.

I knew Bob would be the center of the party as he always was wherever writers and alcohol came together. All the way down the Pacific Coast Highway we talked story ideas. Bob was warming up for the writers who would soon be circling for a chance to talk to him, all of them wanting to break trail for an assignment from *Esquire*, where he was still a contributing editor. Somewhere near Laguna Beach I said something about how anybody interested in journalism (like me) would want to read a piece by someone like Wolfe or Talese or Mailer or anyone good on Bob himself, and what was about to happen to him at the party.

Bob had a way of cocking his head when he was enjoying whatever he was thinking. That's what he did then, and told me *he* thought *I* thought like an editor and we should *both* think about *that*. Think about me becoming an editor. Think about making magazines. "Think about monkeys jumping out of boxes," he said. "That's what

5

good editors do." I had not heard that one but figured he was talking about jack-in-the-box surprises. I nodded. He cocked his head again. I waited.

"Plus," he said, taking another pull from his Tecate, "good editors never have to drive."

-ENDIT-

Word Count (320)

Editing is about ideas, but it is mechanical, too. You have to get under the hood of the language, and editors use many tools. I'll start by leaving the word counts at the top of my chapters because as an editor I always wanted to know how much I was about to read. This helped me evaluate pacing or the lack of it in a piece. Writers were sensitive to this once they found out how I worked, and were generally attuned to length, even if they weren't being paid by the word.

At all the magazines I edited (*Rolling Stone, Esquire, Sports Illustrated,* et al.), feature stories were assigned at a specific length—usually four thousand words—and most writers would take that over five thousand and say they were close. Others would come in under three thousand and say the same thing. It was mysterious why being direct about the number of words they were filing was so difficult but I am sure it had more to do with alchemy than lack of discipline. Before Microsoft Word, stopping to count how many words you'd typed could be refreshing, like stopping to make tea or smoke a cigarette. Now doing a word count can have a slot machine kick to it if you have the discipline not to do it every time you hit Save.

None of this matters if the piece is good—and that's determined by voice and narrative, not length. Going long is always more ambitious and usually more fun. This was true before lengthy pieces became "creative nonfiction" or "narrative journalism," and it is true now that we've finally debunked the simple-minded Web assumption that no one will screen-read anything longer than a news capsule. No writer I ever edited wanted to go short, anyway. Neither do I, but I also know that the best pieces seem to find their own length. That's the alchemy.

-ENDIT-

Jim Harrison (525)

THE FIRST CHAPTER of Jim Harrison's first novel, *Wolf,* begins with a two-page sentence. He says it was vanity, that he wanted to show it could be done because he was a young writer and hungry. That was in 1971. A few years later when I was starting to work with him, I asked if his editor had tried to do something with that first sentence.

"Of course," he said wearily, as if in my tragic inexperience I was unable to grasp the basic construct of editing him. Jim did little revising and was proud of it. Rewriting was for people who hadn't worked everything out early—not for Jim, who insisted that he always thought things through before he wrote anything down. As for editors, why should he let them fool with his choices? They were not, as he had explained to me when we first met, writers. He also liked to note that he was a poet and "editors don't change poems."

"I wouldn't change any of your poems either," I said, but when it came to his journalism I wasn't so sure. Being above editing was a pose some writers found situationally useful, the way some children are "allergic" to lima beans. It was the foot Jim liked to get off on and, sure enough, we tangled over copy our first time around. I was at *Outside* magazine and suggested that his lede on a story about Key West was really the second paragraph and the first paragraph should be the kicker at the end of the piece. He hung up on me.

I got an immediate follow-up call from his agent, Bob Datilla, a tough, reasonable guy.

"You want to pull the piece?" I asked, after his declension of my shortcomings.

"Of course not," Datilla said. "We just want to be on the record about what a dumb shit you are." (Pause.) "But Jim can be difficult, too."

"So we'll all think about it?" I said.

"Exactly."

I'm not sure how much we all thought about it, but I switched the paragraphs to what I'd suggested and we never discussed the piece again. Maybe Jim didn't notice. But I learned to tread lightly or risk being told, as I once was by him, "You lynched my baby." His raw copy was so ambitious that I usually just checked the copy edit and wrote the headline. We talked about other things, like what we were having for dinner, as well as what we were reading. My working relationship with Jim and other writers, my growing friendships with them, was nourished by even the mundane details of their lives.

In *Wolf*, Jim wrote, *Perhaps I'll never see a wolf. And I don't offer this little problem as central to anyone but myself.* Fair enough. As a reader, I took that as a glance at a private mystery. As an editor, I wanted that wolf to be my problem, too. I wanted to ride along. I hoped that was how I could become a good editor, by editing great writers and getting to know them. The ancient Greeks had a word for this: *hubris.*

-ENDIT-

The Other Bob Sherrill (449)

LA HAD FOLDED NOT LONG AFTER Sherrill suggested
I become an editor, and he moved back to New York to work at the
glossy but hip *New Times* until *it* folded, and then home to North
Carolina, where he was doing some newspaper work in Durham. I
had gotten associate editor jobs at *San Francisco Magazine* and *City*
magazine and then become a senior editor at *Outside*.

> *Dear Terror:*
>   *This is the voice of your conscience speaking:*
>   *Fuck you, Terry. By now you are probably saying "piece" and*
> *"superb" and "structure" and you probably even have little slips*
> *of paper that say, "We regret that your submission does not meet*
> *our present editorial requirements, etc. . . ." Abysmal words that*
> *hang empty and impersonal on the giant dark screen of some*
> *poor fool's mind . . .*

He was pitching me for a writing assignment, and that's the way
he opened his query. And of course he was giving me some editing
advice, or a reality check, or maybe it was a test. His first story idea
was a road piece.

> *I'm gonna hit the old Appalachian Trail, I think, as soon*
> *as I'm fired here. Maybe before. The bucolic freeway. Nope.*
> *Greater solitude is to be found in Nathan's on Seventh. Rackety-*
> *rackety. For you I'd want to make a study of the off ramps, and*
> *traffic in general, see how the charismatic fauna is doing. The*
> *point is, perhaps sadly, wild animals have learned to cope.*
> *They've learned how to live with us . . . hawks and groundhogs*
> *happy and fat in a suburbia cut up by tobacco farms.*

I was confused. I looked at a map of the Appalachian Trail, which is a highway as well as the hiking network I'd always thought it was, but what the hell anyway. I knew Bob always saved his best for last and, sure enough, after some rambling thoughts about the American musical theater and a notion he had for a "scientific" musical called *The Big Bop Theory*, starring God, he got to the other idea.

Something on hippiebillies. Hip hicks. Into Drugs of all kinds. Still country but much more sophisticated in strange ways. One is now working on my sixty-fo fo'd (Sky Blue).

I wrote to him that he should hit *the old Appalachian Trail* in search of *hippiebillies* and write the piece. Maybe he could work in some of that *charismatic fauna* coping on the off-ramps. It was *Outside* magazine, after all. Bob wrote back a month later that he was pleased that I was thinking like an editor. The bad news was that he had not been fired so could not take the assignment.

-ENDIT-

Rejection (1,492)

As ADMIRABLE AS IT WAS to be honest and decisive, enemies could be made stupidly and by accident, and terrible mistakes could test friendships. George Plimpton, as editor of the *Paris Review*, once turned down a story from his childhood friend Peter Matthiessen, calling it "risible"—something he regretted as long as they lived. A friend of mine from college became outraged after I rejected one of his poems at *Rolling Stone*. I told him the magazine didn't run poetry anymore, which it didn't. He never spoke to me again.

The second-best answer an editor can give a writer is a "fast no." Most editors are not very good at this and leave writers hanging, sometimes for months. No response is worse, of course, and that's common, too. The arrogance drives writers crazy with humiliation. Some very good editors don't care, but the best ones do. Or maybe the ones who care the most are writers themselves, like Lewis Lapham at *Harper's* and then *Lapham's Quarterly*, and Graydon Carter at *Vanity Fair*.

Some editors, like Bob Silvers at the *New York Review of Books*, wrote thoughtful, useful letters. Others tossed off notes full of veiled irony that was easily misunderstood, often beginning or ending with a sentence or two about how busy the editor was. This preoccupation with their own time ("things are *crazed* here at the magazine") is still a quick jump to the uniform rejection note, a kiss-off engineered to shield the editor from further correspondence or, worse, becoming a target of abuse because he or she has tried to point out to overly sensitive and usually obstinate authors the specifics of how their manuscripts fell short.

This from the *Century* magazine in 1890:

> *Out of nine thousand manuscripts a year* The Century *can only possibly print four hundred or less. It follows that editing a*

magazine is not unlike walking into a garden of flowers and gathering a single bouquet. In other words, not to accept an article, a story, a poem is not necessarily to "reject" it. There may be weeds in the garden . . . but the fact that a particular blossom is not gathered into the monthly bouquet does not prove that the editor regarded the blossom as a weed, and therefore passed it by.

Or this, composed by Hunter Thompson in the early 1970s for pieces sent to him care of *Rolling Stone*:

You worthless, acid-sucking piece of illiterate shit! Don't ever send this kind of brain-damaged swill in here again! If I had the time, I'd come out there and drive a fucking wooden stake into your skull. Why don't you get a job, wino? Like maybe as a night watchman, or delivering the Shopping News. You [insert name of city] cocksuckers are all alike—just like those dope-addled dingbats at Rolling Stone. I could kill those bedwetting bastards for sending me these tedious and embarrassing tissues of delusions . . . and I wouldn't mind killing you, too. Stick this manuscript where it belongs: up your ass.
   Cordially,
   Yail Bloor
   Minister of Manuscripts

Hunter was never an editor but became a magnet for lofty ideas and bad writing about freak solidarity. Many admirers sent him page after page of their ramblings in the hope that he would help get them published in the magazine, where, with a strange and callow glee, many of the editors began using what became known as "the Yail Bloor letter" as a uniform rejection note.

Fifty years earlier, Ring Lardner's advice, in his book *How to Write Short Stories* (1924), was that it was always a mistake for a writer submitting a story to a magazine to enclose the called-for stamped, self-addressed envelope—"too much of a temptation to the editor." After all, why should an editor spend time looking for new writers when he already knew way too many? (As quaint as envelopes sound, the temptation to ignore e-mail from unknown writers can make sending a traditional letter shockingly more effective—nobody gets mail like that anymore.)

Well-known writers have always had the edge, although the wonderfully named Sumner Blossom devised a system to ensure fairness for unknowns when he was editing *American Magazine* in 1934. Manuscripts were evaluated with author's name obscured to make sure they were judged on merit alone. Ha.

The most implacable pieces almost always came from big-name writers on important subjects, with enterprising editors making aggressive assignments serving as the grease. Harold Hayes, then editor in chief of *Esquire*, in a 1964 staff memo to the Other Bob Sherrill, among others, wrote:

> *A passive, inert, dull magazine . . . is usually made up of editors who sit around and wait for writers to send them queries, or pictures, or finished pieces upon which they can react and thus fulfill themselves. . . . Magazine editing is not just the act of choosing, it is an act of assertion.*

Editors have to be optimistic, expecting to get what they ask for from writers and ever hopeful that the next issue will come together not quite so badly as the last one. This has always led to a kind of far-flung enthusiasm in the assigning process that underlines the well-known quip by William E. Rae, editor in chief of *Outdoor Life* magazine in the fifties and sixties: *An editor is a man who doesn't know what he wants but recognizes it instantly.*

John Cheever was more optimistic in his 1969 *Paris Review* interview: *My definition of a good editor is a man I think charming, who sends me large checks, praises my work, my physical beauty, and my sexual prowess, and who has a stranglehold on the publisher and the bank.*

The crime writer, lawyer and newspaper columnist George V. Higgins took it the other way in *On Writing*, his 1990 book on the subject: *Only a seriously disturbed person would sincerely wish to have an editor for a friend.*

I never heard editors talk about how disturbed and insecure writers might become as a result of relentless rejection, living every day with what James Salter called "the feeling of injustice." It was more fun for editors to characterize their jobs as overseeing petting zoos full of needy misfits and narcissists, a point of view that was always amusing to other editors but infuriating to writers. Every writer, of course, has very specific ideas about editors. But writers seldom get the last word on anything.

My favorite exception came from Francesca Bell, a Native American poet who dropped out of middle school but found a way to crack the poetry establishment and its network of small magazines. In 2013, Bell had this poem published in *Rattle:*

I Long to Hold the Poetry Editor's Penis in My Hand

and tell him personally,
I'm sorry, but I'm going
to have to pass on this.
Though your piece
held my attention through
the first few screenings,
I don't feel it is a good fit
for me at this time.
Please know it received
my careful consideration.
I thank you for allowing
me to have a look,
and I wish you
the very best of luck
placing it elsewhere.

Of course editors are mostly men and, fuckers that they are, the obvious observation that they are necessary probably goes back to papyrus. The earliest quote I found was voiced in self-defense by Charles Fletcher Lummis, editor of *Out West* magazine, in 1904; he said simply, *Editors are necessary evils.* Hunter Thompson said the same thing, noting with irony in his interview with the *Paris Review* in 2000, *I've never sent [in] a piece of anything that's finished.*

Specific definitions of editing are tricky, although the thinking divides along two distinct lines. The celebrated *New Yorker* editor Harold Ross and longtime contributor Brendan Gill articulated the extremes. Ross defined editing as *quarreling with writers—the same thing exactly.* In *Here at the New Yorker* Gill wrote, *The work of a good editor, like the work of a good teacher, does not reveal itself directly; it is reflected in the accomplishments of others.* Both Ross and Gill are right.

The most ambitious definition I ever came across was from Norman Cousins, a longtime editor of the *Saturday Review*, when I was struggling to find pieces and cold-calling Jim Salter and other favorite writers to get *Rocky Mountain Magazine* launched. Cousins had written:

Nothing is more ephemeral than words. Moving them from the mind of a writer to the mind of a reader is one of the most elusive and difficult undertakings ever to challenge the human intelligence. This is what being an editor is all about.

This floored me with its combination of clarity and sensitivity. The ambition of it made me suddenly proud to be an editor. Thinking I would compliment Cousins in some editor-to-editor way, I wrote him a careful letter introducing myself. When I didn't hear back I felt like a writer again.

–ENDIT–

Ed Abbey (2,633)

COLD-CALLING WRITERS I ADMIRED and offering them assignments was impertinent and I knew it. I built up my nerve before making a call by telling myself what I liked about their writing. And I wouldn't call without a story idea that I could be specific about. This worked out more often than not if I followed up right away with a letter and contract in the mail. Sometimes the hardest part was getting the phone number.

Ed Abbey didn't have a phone but was easy to recruit, once I tracked down his post office box in Oracle, Arizona. His novel *The Monkey Wrench Gang* was then the defining document for the wild-ass splinters of the environmental movement as it turned belligerent— birthing the militant Earth First! and Sea Shepherd. More important to me, his first nonfiction book, *Desert Solitaire*, read like observational sorcery, which is the kind of language Ed would make fun of but it's what I told him when he called me collect after getting my postcard offering whatever assignment might interest him.

"The last thing I need is another editor," he said. "But I suppose I could use the money."

This was in 1977, when I was at *Outside*, and for the next ten years Ed and I usually had a piece going or at least percolating. He was a prickly edit, but funny about whatever I suggested, which always involved him writing more. He was usually on the road and I'd call him at a prearranged number, a bar pay phone in Moab, Utah, or wherever, and we'd talk through the piece. A week later I'd get whatever I'd asked for in the mail.

We got together in person for the first and only time two years later, when Ed visited me in Denver, where I was editing *Rocky Mountain Magazine*. "Passing through," Ed said, but he was also making a speech at the University of Colorado in Boulder. I was living in a solid little red brick house just south of Colfax Avenue, where the Denver dive bars and strip clubs were then.

Ed didn't call first, just rang my doorbell. Much taller than I expected, standing on the porch with a cragginess that didn't make him ugly, but he was not handsome, either. He looked strong and difficult and more than anything like the cowboy he always insisted he wasn't. An anarchist was what he was, from the confusingly named Indiana, Pennsylvania, who had left home after high school to find, as he put it, *the West of my deepest imaginings—the place where the tangible and the mythical became the same.* He could write cowboy better than anybody.

Ed's early novel *The Brave Cowboy* became the last black-and-white cowboy movie, *Lonely Are the Brave,* starring Kirk Douglas, who said it was his favorite film. I saw it on television not long after my first conversation with Ed. It was the kind of movie that made romantics want to mount up—about a young cowboy at odds with modern society, rejecting technology, cutting down barbed wire, and as true to the West as sage. When his friend is locked up for refusing to register for the draft, he gets himself arrested, in order to break his friend out of jail, but winds up on the run on horseback, with helicopters chasing him. It does not end well, but Ed's cowboy is true to himself (refusing even to carry a driver's license or Social Security card) and wildly heroic. By the time Ed was standing on my porch, however, he was writing and giving speeches about how *the beef industry's abuse of our Western lands is based on the old mythology of the cowboy as a natural nobleman, the most cherished and fanciful of American fairy tales.*

Ed said he had been asked to speak about something goofy like "literary environmentalism" but that he always just talked about whatever he felt like when the time came and nobody ever seemed to mind. He was to appear the following afternoon on the University of Colorado campus, but tonight he was invited to a dinner party at the home of an important academic who had something to do with him getting invited to speak. After my deputy at *Rocky Mountain,*

Karen Evans, came by my house for a drink, Ed insisted that we both go with him to the dinner. Karen, a polished woman with beautiful style, was skeptical, saying we would be imposing on what was surely an important dinner party for someone. Probably seated. Ed said he didn't "give a hoot."

The hostess, a young academic wife in a short skirt, met us at the door with a smile for Ed—and wary accommodations would be made for Karen and me. Among the faculty guests, we met a handsome young guy in hiking boots and a tweed blazer who said we should give Buddhism a try. I thought *try* was a peculiar word to use, but Karen said he probably meant meditation, not Buddhism. Ed, meanwhile, was being monopolized sequentially by our host, an older professor, and the other important PhDs. After more than an hour of drinks, we were all squeezed around a long table under a bright chandelier in a formal dining room.

Ed was at the head of the table, Karen and I next to each other on extra chairs wedged in at a far corner. Carefully seated up and down were obviously well-meaning people, and I inferred from the small talk that they wanted Ed to tell them about the spiritual importance of nature and the enlightenment he'd found as a back-country ranger in Arches National Monument, in Utah, when he was writing *Desert Solitaire.*

One of the guests had a first edition that I could see had passages underlined on many pages, and he knew some of them by heart. He wondered if Ed could expand on his idea that *There are no vacant lots in nature.* Better yet, could Ed tell the table what he was think-ing when he first saw *the flaming globe, blazing on the pinnacles and minarets and balanced rocks.* It was impressive, but Ed just shrugged and said, yes, that's what he had written. Someone else suggested that Ed had become a "philosopher of nature," but it was clear to me when I caught his eye that Ed wasn't feeling very philosophical.

Finally, in response to an achingly long question about the impor-tance of saving the beauty of the desert canyons, Ed asked about what he had heard to be excessive drinking, drug use and sexual promiscuity among the Buddhists at their nearby Naropa Institute. It was a question to silence any dinner party, especially one with Naropa connections to some of the guests. But then, as several people finally pointed out in a low-key but surprisingly aggressive chorus, there really wasn't much *to* all those rumors. The young Buddhist in the hiking boots said he could vouch for that, but his voice broke when he tried to say something about being misunderstood himself.

"Well, then, just kidding," Ed said, to everyone's relief, but he was not smiling.

Changing the subject, someone asked Ed to characterize his work—what was he going for in his writing? Ed frowned and said that wasn't his job. "Maybe you should ask Terry," he said, disappointing everyone. "He's the editor."

This surprised me a little, but then I stepped into it. "Ed's a dangerous writer," I said, probably taking another drink. "He scares people like you." It was a belligerent thing to say, and I was immediately sorry, but there it was. I think I then made some preposterous jump from the environmental movement to the anti-war movement and the Black Panthers and back to the radical environmental movement that Ed had inspired with *The Monkey Wrench Gang.* The table was turning from surprised to resentful, but now Ed was smiling.

"The Black Panthers are criminals," our host said. "'Thugs,'" he had read in the *Saturday Review.*

I said the Panthers did a lot of good things, although some of them were gangsters for sure.

"And you know all about that, I suppose," said our hostess.

"I was in SDS at Berkeley," I said, compounding my silly trucu-lence.

"How unattractive," said our hostess.

My memory of the details of what followed fails, but I may have mentioned Tom Wolfe's *Radical Chic & Mau-Mauing the Flak Catchers.* Perhaps I said something more aggressive. What I do remember, distinctly, was the reddening beautiful face of our hostess.

"You're insulting," she said. "You should apologize to everyone here, including our guest of honor."

"I should just go," I said. "I'm sorry to have ruined your dinner."

The hostess smiled tightly and stood up, making it clear that this would be fine with her. Karen and I stood up too, but all eyes were on Ed.

"Well, then," he said, also rising. "I'll be going, too."

WHAT SHITS WE WERE, I thought, getting into my car, and I could see that none of us were feeling especially noble. Ed said he thought that the Buddhist kid had been about to cry, and he was sorry about that because he kind of liked Buddhists. Academics not so much. "I only asked about Naropa because I was interested in the sex," he said.

We drove to one of the bars on Colfax Avenue, and ate pickled eggs and drank boilermakers. Ed spent the night at my house, and we were up late, talking radical talk about what was wrong and maybe a little right with blowing up dams to save rivers. *The Monkey Wrench Gang* was about that, and so was Jim Harrison's *A Good Day to Die*, an earlier novel Ed admired. None of this was ironic except that Ed did say what he was thinking when he first saw *the flaming globe, blazing on the pinnacles and minarets and balanced rocks.* He said he hadn't been thinking at all.

He also said he thought the FBI might be keeping a file on him because when he was in college at the University of New Mexico he had posted a letter urging other students to throw away their draft cards. "How paranoid is that," he said, and poured another drink.

NOT LONG AFTER, I sold a novel and left Colorado and *Rocky Mountain Magazine* for Montana, where I planned to write for a while. Ed approved and blurbed the novel when it came out, saying, with his characteristic kindness to other writers, that *"California Bloodstock* is most stylishly composed, in the cool, nihilistic manner of Joan Didion."

Ed knew I loved Didion, and I loved *nihilistic* too, because it was not one of Ed's words and he had obviously thought about it—even though he'd just been composing a blurb. His own writing was never that mannered. He hid the craft but never the beauty of the words— words like *chaparral* and *blue columbine* and *mosquito*—that he set in place, all in the voice of an outraged populist poet. Ed was against development and tourism and earnest engineers, nostalgia for the lost America, cattle shitting in the watersheds, daily routine, and, in his own words: *the* insufferable *arrogance of elected officials, the crafty* cheating *and the* slimy *advertising of the business men . . . the foul, diseased, and* hideous *cities and towns we live in, the constant* petty *tyranny of automatic washers and automobiles and TV machines and telephones!*

I reread Ed often, like I did Mark Twain, grinning at the contrarian spirit and showmanship. He threw homilies like roundhouse punches: *One man alone can be pretty dumb sometimes, but for real bona fide stupidity, there ain't nothin' can beat teamwork.* He didn't talk like that, but he wrote that way when it served his purpose—like here, from A *Voice Crying in the Wilderness* that he published in 1989: *When a man's best friend is his dog, that dog has a problem.*

As the Other Bob Sherrill would sometimes say when he liked the way the words worked: "There is a small revolution going on in that sentence."

SEARCH FOR EDWARD ABBEY on the FBI website (fbi.gov) and you can find a 1952 memo from J. Edgar Hoover outlining "A Loyalty of Government Employee investigation" to be conducted when Ed was working for the National Forest Service. It was triggered by that college letter about throwing away draft cards. Ed was on the FBI's watch list from then on, and when I looked it up years later I found notations like "Edward Abbey is against war and military." And the agency continued adding to his profile, keeping track of him, although probably not at Boulder dinner parties. Toward the end of his life, when Ed's FBI file became public he told friends, "I'd be insulted if they weren't watching me."

The day Ed died in his home, Fort Llatikcuf (read it backward), near Tucson, close friends put his body in his old blue sleeping bag and loaded it into the bed of a pickup packed with dry ice. After stopping at a liquor store in Tucson for five cases of beer and some whiskey to pour on the grave, they drove deep into the Cabeza Prieta desert— all according to Ed's wishes, and disregarding all state burial laws.

I want my body to help fertilize the growth of a cactus or cliff rose or sagebrush or tree, Ed had written. And for his funeral: *No formal speeches desired, though the deceased will not interfere if someone feels the urge. But keep it all simple and brief.* He also requested gunfire and bagpipe music, a cheerful and raucous wake, *and a flood of beer and booze! Lots of singing, dancing, talking, hollering, laughing, and lovemaking.* Doug Peacock wrote later in *Outside* that the last time Ed smiled was when Peacock told him about the place he had come up with for Ed to be buried.

That location remains secret, but there is a hand-carved marker on a nearby stone:

Edward

Paul

Abbey

1927-1989

NO COMMENT

KAREN EVANS HAD STAYED in loose touch with Ed and interviewed him by mail not long before he died. I don't think that interview was ever published, but I found Ed's long letter to her in a posthumous collection of his correspondence, *Postcards from Ed.* Apparently, like the guests at that unfortunate dinner party, Karen had asked him to characterize his work and what he was going for in his writing. But Ed liked Karen, and he answered:

What I am really writing about, what I have always written about, is the idea of human freedom, human community, the real world which makes both possible, and the new technocratic industrial state which threatens the existence of all three. Life and death, that's my subject, and always has been—if the reader will look beyond the assumptions of lazy critics and actually read what I have written. Which also means, quite often, reading between the lines: I am a comic writer and the generation of laughter is my aim . . .

. . . I now find the most marvelous things in the everyday, the ordinary, the common, the simple and tangible. For example: one cloud floating over one mountain.

At the end of the letter, Ed instructed Karen to revise and colloquialize what he had written, as she saw fit, to make it read like a conversation. It was all up to her. And she could write and ask for more if she thought she needed it. Or Karen could just come to Tucson for a day or two, because it didn't look like he was going to be getting out of there that summer.

-ENDIT-

Sans Serif (1,120)

I OFTEN PAGED THROUGH MAGAZINES wondering why some editors would run headlines over dark, muddy photographs that made the type difficult to read, or insert a gigantic drop cap that overpowered the lede paragraph of their cover story. Then I'd run into the editor and he or she would bring the layout up as evidence of the difficulty managing the belligerent art director or design director or creative director or whatever the top designer was called at that particular publication. Sometimes I felt sorry for these editors, but it was a feeling that never lasted.

The art directors I worked with were always co-conspirators and often my best friends on the masthead. The art director at *LA* was Roger Black, who was then a fresh-faced twenty-two-year-old with a d'Artagnan haircut and preppy clothes. He was just out of the University of Chicago and *Print Project Amerika*, a hip, politically radical (or trying to be) magazine I knew from Mayday—which was what we called one of the last Washington anti-war demonstrations, held in the spring of 1971. Roger had been the editor of *Print Project Amerika*, an experience that had convinced him that design was by far the most fun part of publishing, so he'd immersed himself in typography and a year later, there he was in Los Angeles. He told me this when we met, sharing a joint in the parking lot of the *LA* offices in Westwood.

I was still a reporter then, though I also took pictures and was increasingly interested in design. I had never worked closely with an art director before, but I figured I wasn't coming into it cold because my degree was in art, which I told Roger. He told me his was in English and he might write something if "you don't watch out." I didn't know quite how to take that but Roger struck me as amplifyingly cool. He was married to a sweet, red-haired woman of perhaps thirty called Pinkie Black who liked to talk about fashion as art and once came to a party wearing pots and pans over a bodysuit—which everyone thought was way hip. Roger was also starting a little business on the side called "the FBI" which stood for "the Font Bureau Inc." I started stopping by Roger's desk to look at his layouts, in various stages of progress, and cover mock-ups. Very quickly I began to think I knew *why* I liked this or that graphic, not just that I liked it. I also learned what *sans serif* meant.

One day, after clearing it with our boss, the Other Bob Sherrill, I told Roger I was going to be *LA*'s photo editor, along with my other duties. We hadn't published our first issue yet, still doing run-throughs, and I was enjoying the time I was spending in the art department.

"Good," Roger said. "Or we can just have an in-box."

I didn't have to think much about that. Roger was telling me that he wanted to make the decisions about which photos were used, no matter where they came from, as well as choosing the caption length and typeface—in other words, he wanted complete control of all visuals. I learned later that the best art directors are all like that.

I also learned that if you've got great images, you win easy, but typography can save you if you're stuck with bad ones. Then again, even great photos sized to the same aspect ratio on every page make the pages seem identical no matter what else you do. You also need scale shifts to differentiate the notes you want to hit, story to story, in your mix. So-called white space (empty space on a page) can help too and is the key to running those gigantic drop caps I usually don't like much. And you need *hierarchies* and *protocols*—I still love using those terms—and a distinctive color palette, but one with colors that exist in nature or whatever you do will look like you're selling cheap toys or fast food.

For designers, making decisions about what to do with what you have to work with is infinitely more interesting than collecting the various elements of a page. A lot of magazine work always was (and still is) about fetching—especially in fashion and at service magazines, where sub-editors deliver cupcake after cupcake of Must-Haves, How-Tos, Where-Tos and What-Fors. Roger was right about that. And putting what has been fetched together with *other* ideas was (and still is) where editors and art directors get to show off.

For a profile of "Jimmy the Greek," a popular commentator who was bringing gambling to the mix of TV sports, the art director at *City* magazine, Mike Salisbury, simply paper-clipped the Greek's cheesy business card to a lame PR photo of the weird old bookie and thereby transformed the piece. It was like the layout was winking at the reader. The card had Jimmy's Vegas phone number and that was it, so . . . *Give The Greek a call if you feel like it!* You didn't even need a headline. I admired Salisbury for that but knew the layout had needed editor Warren Hinckle's final approval and thought maybe it had been his idea. He was the one who had gotten the card in the first place.

"Of course it was my idea," Warren said when I asked him about it a few years later. "I was the editor!" I was running a magazine by then myself and felt eerily proud of how clearly I understood what Warren was telling me.

Editors and art directors pivoting off each other's ideas is a beautiful thing, but the editor has "the conn," as we called it at *Newsweek*—a goofy reference to being in command of the *Enterprise* on *Star Trek*. And that was the way it had to be, as I learned over and over, not just working closely with Roger—as I did at five magazines—but with every other art director I came to know. By the late 1980s, I was sitting side by side with them at their computer screens. They all wanted to make the decisions, and that's the confidence I wanted from them.

There was one designer I tried to hire at least twice. He said he had heard how "hands-on" I was as an editor when it came to design and that he'd rather we just stayed friends. I felt a little busted for maybe grabbing too much credit or perhaps, as Roger once put it, "riding designers like racehorses," but, like feeling sorry for editors who lost control of their art directors, that didn't last, either.

-ENDIT-

Peter Matthiessen (2,157)

W<small>E WERE IN A CANOE</small> on the Yellowstone River, near my house in Montana. Peter pointed to the riverbank, where a bird with a tough-looking black bill and a rufous band extending down its flanks was perched on a cottonwood branch overhanging the water. We had fly rods with us but were mostly watching birds.

"Belted kingfisher," Peter said.

There was no wind. The kingfisher shifted on the branch.

Peter's voice dropped. "Watch," he said. "She will probably fall."

We watched, our canoe sliding slowly in the current, and the bird did fall, recovering to the bank after a noisy splash. I had lived on that river for a year and had spent time on many others and had never seen a bird fall into the water, never thought of such a thing.

"Young birds have to learn simple lessons," Peter said, feathering his paddle in the water. He told me he'd known it was a juvenile female because that reddish-brown band was mottled thinner than on adult females.

All of Peter's bios said he'd been obsessed with birds as a small boy, and that he took ornithology, zoology and marine biology courses at Yale alongside his work as an English major. There was more to it. Peter had many obsessions, and his connection to what he called "the transience" of what is wild and beautiful was something you saw just watching him scan the horizon beyond the river, but you saw it other places, too.

Peter was born in 1927, the day after Charles Lindbergh landed in France after flying across the Atlantic in his *Spirit of St. Louis*. This meant that Custer's Last Stand was closer to Peter's birthday than his receiving the National Book Award for *The Snow Leopard* in 1979 — a calculation that amused him as he got older. He had grown up before television, mostly outdoors overturning rocks, listening to birds and catching snakes, as he described it. When his mother found out he was keeping poisonous copperheads in homemade cages she told Peter to kill them, but he let them go.

When he told me about the snakes, he smiled. Maybe the inevitable momentum of Peter's life started there. The work that trailed behind him echoed the loss of every extinct creature and ruined habitat he learned about, and he learned about all of them. His *Wildlife in America*, published in 1959, grew out of a *Sports Illustrated* assignment to report a three-part series on the connections between extinction and disappearing habitat. When the series ended, the unused reporting resulted in the prototype of modern environmental journalism, and even calling attention to global warming as well as the ruinous relationship between man and animals.

There's an elegiac quality in watching [American wilderness] go, because it's our own myth, the American frontier, that's deteriorating before our eyes. I feel a deep sorrow that my kids will never get to see what I've seen, and their kids will see nothing; there's a deep sadness whenever I look at nature now.

You didn't get that sadness from him in person, especially surrounded by nature, like on the Yellowstone River. He was in his early fifties then and his parallel careers as a naturalist and writer had come together in commercial success with *The Snow Leopard*, his meditation on the wildlife and landscape of the Himalayas, made lustrous by his deeper contemplation of life and death as a student of Buddhism. There were several of us on the river with Peter that day, and we had all read *The Snow Leopard* and found it to be full of lessons that took work to understand. Yet that night, drinking wine and soaking in a hot spring in one of the creeks that fed the Yellowstone, there was only celebration of where we were and what we had seen. That was the work.

LAUNCHING *ROCKY MOUNTAIN MAGAZINE* in 1979, I had called Peter's Sagaponack number and spoken with his future wife,   29

Maria Eckhart, who was appropriately skeptical and protective: "Another new magazine, really—well, Peter's not only not here, he's out there somewhere and, as you can imagine, very, very busy." Her words were discouraging and a little ironic, but she had a lovely Tanzanian accent and a kind tone, a combination that I learned eventually to translate into advice. She took my number.

Peter did call back, from a gas station on the Hopi Reservation in Arizona. He was in the middle of three years of reporting—traveling Native American reservations gathering stories and details that would become *In the Spirit of Crazy Horse* in 1983 and, a year later, *Indian Country*, both expressive and painful looks at Native Americans. With him much of the time was Craig Carpenter, a self-described "half-baked detribalized Mohawk from the Great Lakes country trying to find his way back to the real Indians." It was the disappearance of traditional cultures, along with the loss of wilderness, that most interested Peter, and his outrage was making him enemies, especially his defense of American Indian Movement leader Leonard Peltier.

Peltier had been convicted of murder and sentenced to life in prison for the 1975 killing of two FBI agents, in what would be known as the "Incident at Oglala." Peter's work to free Peltier would become an enduring commitment, but for *Rocky Mountain Magazine* he wanted to write about trouble among the Indians themselves, a range war developing between the Hopi and the Navajo over land use and water rights in Arizona. Was I interested in that? It was one of those moments all editors fear: a great writer pitching a story about . . . water rights?

Peter told me that *Hopi* translated to "peaceful ones" and that they were a traditional people living in an area called Black Mesa, a plateau rising six thousand feet above the surrounding grasslands. The Hopi referred to this place as sacred, the center of the universe, although they were entirely surrounded by the much larger Navajo reservation, and the Navajo were about as traditional as ATVs and slot machines.

"How many words are you thinking?" I asked.

"Long," he said.

"Five or six thousand words?"

"More like ten . . ."

Two weeks later, he filed fifteen thousand, twice as many as I had ever run in any magazine. I combed through the piece with a careful line edit, bringing it down to twelve thousand, cutting only one complete section—about the brutality of the Navajo Police. My problem with that section had less to do with length than reporting; it didn't have denials from the police. Peter resisted every change with patience and grew finicky only when it became necessary, realizing that he could not wait me out because of the deadline. But he would not agree to lose the section on the Navajo Police, for which his primary source was Carpenter, the "half-baked detribalized Mohawk" he had been traveling with.

"You have to trust your writers," Peter said.

I could hear the humor in his voice. He was an amused Buddhist, and I think Peter regarded me then as he regarded most editors—as a failed writer. And as a serious Buddhist, he thought of himself as a teacher—perhaps not when it came to his editors at Viking and the *New Yorker*, but certainly with me in a little house in Denver crawling over his fifteen thousand words on the Hopi. I had never edited a writer who knew so much about so much beyond his own writing and it was easy to become his student, especially after I fact-checked the passages about the Navajo Police. They were brutal.

When we were finished with the edit, I made some notes for the short bio of Peter that would run with the piece. I found those notes years later in my worn copy of *The Snow Leopard:* "Novelist, journalist, editor, activist, naturalist, explorer, anthropologist, zoologist, ornithologist, ichthyologist, entomologist, oceanographer, fisherman, waterman, charter boat captain, shark hunter, linguist, adventurer, scientist, LSD pioneer, Vietnam war protester, radical, Buddhist," and so on, finally getting to "shaman," underlined at the bottom of the page. It seemed as if what I had written was for a sixth-grade report, trying too hard not to miss anything—a list impossibly naïve in its comprehensiveness. Peter wasn't there at all. When I checked the old magazine, I saw that the bio I had run said simply that Peter was "the author of *The Snow Leopard*."

When the Hopi piece went to press (fourteen thousand words), Peter was still on the road.

PETER TRAVELED WITH UNIVERSAL NOTEBOOKS, taking notes on the right-hand pages, leaving the left blank until he used them for his first run at usable copy—usually in the evening after a day of reporting. It was an efficient system that made him productive on the road. The notebooks were artifacts too, and I think they meant as much to him as the research they held, although he insisted that this was a silly idea.

He lost one of those notebooks once, at the San Francisco airport, while returning from reporting in Klamath National Forest in Northern California. Those were the days of pay phones, and Peter had left the notebook at one in the main terminal—for only a few minutes, but when he realized what he had done and quickly returned, it was gone. Hans Teensma, who was the art director at *Outside*, had driven Peter to the airport and was seeing him off. They went on the search together. Then as now, there was no effective Lost and Found at any airport, so that took about five minutes before they started reverse-engineering the trash-disposal procedure. They found rooms full of sorted garbage but Peter, forlorn and increasingly resigned to the loss, had a flight to catch.

Hans continued the search, with no luck. Driving home that night empty-handed, he figured that only a crazy person would look at one of Peter's notebooks and not understand that someone had put a lot of work into it. They might not want to go to any trouble to find the owner, but something like that would be very difficult to just throw away. Hans returned to the airport the next afternoon and tracked down the notebook in the janitors' changing room. One of them had picked it up and just stuck it on a shelf before he went home.

Hans called Peter, and then Peter called me to tell me what a brilliant and wonderful thing Hans had done. Hans and I worked together again at *Rocky Mountain Magazine* and then lost touch, but for all the years that followed Peter and I would talk about how Hans had gone back to the airport and found that notebook. Peter always implied some kind of tangential credit for me, the way he often did with his friends when something they'd had very little to do with went right in the world. It was a way for us to talk about the value of work and friendship.

OUR CONVERSATIONS, especially when I'd reach him driving one of his numerous loops through the deep West, never started with where Peter was but where he was going next. All the travel, all the reporting were central to his work. "I like to hear and smell the countryside, the land my characters inhabit," he said, when he talked about writing. "I don't want these characters to step off the page, I want them to step out of the landscape." And they did. His detail was so unblinking that he put you inside those landscapes too, no matter how uncomfortable it was to be there with him.

In my copy of *The Snow Leopard*, where I found those bio notes, I had underlined the second paragraph of the first chapter, in which Peter's expedition stages out of the Nepalese village of Pokhara—where the last road ends.

> *We are glad to go. These edges of Pokhara might be tropical outskirts anywhere—vacant children, listless adults, bent dogs and thin chickens in a litter of sagging shacks and rubble, mud, weeds, stagnant ditches, bad sweet smells, vivid bright broken plastic bits, and dirty fruit peelings awaiting the carrion pig; for want of better fare, both pigs and dogs consume the human excrement that lies everywhere along the paths. In fair weather, all this flux is tolerable, but now at the dreg end of the rainy season, the mire of life seems leached into the sallow skins of these thin beings, who squat and soap themselves and wring their clothes each morning in the rain puddles.*

Peter's writing is full of such passages, somehow beautiful in their harshness. He was a realist that way, writing about life as he searched it out, but then spending time with him, you saw something else, something his friend Kurt Vonnegut described as "charm completely devoid of narcissism, like animals have."

-ENDIT-

Learning Curve (406)

As my confidence increased, I began to say that the definition of a good editor was a person with no friends. I was talking about dealing with writers, editing them with "a firm hand and terrifying clarity." That always got a laugh, but it was posturing. To be a good editor you need friends, or at least writers who like you enough that you can talk them into doing what you want them to do. At least that was a lot of the job for me.

I found that you only irritate good writers if you try to flatter them into working for you. I had this problem with a lot of writers because I loved their work so much. Joan Didion was flawlessly gracious, but not a fan of ass kissing.

With Hunter Thompson and George Plimpton, I began to think that I had to try to be somehow as interesting to them as they were to me. That was how Hunter and George worked with the Hells Angels or the Detroit Lions or politicians or circus midgets or whomever. George invited everyone he wrote about to his parties. Hunter wrote careful, hilarious letters and schemed relentlessly to make himself interesting to his biggest subjects, like Muhammad Ali and Bill Clinton. It was obvious. But I also found that just paying Hunter more money made me more interesting to him.

Even after the money was set, I learned never to suggest that another writer was coming on strong. I remember once mentioning to Tom McGuane that a couple of writers who were teaching in the writing program at the University of Montana in Missoula were turning out some sharp and tricky essays about the West. "I've done a lot of things in my life I'm not proud of," Tom said, seemingly without guile. "But I ain't never taught no creative writing."

Telling this story is not fair to McGuane, who is both generous and hilarious, but going into dialect as he did then was deadly. After Tom used that same line on a newspaper reporter doing a profile of him,

35

Never teaching no creative writing became a badge of professionalism in the movie business, and among hard-core freelancers in New York. It cracked me up, and was one of the jokes that led to a kinship with this or that writer as we built out our working relationship—and our respective mythologies about working together.

-ENDIT-

Boy Howdy! (1,197)

Gonna get me a pony
and an ounce of cocaine
goin' out to Montana
to fuck Tom McGuane

—ANONYMOUS

IF YOU WERE A WRITER from Montana, or had a place there, you somehow earned immediate status in both New York and L.A. After I moved there in 1980, I sometimes wondered why we were all so proud of it, but I loved the eccentric solidarity and the many writing and movie connections. Some were brief; others grew out of love affairs and rivalries that lasted until someone died. And even before anyone was dead (Richard Brautigan, suicide at forty-nine, 1984), Montana was a literary force field of those connections doubling back on themselves. I think in the beginning only Tom McGuane saw the celebrity overload on the horizon. Or maybe he just saw it coming when he looked in the mirror.

Tim Cahill moved to Livingston to write a book about McGuane but became his neighbor instead. He found a place outside town up Swingley Route at Poison Creek. Swingley Road, as it is called now, was a bouncy track of unpaved road that still runs up the edge of the Absarokas to the Boulder River and Big Timber. Poison Creek wasn't poison but the name spoke to the problematic past of ranching cattle up there. Cahill had been there for six months when I drove up from Denver, where *Rocky Mountain Magazine* had just launched.

Cahill's wife, Susan McBride, had progressive rheumatoid arthritis and just moving around the house was difficult for her. The Montana weather didn't help, especially compared to how it had been on the acre or so they had left behind in Northern California, but you never heard about that. When you talked to Susan, she talked about you.

She had been a beauty and carried herself like a wounded hero— which she was to all of us. She was a poet too, with a fast mouth that could turn even short conversations into games of meaning. If you wanted to talk about love, say, or getting high or drinking, Susan was your girl. She drank every day, usually from early afternoon into the night. She called Cahill "Cahill," and he bought her Jim Beam in half gallons and called her "McBride." The rest of us called her Susan.

IT WAS SPRING, and still cool in the evenings, and I arrived to find that she and Cahill had organized a dinner with Tom McGuane and some other writers, including Gatz Hjortsberg, and the painter Russell Chatham. The actor Peter Fonda and his wife, Becky, were there too, and we sat around outside watching the sky fade into one of those glories that explains the motto on Montana license plates. When the woman I had brought with me from Denver complimented Susan on the sunset, she said it went with the territory and took off on one of her tears about writing and journalism and where we were all headed and where she fit into things—her status in the *tribe*, as it were, because it was the West, after all.

"Boy howdy!" she'd say after making a point.

So *sure*, she said, she might be a big drinker but she was never confused about it, like some others she could mention. *Boy howdy!* on that. And by the way, she was enjoying the best possible weather in her head. We could all go racing from summit to summit or across the moors or wherever, and so what if she couldn't walk a mile down the road even if she had been sober. But there was never any self-pity in her *Boy howdy!* Susan would give you a wink and lift you with it. The wilder the better, she'd say, but she was never going to make it into the backcountry, the high windy places we all wrote about, the places where rock and water and sky hammer your eyes. *Boy howdy,* never going there. Better to look for trouble in town, forget the cliffs behind the house, more interesting to find a seat at the bar at the Mint or the Murray or the Wrangler. Or like that time in Mexico, the rest of us going fishing, leaving her on the porch with enough ice.

"The nature of wildness eludes me not," she said slowly. "And I don't have to jump out of *no stinkin' airplanes . . .* " She and Cahill both loved the "stinkin' badges" line from *The Treasure of the Sierra Madre*, and everyone laughed. We all knew that Cahill had written a piece for *Outside* about what it was like to skydive for the first time.

EVERYBODY LOVED CAHILL, especially Susan except sometimes she gave him a hard time, and this night was one of those times. She rattled the ice in her glass at him for another drink and started talking about what a genius McGuane was, starting with a line Tom had written somewhere about a debutante "committing experience" with shrimpers in Key West. *Boy howdy!* to committing experience.

"You're the best writer," she said looking at Tom and, ignoring his deflections, marched through an argument praising his novels *Ninety-two in the Shade* and *Panama*, which was just out and was drawing attacks for McGuane's having "gone Hollywood." *Boy howdy! And fuck that!* And by the way, Hollywood was a good place to go to get the money, something some other writers she could name had a little trouble doing.

Cahill just shrugged, but McGuane didn't like this, and neither did anyone else. It opened a bad drawer. No one ever talked about who was the best writer. That was for *New Yorker* writers to talk about in New York. Out here in the Writerly West, McGuane's surmounting success was either not discussed or was written off in jokes about his luck—if Tom were broke and stumbling around some fallow sugarcane field like the bums did in Florida, he'd probably fall and hit his head on a priceless conquistador breastplate.

The sky was darkening and we all kept drinking.

When Susan didn't let up, Cahill said she was right. So did Gatz and Chatham. Yes, Tom was the best writer. You could see it upset everyone, but maybe it relieved them too—like finally saying you're sorry to someone at your high school reunion. We kept drinking and Susan kept pushing, like some kind of reverse AA facilitator, asking questions and riffing. She was a writer too, but nobody read the poetry she wrote except Cahill. How did everyone feel about that? Fonda chimed in that Tom was better than he was at everything, which was interesting on some aberrant level because his wife, Becky, had been Tom's first wife.

Quoting *Panama* again, Susan said our little western barbecue was getting *too Cuban for words.* She was right, of course, and it went deeper into the night. More drinking. Someone got sick under the big yard light, throwing convulsive shadows up the dirt driveway. Nobody drove home. There we were, some of us lying drunk on our backs in the dirt, passed out or just staring up at bright stars in the cold Montana sky.

-ENDIT-

Tom McGuane (3,603)

WHEN McGUANE MOVED TO LIVINGSTON in 1968, he said it was because he didn't want his sporting life (hunting and fishing) to be "expeditionary" anymore, which meant he wanted it in his own backyard. Livingston was perfect, a railroad and ranching town on the Yellowstone River at the bottom of the Paradise Valley—a tough but friendly place that still had counter checks, unlocked doors and Dan Bailey's famous mail-order fly-tying business.

Tom's career was forming up, and he was married to Portia Rebecca Crockett, who had money of her own. They made friends easily and everybody loved Becky, who was petite and sexy, with old-fashioned manners. Becky described Tom's "beautiful, long back" as something he passed to their infant son, whom everyone called Young Thomas. Big Tom was strong-looking, and he sometimes explained himself by saying he didn't want to have "writer hands," a slap at his own MFA in playwriting from Yale and his Wallace Stegner Fellowship to Stanford, where he finished his first novel, *The Sporting Club*, the movie sale of which bankrolled what he named "the Raw Deal Ranch," just outside of Livingston.

Writing and fishing friends followed, with some—Hjortsberg, whom he had met at Yale, Brautigan, and Chatham, from Northern California—moving nearby. Jim Harrison visited often, driving in from Michigan. With McGuane and Becky as de facto gatekeepers, the Paradise Valley was increasingly visible as a hideout for creative work and good times. The locals welcomed everyone and were not yet cynical.

"SURE," the operator said, "Tom," . . . sounding like she knew him, when I called Livingston information. I was working on the start-up of *Outside* magazine out of the *Rolling Stone* offices in San Francisco, where I had landed the job by saying I would get interesting novelists to write about the natural world and whatever intrepid, enlightened young men and women were doing out there in it. This meant covering "adventure travel" and the new "extreme sports." We had a statement of purpose proclaiming a commitment to *the people, activities, literature, art and politics of the outdoors* . . . which I rattled off to Tom on the phone that morning.

"You probably don't want anything about hunting," he said.

He was right, but I said hunting would be fine, wonderful really, "whatever you want to write about." Getting him in the magazine would send out a literary signal. I had read his novels and the journalism he had done for *Sports Illustrated* and figured whatever he wrote would be ambitious. The problem would be that hunting was looked upon with horror by most of my new colleagues, as well as by the readership the *Rolling Stone* circulation department had identified as the ideal demographic for *Outside*.

I didn't know yet that "biting the hand that feeds you" was at the bottom of Tom's work philosophy—which in retrospect seems related to how we didn't talk about money except when he said, "Your top rate, right?" I was grateful to get off easy like that. We were paying two dollars a word, and I was embarrassed saying it out loud. Other magazines—*Esquire*, the *New Yorker*, *Rolling Stone*—were paying double that. Such specifics seemed like the last things on his mind.

McGUANE'S SECOND NOVEL, *The Bushwhacked Piano*, had come out in 1971 with the *New York Times* announcing "a talent of Faulknerian potential." The last sentence of the novel read: *I am at large.* More than being at large, Tom was lifting off. Every writer I knew was reading him. Saul Bellow described him as "a language star." The opening sentence of his third novel, two years later, *Ninety-two in the Shade*, felt generationally intimate. It was ominous and hilarious at the same time, articulating more or less the national mood in the mid-1970s: *Nobody knows, from sea to shining sea, why we are having all this trouble with our republic* . . . It was a very fast read with an exactness of intent reflected in the dedication: *for Beck for Beck for Beck.* Every word seemed perfect, both obvious and nuanced, "hinged and sprung," as Thomas Carney wrote in *Esquire.*

When the producer Elliott Kastner came to visit at Raw Deal to talk about projects, he took Tom's *Rancho Deluxe* screenplay upstairs to read while Tom fed the horses. Less than an hour later, Kastner was back down at the kitchen table announcing that he and Tom were going to make the movie and they were going to shoot it in Livingston. Already a local celebrity, Tom was now a rainmaker. The movie brought several million dollars into town. It also brought Frank Perry, who had directed *Play It As It Lays,* and a hipster cast—Slim Pickens, Sam Waterson, Harry Dean Stanton and Elizabeth Ashley—who all thought Livingston was a hoot and invited friends to visit. The leading man, Jeff Bridges, fell in love with a local girl named Susan Geston and bought a place up the road from Tom. Jimmy Buffett wrote the score, including "Livingston Saturday Night":

You got your Tony Lamas on, your jeans pressed tight,
You take a few tokes, make you feel all right,
Rockin' and rollin' on a Livingston Saturday night.
Pickup's washed and you just got paid.
With any luck at all you might even get laid,
'Cause they're pickin' and a-kickin'
on a Livingston Saturday night.

Livingston was still authentic, but now there were movie stars on the next bar stool at the Wrangler and playing pool at the Long Branch ("the Short Stick"). Lots of people were flying in to what Tom called "flyover country" to check out the scene. The director Sam Peckinpah, who didn't have anything to do with *Rancho Deluxe,* moved from L.A. into the Murray Hotel, where there was a high-stakes poker game every night, and producers and directors were showing up with offers for Tom. He wrote *The Missouri Breaks,* which Arthur Penn made with Jack Nicholson and Marlon Brando, but first there was *92 in the Shade,* the movie—shot in Key West starring Peter Fonda, Margot Kidder and Warren Oates, along with Ashley and Stanton. Tom stepped in to direct when Robert Altman pulled out at the last minute.

Key West had been on his circuit since boyhood fishing trips with his father, and by the late 1960s he was back, hanging out with guides but often spending days on the water alone, learning the complexities of the tides and tarpon and permit. It was a fishing-and-writing life, with plenty of dope and prowling the bars with old friends Guy de la Valdene, the poet Dan Gerber and Chatham and Harrison. The movie was tangentially about that life, and directing it kicked Tom's intensity up several notches. Chatham had given him the nickname "Captain Berserko" for his up-all-night antics in Marin County, where they were steelhead-fishing buddies, but that had been just the beginning; 92 *in the Shade* was Captain Berserko time for everyone on the set, especially the actors. "Maybe there was too much acid" is how Becky once explained it to me.

Tom was prone to tangents and distracted by his sexual escapades. His raucous public affair with Elizabeth Ashley made tabloid headlines and led to his split from Becky, who took off with Warren Oates, then Fonda. By the time the film wrapped, Tom was with Margot Kidder, who was soon pregnant. There is a photograph of Tom with Tennessee Williams and Truman Capote at the wrap party. Tennessee and Truman are both laughing. Tom, drink in one hand, cigarette in the other, is between them, staring into the camera. People sometimes said Tom had warm eyes, calm and friendly. Not in that picture.

Tom's first divorce (Becky), his second marriage (Margot), the birth of their daughter (Maggie), and his second divorce (Margot) all happened in less than a year. Becky went on to marry Fonda, moving with him to Indian Hill Ranch, next to the Raw Deal, where Tom was then living with Margot. Peter started calling Tom his husband-in-law, and maybe sometimes it was that simple. Tom's bad luck was that his life was getting more attention than his work. There was even a gossipy piece about him in *Esquire* with the headline

"McGuane's Game," and a subhead that asked, "This crazy life that novelist Thomas McGuane has been living—is it a dream? Or a nightmare?"

When *92 in the Shade* got a terrific review in the *New York Times* but flopped at the box office, Tom told *People* magazine, "I know it's a good film, and as Fidel Castro once said, 'History will absolve me.'"

THAT FIRST PIECE TOM WROTE for *Outside* was "The Heart of the Game," an almost cinematic contemplation of hunting that snuck up on you, a technique I understood later was instinctive to him. The first sentence: *Hunting season in your own back yard becomes with time, if you love hunting, less and less expeditionary. This year, when Montana's eager frosts knocked my garden on its butt, the hoe seemed more like the rifle than it ever had before, the vegetables more like game.*

At first read, it seemed confusing. I told Tom I was thinking the piece should start with the second graph, which began, *My son and I went scouting before the season and saw some antelope in the high plains foothills of the Absaroka Range.* All we would have to do, I said, is add *hunting* before *season.*

"I wrote it on purpose," Tom said.

"Well . . ." I knew that, of course, but had never thought much about writers' intentions. I was proud of making quick decisions about ledes. I could work through my reasoning—something about telling the readers where you're taking them, getting right to it, whatever *it* happened to be. But what if I was unthinkingly undermining the ambition of the writer? That set me straight. An editor could do nothing worse.

"And you asked for it," Tom added.

Tom made his killing shot in the piece with the buck *bounding toward zero gravity, taking his longest arc into the bullet and the finality and terror of all you have made of the world, the finality you know you share even with your babies and their inherited and ambiguous dentition, the finality that any minute now you will meet as well.* I was

45

stopped cold by *ambiguous dentition* and have never read anything like it.

The piece ended with Tom dressing out the buck he had hung over a rafter in his woodshed with a lariat: *I could see the intermittent blue light of the television against my bedroom ceiling from where I stood. I stopped the twirling of the buck, my hands deep in the sage-scented fur, and thought: This is either the beginning or the end of everything.*

I didn't change a comma, top to bottom, and the piece ran in the first issue and set the literary tone for the magazine. Tom wrote a dozen pieces for *Outside* over the next couple years, lifting the magazine with his tight control of language, humor and what one critic called his mastery of "macho angst," whatever that was. He wrote columns about fishing and dogs and growing up in Michigan, and longer pieces about rodeo and team roping (*I like to get a leetle loaded and rope horned cattle*) and taking his horses *to contest.* I sent him an *Outside* T-shirt, and he wore it to a cutting. He told me once that he liked "long reaches," and the reach he was proudest of was the one between being nominated for a National Book Award (*Ninety-two in the Shade*) and winning the team roping at the small local rodeo in Gardner the same year, 1973. We were on the phone maybe once a week then and finally I asked him about the new novel I knew he had going.

"It's not for you," he said, meaning *Outside.* "Maybe it's not for anybody."

Odd, I thought. Not like him. He told me he had a hangover. Later, when I got a bound galley of *Panama*, it was a relentlessly funny read, even as it was about loss and depression. Tom let you know where he was going in the lede: *This is the first time I've worked without a net. I want to tell the truth. At the same time, I don't want to start a feeding frenzy. You stick your neck out and you know what happens. It's obvious.*

Tom thought it was his best novel although, except for the *New York Times* and the *Village Voice*, it was reviewed as various combinations of self-indulgent, self-absorbed and self-destructive. It was in fact a tremendous high-wire act of honest writing but the critics gnawed on Tom's celebrity as if he had betrayed some monastic tradition of keeping your head down. It didn't help that his main character and narrator, Chester "Chet" Pomeroy, was a performance artist and rock star who sometimes did the wrong thing trying to save himself. At one point early in the novel Chet says, *There was as much cocaine as ever. I had a pile of scandal magazines to see what had hit friends and loved ones.* The critics' expectations smashed head-on into Tom's life as tabloid fodder.

Tom's was not an unknown predicament for a writer and, as with Hemingway and Fitzgerald, the equation is always Writer + Drinking + Fame = Squandered Talent. But his Captain Berserko persona didn't prove the equation and Tom knew it. Visiting Key West years later, he was asked if he thought it possible for a person to write like an angel and yet in every way be despicable. He said it was highly probable and in many cases a fact.

AFTER *OUTSIDE*, I edited Tom at *Rocky Mountain, Smart* and *Esquire,* but then we didn't work together for more than ten years, until he wrote a piece for me at *Sports Illustrated.* No one was better at decoding the redeeming value of sporting ritual, and Tom was interested in writing about fishing again — not for his beloved trout or tarpon but for snook. Snook, he explained, were covert, suspicious and sneaky even if they did crash bait. *Sleazy* was another word he used. Snook humiliated anglers. *Hard to see, hard to hook, hard to land and, because they are so good to eat, hard to release.* Tom always had trouble catching them. Plus: *When they're at the threshold of death, a translucent window appears in the top of their heads.* So the twenty-eight million or so NFL-obsessed *SI* readers got close to eight thousand words on snook.

But not just snook. Toward the end of the piece Tom wrote that he had *once had an episode of serious depression, and its onset was marked by a loss of interest in fishing.* This was the sort of hairpin

47

turn he was so good at, as if he were driving with one of those spinner "suicide" knobs from the 1950s on the steering wheel of his prose. He wrote on that he marveled at people *discussing depression, gnawing the topic of their own malaise like dogs on a beef knuckle. My experience of it was a disinclination to speak at all. I had the feeling of being locked in a very small and unpleasant room with no certainty of exit, and I recall thinking that it was the sickest you could possibly be and that my flesh had been changed to plaster. My business at the time was flight from expectations.*

He had knocked me over again, and I read on as he *thought of incessant-angler pal and novelist Richard Brautigan, who relinquished his fly rod as he spooled up for suicide. Fishing, for many, is an indispensable connection to earth and life, and it matters little that the multitude that practices it is incapable of translating its ambiguities to another idiom.*

That's not writing you edit. As always with Tom, though, when I sent him the galleys, he came back with detail work that he approached like finish carpentry. In one passage he said to *change "helpful" to "optimistic." It was supposed to be "hopeful" but "hope" appears a line or 2 later for an "awk rep."* It was like that with Tom every time.

When Tom found something he wanted to do, he worked at it systematically. He studied. He could fish, hunt, sail, ride, rope, cook, whatever . . . all better than anybody anyone knew. By this time he was a member of the American Academy of Arts and Letters, the National Cutting Horse Association Hall of Fame and the Fly Fishing Hall of Fame. On the occasion of that last honor he e-mailed that it was *a consequence of unscrupulous self-promotion.* I wrote back that as editors are always looking to take credit I wanted to get in on the festivities, no matter how distasteful.

He had written a lot about fishing, which is, I suppose, what he meant. I had run his journalism about fishing as well as most all else he was interested in writing about, including a little cooking and even some golf (chiefly wading for golf balls), and before the snook piece he had sent me what he called a souvenir of our work, a beautiful, slipcased limited edition collection of his fishing pieces called *Live Water*. Directly following the title page I read an acknowledgment to me as an editor *whose conviction that those whose stories he most wants to read usually don't feel like writing them enabled him to pry most of the following out of me.*

Ha! I thought. But he had precisely defined one of the truths of editing. It was always that way with the best writers. If you could match them up with the right idea, all you had to do was hook paragraphs.

LONG AFTER MONTANA SEEMED IMPORTANT to anyone who didn't live there, Keith Kelly started calling me "Big Sky" in his media column in the *New York Post*. It was pejorative, mocking, and I finally called Keith and asked him to lose it. Keith said he thought it was funny but if it was a big deal to me . . . I said it was, and after I hung up I thought about flying out of Bozeman to New York to take the *Rolling Stone* job. I remembered sitting next to Jeff Bridges, who was reading a script. I was looking down at the Yellowstone flowing out of the valley like a silver ribbon and telling myself that it was important to remember what I was leaving because I wouldn't be coming back for a long time. I don't know how I knew that.

When I did finally return it was for the wedding of Young Thomas, who had grown up to be famous on his own terms as a knife maker in the Samurai swordforging tradition, an artist, with a studio in Bozeman. Much else had changed too, not that everyone had grown up. Sam Peckinpah had died, but he was still talked about for moving to a place up the valley and then buying the local cab company to ensure his late-night rides home from the poker game. Real estate was soaring, and another wave of movie stars was arriving. Dennis Quaid was building a house near the old Raw Deal with his new wife, Meg Ryan. With very little evidence of a counterculture hangover, Livingston was turning into one of those towns that make Ten Best Places to Live lists. Russell Chatham had his own art gallery, publishing business and restaurant. There were rumors that Robert Redford was coming. 49

Tom had been married to Laurie Buffett, Jimmy's sister, for more than a decade by then, and they now lived one watershed over on an immaculate ranch in the Boulder River Valley, outside of tiny McLeod, in Sweet Grass County. He was raising cattle, working his cutting horses and fly-fishing all over the world. He had quit drinking, just stopped by force of will like he did everything. He always had what Bill Kittredge, who ran the writing program in Missoula, called a "genius for living well," and now his reach was about that and family, too.

At the wedding he looked the perfect father of the groom, tall and calm and handsome, any tempestuousness lifted off him. When we shook hands that night, his eyes were warm, deep but untroubled. The reception went late into the night and at one point Susan Bridges and I were talking outside. Men in boots and hats were smoking in the moonlight with sophisticated women. Montana was different now; we agreed easily on that. She wasn't sure which had changed more, the people or the place, but they had changed each other. "Friends are still friends," I said lamely. I wondered if the locals were finally turning cynical about all the people who had come and gone.

"I'm a local," she said.

"You live in Santa Barbara."

"Everybody grows up," she laughed.

Like Tom, I thought.

"Even Tom."

WHEN I READ A TOM McGUANE story now, mostly in the *New Yorker,* his talent spins me like it did when I first read *Ninety-two in the Shade.* It's all there, the uncanny language, the surprising specifics that made me a better editor just by reading his sentences. Before I had the chance to edit any of the fine writers I worked with later, that first go-around with Tom set me straight.

–ENDIT–

Cahill (1,025)

W<small>IDE-SHOULDERED AND TALL</small>, Tim Cahill had been a scholarship Division I swimmer at Wisconsin. After college he put on a little weight, which gave him a powerful presence, but he was gentle and could hold his liquor and never got too high, either. When you saw him in the water, you thought of dolphins—at least that's what Susan McBride said about him once. She said she liked that, and that he had called her McBride when they first started going out and still did even though they'd been married for a while. Cahill had friends who were cartoonists and that was cool, too, and not surprising when you read his copy.

Cahill was there, grinning, at the editorial meetings when *Outside* incubated out of *Rolling Stone*'s "Men's Issue." (As if every issue of *Rolling Stone* wasn't already . . .) And at *Outside* he soared as a writer, developing a recognizable voice in its own evolving, hybrid hipster-environmentalist-investigative-travel-adventure-humor genre. Whenever he was asked about his job, he said it was simply to "create great literature that will live forever in the minds and hearts of men and women for time immemorial. Goddamn it."

We sent him to Peru in search of the Lost City of the Cloud People, and he called in from Lima after three weeks in the Amazonas jungle. The assignment had started on the come. We had never expected him to find any "stinkin' Lost Cities" (as in "stinkin' badges"). The search would be the story; we had agreed on that. And if he got sick, as most travelers did in Amazonas, he would write about that. But he didn't get sick, and with the aid of local coca leaves and shrewd management of his guides, the *four* Lost Cities of the Cloud People were no longer lost, and he would henceforth be known as the great explorer Don Timoteo.

Our machetes swung by our sides. . . . Old women gathered up the children and shooed them indoors as we passed. We had come from Congona, and something in the eyes of the people begged us to swagger. We were brave men, foolish men.

Another early piece found him in a Northern Cheyenne sweat lodge chanting *hi-how-are-ya, hi-how-are-ya, hi-how-are-ya* with tribal elders. He also found exploding bat shit while spelunking in Kentucky. Cahill had range, too. In the winter of 1977, when he went down the west coast of Mexico to swim with the sea turtles, he came back with evidence of the slaughter of an endangered species: *Thousands upon thousands of eggs, all rotting in [an] evil heap . . . 90 million years of evolution going to waste on the beach at Escobilla.*

He hit hard again for *Rolling Stone* a couple months later with a dark reconstruction of the Jonestown massacre in Guyana, where 920 people died in a sickening mass suicide organized by Peoples Temple leader Jim Jones. This was the greatest single loss of American civilian life in a nonnatural, nonaccidental disaster prior to September 11, 2001. Cahill's fine-toothed reporting of the gruesome details resonated with a horrifying humanity:

A woman in her late twenties stepped out of the crowd. She was carrying her baby. The doctor estimated the child's weight and measured an amount of the milky liquid into a syringe. A nurse pumped the solution into the baby's mouth. The potassium cyanide was bitter to the tongue, and so the nurse gave the baby a sip of punch to wash it down. Then the mother drank her potion.

Death came in less than five minutes. The baby went into convulsions, and Jones—very calm, very deliberate—kept repeating, "We must take care of the babies first." Some mothers brought their own children up to the killing trough. Others took children from reluctant mothers. Some of the parents and grandparents became hysterical, and they screamed and sobbed as their children died.

Like every good reporter I ever knew, a shocking first look at the dark side drew Cahill further into it. His book about the murderer John Wayne Gacy, *Buried Dreams: Inside the Mind of a Serial Killer,* was as riveting as it was disturbing, unmasking the motivation of a horrific madman. But adventure travel was the genre he would ultimately own. Traveling, as he put it, *like a hysterical monkey,* always with a bottle of Tabasco sauce because *roasted beetles can be bland,* he roamed from the Pantanal swampland in Brazil to the Hecate Strait in the far Pacific Northwest.

I could go on and on . . . like Tim did—floating the Ganges River; riding horseback across the steppes of Mongolia; dropping in on the Karowai hunter-gatherers in what was then Irian Jaya (now West Papua); surveying active volcanoes, salt mines, toxic-waste dumps; tracking the Caspian "ghost" tiger on Turkey's southeastern borders and finding that war between Iran and Iraq was, however absurdly, wildlife's best ally against extinction. He wrote stories, not issues, but the politics always came through. All of the above, including the politics, is hard, often uncomfortable, and sometimes dangerous in very fundamental ways. But I have never wondered why Cahill did it. He did it because it was so much fun.

Getting in and out of trouble was what made Cahill's stories work, and that led him to his own definition of fellow travelers. A decade or so after we launched *Outside,* he and his professional partner, Garry Sowerby, set a world record in speed for driving the length of the American continents, from Tierra del Fuego to Prudhoe Bay, Alaska. By then he was already known for lines like my favorite: *A journey is best measured in friends, not in miles.*

WHEN OUR CAREERS TOOK US in different directions Cahill and I lost touch, at one point for more than twenty years. I kept up by reading everything he wrote. And then, when Susan McBride was dying in a hospice in California, Tim e-mailed a lot of us, letting us know the bad news and how we might contact her. Looking after her to the end.

-ENDIT-

Pygmalion (1,672)

IN A LOG HOUSE on the Yellowstone River in the Paradise Valley, Arnold Schwarzenegger sat on the floor in front of a stone fireplace smoking a cigar. He would take a puff and then stare at the cigar ash, closed into himself. Charles Gaines, who had brought Arnold to Montana, was in the open kitchen working on dinner with friends who lived close by. A couple local writers were there too, all of them standing around Charles, reluctant to engage with Arnold.

"What are you thinking over there by the fire?" Charles called into the living room.

"I am thinking, 'What a *vunderous* thing to be Charles Gaines,'" Arnold said, mocking his own accent. "He is so handsome, so brave . . ."

Everyone laughed. Being Charles Gaines did look good: promising novelist, television sports correspondent and, now, discoverer of Arnold. The next day they were going into the Yellowstone backcountry to shoot a segment for ABC's popular *American Sportsman* with Doug Peacock, who was known then for talking to grizzlies, even shouting them down. It was crazy, but Peacock had done it.

The segment was about Arnold too, of course, part of the exposure and polishing Charles had been giving him, taking him home to meet his family in Alabama, introducing him to Andy Warhol at the Factory, having late dinners at Elaine's in New York. It was 1984 and most of what I knew about Charles came from his novel *Stay Hungry*, about a son of southern gentry who finds his identity in the decidedly unliterary culture of bodybuilding. What I knew about Arnold came from *Pumping Iron*, the documentary Charles had made with George Butler. The film ended with Arnold being declared Mr. Olympia and celebrating by smoking marijuana and announcing his retirement. Butler was quoted widely calling Arnold "our Pygmalion." Charles never said anything like that.

Joints were passed at dinner, but Arnold smoked only cigars. The wonders of fly-fishing were discussed interchangeably with literary gossip and recent assignments. Arnold listened quizzically, refusing to be drawn in, but you could see his sharpness. At the end of the dinner Charles proposed a toast to him.

"No," Arnold said, raising his glass. "To Charles Gaines, and the rest of the American grizzly bears who want to eat me up."

A COUPLE YEARS AFTER that dinner, Charles called with an idea. The "Survival Game," as he explained it, had been inspired by "The Most Dangerous Game," the 1924 short story by Richard Connell about a wealthy big-game hunter from New York who winds up in an isolated preserve, where he becomes the quarry of a bored aristocrat. In Charles's game, players armed with those Nel-Spot pistols used by ranchers to mark trees and livestock with splats of paint would stalk one another through the woods, testing their various survival skills as they tried to capture a home-base flag.

"And they blast each other?" I asked.

"They can eliminate one another," Charles said. "But I'm interested in which skills will win out." The first players would include a Vietnam vet, a New England forester, a turkey hunter, a doctor and an investment banker. They would compete in the woods surrounding his farm in New Hampshire, and I was invited—or should at least send a reporter to cover it. (The forester won.)

Paintball, as it came to be called, grew into a billion-dollar sport played by millions around the world, but Charles sold his interest after a year and never seemed particularly bothered by his timing. He said he would always be a writer first. For a while it seemed like every writer I knew wanted to write about fishing, but none more than Charles, and editing him became an exercise in channeling his angling enthusiasms. Most great fishers *win ugly*, which means they simply will not be denied their chosen fish on any particular day. Charles went the other way. He was not obsessed but, rather, so graceful in his fishing life as to pass from time to time into what his friend the sporting writer Vance Bourjaily called "the trance of instinct." Charles said this was where his life was most vivid—sacred, even. But he was funny about it, calculating that the amortization of the market value of the fish he caught some years would run to $500 a pound.

His writing alluded to Hemingway and Zane Grey in both anecdote and spirit, and he got them into the same piece with musical references to "Bayou Pon Pon" or Dion and the Belmonts. He would introduce you to the "Hegel of fishing guides," and he knew his fish. For example, most saltwater game fish lived *like Greek playboys, following pleasure and abundance from one sunny spot to the next.* Charles had a lot of that in him, too. Beyond the reflective silences of the tiny trout stream, he knew all about the *nonstop wet dream of fun in a faraway place catching huge fish to loud music with a buzz on,* as he described it in an *Esquire* piece about marlin fishing in the South Pacific.

As a sidecar to his journalism Charles started a travel business, identifying and booking high-end fishing and hunting destinations. His criteria for the lodges started with excellent game, but he also demanded that days spent have *symmetry, excitement, and spiritual comfort to them.* His job as CEO was both the scouting and the quality control—his market rich, middle-aged white guys eager to boast that they had enjoyed a drink with Charles at Ballynahinch Castle in Connemara or Wilson's on the Miramichi, or maybe even Perry Munro's smallmouth spike camp on the Black River. His life was so full of sport, travel and action that boredom had to be a sitting duck. If you looked at Charles from a distance he was like those playboy game fish, *following pleasure and abundance from one sunny spot to the next.* But he was writing less, and his time on the road pulled at the seams of his life.

LIKE HIS OTHER EDITORS, I was invited to visit, first at his New Hampshire farm, where he and his wife, Patricia, entertained streams of houseguests—writers, movie people, artists, athletes, charter captains, venture capitalists, academics . . . Patricia was beautiful, a former Miss Alabama, and an artist. Charles was tall and assured, vigorously handsome. When they separated, it was as if the good life was taking revenge on them—victims of the fast lane that had run through their farm.

Charles stayed in New Hampshire, alone and depressed, brooding about his failures as a husband, how vain, feckless and bullying he had been. He called me once during that time. Painting alone in her apartment on the Upper West Side in Manhattan, Patricia had fallen into despair and given away all her jewelry, including her wedding and engagement rings, to homeless women on the street. Did I know anyone in the NYPD who could help get it back? More important, he wanted *Patricia* back.

When she agreed to give the marriage another chance, they found 160 acres of wild land on the northeast coast of Nova Scotia and wove a plan. It had forests and meadows and cliffs overlooking the sea. They would build a house there with their children over the coming summer, and they would build it with their own hands.

The book that came out of that summer, *A Family Place*, was careful, heartening. Charles's narrative followed the house building, living in tents without electricity or running water, relearning the pleasures and limitations of a simplified life. It was as far as you could get from flirting with movie stars and the carelessness that left incriminating debris. Patricia had once walked in on Charles to find the wife of one of his best friends blowing PCP up his nose with a straw. Charles had found letters to her from another man not meant for him to read. Now, echoing on every page, was the story of two people who, unconsciously and not, had been bent on destroying their marriage but had found a way to save it.

IN 2009, WHEN THE MANUFACTURERS and promoters who'd profited most from paintball decided to establish a Hall of Fame, they wanted Charles to be in the first class. I talked him into writing a piece for *Sports Illustrated*. It had been almost thirty years since that first game on his farm in New Hampshire. His lede was *One way of measuring a life—maybe as good a method as any other—is on the basis of how much peculiarity you have helped to generate.*

Perfect, I thought; not cynical but with an edge. It was the same voice you read in his sporting journalism, and it made you smile. His collection of pieces, *The Next Valley Over,* was the book Meriwether Lewis might have written about fishing if he had had a sense of humor— or maybe just been a better writer and as good a fisherman as Charles, which he was not. Reading it, you saw Charles leading his own personal Corps of Discovery, exploring life's possibilities way beyond shooting jawbreakers of paint at your friends to get your adrenaline rush.

Because I had edited many of the pieces, Charles asked me to write an introduction. I wrote that Charles was an animist who believed in the ritual of fishing, but I was thinking about that house in Nova Scotia, and what it had taken to rebuild his family with it. When Arnold was elected governor of California in 2003, Charles wrote a story for me at *Men's Journal* that called Arnold a *wizard of his own growth,* saying that his story is *like Gatsby's . . . not because of its payoff of riches and fame, but because it says unequivocally what we all want most to believe about ourselves: that we can be our own Pygmalions.*

Like Charles, I thought, who in his own words had been *caught and released.*

-ENDIT-

P. J. O'Rourke (607)

P. J. O'ROURKE LIVED IN A TRIANGLE-SHAPED apartment above the Queens-Midtown Tunnel in Manhattan. The living room came to a point like the bow of a ship heading uptown on First Avenue. Other writers knew P.J. as an editor at the *National Lampoon*, where they had put a dog with a pistol in its ear on the cover with the headline "If You Don't Buy This Magazine, We'll Kill This Dog." I'm not sure why, but that cover line and that pointed apartment seemed to make sense together.

We often wound up at the same bar or table or party—sometimes in that order over a single night. He looked a little like Ringo Starr, but in a handsome way, and he had lots of girlfriends and writer friends, too. He told me that whenever he had a little money in the bank he applied for higher credit lines and that I should, too.

"It's not like we've got a secure future," he said, but it was also clear that he was going to figure out something smart for himself—maybe even as a writer. He had just gone freelance. "Time to grow up," he said. "We're screwed."

P.J. had been a liberal with long hair and underground newspaper credits—his politics formed by the Vietnam War, the subtext of which, he said, was "saving one's own butt." That changed at the *Lampoon*. His most famous piece was "How to Drive Fast on Drugs While Getting Your Wing-Wang Squeezed and Not Spill Your Drink," which P.J. used as a liftoff to become what he called a "pants-down Republican":

I think our agenda is clear. We are opposed to: government spending, Kennedy kids, seat-belt laws, busing our children anywhere other than Yale, trailer courts near our vacation homes, all tiny Third World countries that don't have banking secrecy laws, aerobics, the U.N., taxation without tax loopholes, and jewelry on

60

men. We are in favor of: guns, drugs, fast cars, free love (if our
wives don't find out), a sound dollar, and a strong military with
spiffy uniforms.

P.J.'s work as an editor and writer at the *Lampoon* nailed a sensibility many of his colleagues cashed in on when they stepped easily into
the movie business, starting with *Animal House* (1978). P.J. took his
shot with a Rodney Dangerfield vehicle called *Easy Money* and used
the payday as a down payment on a small house in New Hampshire
and a Porsche. Problem was, he hated the work as much as he loved
that 911 Turbo.

"It's just a stupid movie," P.J. said when we were driving from New
Hampshire to Boston. He was going to drop me at the airport and
then spend the day working with Rodney on the script.

"Come on . . ." I said. Like everyone I knew in journalism, I was
envious of movie money.

"I should know how bad it is," he said. "I'm writing it."

There were three other writers on *Easy Money*, including Rodney.
The setup was that a hard-drinking, pot-smoking, obsessive gambler
had to change his ways to inherit $10 million from his puritanical
mother-in-law. The marketing language would read: *No Cheating!*
No Gambling! No Booze! No Smoking! No Pizza! No Nothin'! We're
taking all the fun out of life—and putting it into a Movie!

P.J.'s script called for Rodney to lose thirty pounds as he got healthy
over the story arc.

"He's never going to do that," P.J. said.

"Good luck," I said, getting out of the Porsche at the shuttle
terminal.

"No more movies," P.J. said.

I wondered how high he had pushed his credit lines.

-ENDIT-

Money (1970)

MONEY WAS ALWAYS A PROBLEM. There was never enough and it was always late, making the life of a magazine freelancer problematic at best and impossible for many—a special kind of pride-killing hell that grew out of the worst combination of ambition and disappointment.

Money was key to making most assignments, although some established writers who were doing well with novels or in the movie business would sometimes work cheap if they liked the idea. They just didn't want to feel stupid about the money. But many writers, some more than competent, couldn't make enough writing for magazines to have anything like a sustaining career. Editors didn't talk about this, probably because as editors on someone's payroll they never felt that pain, even though they knew it to be real.

Big talent was no guarantee of success, although sometimes everything worked out well if you had it. When she was just beginning to write, Elizabeth Gilbert sold me (at *Esquire*) a short story about a truculent cowboy falling for a female ranch hand in Wyoming. The story was called "Pilgrims" and under the title I put: "The Debut of an American Writer: The first unpublished short story writer to debut in *Esquire* since Norman Mailer." I loved that story.

"Are you kidding?" she said the morning I bought it, sitting across from me at my desk. I had invited her in for a meeting, but my assistant had made the appointment without telling her why.

"Four thousand bucks," I said, showing off, and then quoted Samuel Johnson: "'No man but a blockhead ever wrote, except for money.'" Not funny.

"I just want to write," she said, as uncynically as I have ever heard that said.

She was twenty-three then and she didn't know it but her career was going to take off with magazine pieces leading to best-selling books and movies (*Coyote Ugly*; *Eat, Pray, Love*; *The Signature of All Things*). But even as a rising success in magazines, she was sometimes short of cash. That wasn't funny, either.

AT EVERY MAGAZINE THERE WERE unending fire drills to get writers paid. Money had to be wired to places like Woody Creek and Missoula and Key West. Everyone had their own values and cash-flow problems, and they worked them out like gypsy states as best they could with shifting alliances, more or less braiding ropes to rustle what the very successful freelancer Jon Bradshaw called "donkey money" from the rich caravans of greedy, expense-account publishers.

Let me edit that over-written sentence: Everyone had ~~their own values and~~ cash-flow problems, and ~~they~~ worked them out ~~like gypsy states~~ as best they could with ~~shifting alliances, more or less braiding ropes to rustle what the very successful freelancer Jon Bradshaw called "donkey money" from the rich caravans of~~ greedy ~~expense-account~~ publishers. Notice that fifty words just became sixteen. If you were getting paid by the word, that is significant math. Writers were always on the short end except, in this case, where I kept the redundant word "greedy."

What makes this even worse is that word rates have dropped like rocks in draining ponds. Paying three dollars a word was no problem for me at *Rolling Stone* and *Esquire*, and there were many writers at Condé Nast magazines getting five dollars. Twenty years later, a dollar a word makes writers almost happy, in light of what they might get from even a thriving website like the Huffington Post. Understanding traffic formulas tied to compensation, and conversations about the importance of exposure do not make writers feel better.

Getting paid on time and having expenses reimbursed could be the most difficult and frustrating part of the business, much harder than landing the assignment in the first place. It's worse now, especially when dealing with big publishing companies that string out freelance payment as a matter of policy. This is "the float" bankers talk about. The number of necessary approvals on a fixed timeline

63

from the day the editor accepts the piece takes beyond six weeks at many magazines. So the writer calls the editor, the editor calls accounting, which circles back with the news that the general manager or whomever has not signed off yet.

In the days when I was coming up, top editors and publishing executives enjoyed lavish expense accounts and numerous perks: country club memberships, first-class travel, black radio cars on constant call. The top women fashion editors and publishers had wardrobe allowances (as well as discounts from designers). An editor I knew at *People* joked one Christmas about expensing $20,000 of veal piccata that year. Writers would hear about such high-handed excess and complain to their editor, who would likely take them out for some veal piccata, and that would be that.

Most writers were bad negotiators, some even bragging about being bad at business as if that elevated their writing careers to an admirable level of idealism. Agents could be useful but never wanted to be bothered with their 10 or 15 percent of what magazine pieces paid unless they were important to their client, which was true only if the client had nothing better going—a book most often, or a movie or TV project. There were exceptions, of course, but those were all love stories, like Barry Levinson, who always wanted to write about Baltimore sports, or Tom Robbins on Debra Winger, and those guys were already rich.

Almost every writer I edited had a moment, or many, when they were tapped out. Even Tom McGuane, who always seemed flush, told me once that he was going to "sell Laurie's silver." Tim Cahill signed his letters "Wolf at door." I lost track of the disconnected phones. Hunter Thompson turned getting paid into theater, stopping just short of sending dead cats in the mail.

-ENDIT-

Bob Ward (1,550)

WARD CALLED ME at my office at *Rolling Stone* and asked if I knew what Lee Marvin's last words were.

"You do," I said, "or you wouldn't be calling about it."

"'At least I outlived that motherfucker Danny Kaye.'"

"You made that up."

"Well, those were his last words *to me* . . . on the phone, when he told me how sick he was."

Lee Marvin, the baddest, coolest movie star of the 1960s and '70s, had died that week at sixty-three in Tucson, where he'd been living with his high school sweetheart and second wife, Pam, and where Ward had visited them for a profile for *Rolling Stone* ("Drinks with Liberty Valance"). Like most of the people Ward wrote about, Lee and Pam had become his friends. He had also written about Marvin's only rival for Hollywood cool, the hipster leading man Robert Mitchum ("Mr. Bad Taste and Trouble Himself"), in what he was calling his "Tough Guy" series, which would become part of a collection called *Renegades*, published by Tyrus Books long after he had left journalism for television.

In the book's introduction, Ward described himself as having been a *mustachioed, cowboy-haired, ill-kempt, bourbon-drinking, wild man who would go anywhere at a moment's notice, meet total strangers, get them to reveal crucial things about themselves, sleep two hours a night, come back home on the red-eye with a filled notebook and then sit down and lash together a ten-thousand-word story over the weekend, while still finding time to play the guitar, go to all-night discos with . . .* I remember bars, not discos, and the talent beneath all that swagger. Ward was a sensitive guy, but he didn't let you see much of that, at least not in the beginning.

When he turned to journalism, Ward had already written *Shedding Skin*, which had won a National Endowment for the Arts first novel award and had gotten him a solid teaching job at Hobart College, in upstate NY—which he walked away from, saying he was bored. Journalism came easily to him. He picked up sharp details (Vietnam strongman Nguyen Cao Ky wearing *a heroic black jump suit, his lithe body strung like a bow, his lavender scarf trailing war mythology like a Sam Peckinpah dream,*) and was a natural storyteller and a deceptive listener. People told him things before they knew they were opening up. Secrets flowed—like how tough and closed off and dangerous Lee Marvin's father had been with him, and how, *literally* how, Lee had killed Japanese soldiers during the war with his father's .45. And deeper secrets too, about fathers and sons that Ward saved for himself.

Sometimes after he filed, I'd call him and start quoting his piece back to him as a compliment. Ward's first sentence about Robert Mitchum told you just how wild the piece was going to get: *A big, crazy, sexy, sixty-five-year-old little boy who can't get used to the idea that he's supposed to act like, like* Ward Cleaver, *you dig?*

And in the next paragraph you learned: *All he drinks nowadays is tequila—and milk, though not together.* A little later, Mitchum's *eyelids hang down his face like two broken blinds in a flophouse.* At another point in the piece Mitchum tells Ward that Marilyn Monroe *"had the guts of a lion."*

Ward's pieces were all like that, hallucinations of a *newer* New Journalism, and Ward cranked them out for eight years, writing two more novels along the way, *Cattle Annie and Little Britches* (1977, as well as the screenplay) and *The Sandman* (1978), and working long and hard on a third, *Red Baker.* But the novels were in line behind Ward's big-game profiles, and he went after the biggest: Clint Eastwood, Larry Flynt, Reggie Jackson, Waylon Jennings . . .

Covering celebrities—more specifically, talking them into cooperating for pieces and photo shoots, getting the all-important access—was an ego-triggered minefield that usually fell to editors to negotiate, and almost never with the stars themselves. It was always easier if you knew them or knew someone who did—usually by working with them. Richard Price was able to profile Richard Gere because Gere had starred in the film of Richard's second novel, *Bloodbrothers*. Jim Harrison once called Jack Nicholson to ask him to cooperate for a piece Tim Cahill was doing for *Rolling Stone*, and Jack sat in a lawn chair in his yard in Aspen during a snowstorm for the cover photograph.

Ward always took care of all that himself, even as it got harder and harder. Publicists were rising as the gatekeepers of journalism, but Ward seemed to blow through them, and once he got to Clint Eastwood or whomever, the filters came off. Ward said his only dread was of a subject telling him he "owed everything to Jesus Christ."

RED BAKER WAS A MONSTER of a novel when Ward finally finished it. The title character was a Baltimore steelworker, laid off and running wild—boozing, screwing around, finally turning to crime—trying to build a new identity on the bones of the one taken away from him. Michiko Kakutani wrote in the *New York Times*, "Mr. Ward writes with a directness and sincerity that is increasingly rare in these days of fashionable irony and high-tech literary pyrotechnics." *Time* magazine noted, "Ward has no manifesto and wisely refuses to use Red as a convenient symbol of the wronged working class. With patience and faith, his hero emerges cold—forged by tragedy, observing that what sets one man apart from another is not brains or money but 'what he will risk for love.'"

Ward's friends were happy for him and what they all said was that *Red Baker* had soul—like Bob. But it had taken him six years to write and made him only $10,000. Bob and I had gotten to know each other by then—at dinners, parties, a few days together in the Bahamas—and I told him he could write whatever he wanted for *Rolling Stone*. But he was uncharacteristically down about writing in general. I think I called to ask if he was interested in doing a piece about Harrison Ford. Or maybe it was Keith Richards.

"Thanks," he said, "but what the fuck."

"You don't sound very chipper," I said.

"What the fuck."

He didn't want any assignments, wasn't even sure he wanted to write anymore. That's when what Ward called his "run" started. *Red Baker* got optioned and Ward wrote the screenplay, which got stalled in development, but one night at Elaine's, his agent, Esther Newberg of the powerhouse ICM agency, passed it to the television writer-producer David Milch, who read it and offered him a shot at a script for *Hill Street Blues*. When Ward aced that, he was offered a staff job. He married his girlfriend, Celeste Wesson, an NPR producer, moved to Laurel Canyon, and by his second season on *Hill Street* was making $250,000 a year.

When *Hill Street Blues* was over, Ward moved to *Miami Vice*. I had left *Rolling Stone* for *Newsweek* and then quit after a year to raise investor money to start *Smart* magazine—and I was freelancing. Now I was the one looking for writing money.

"You don't sound very *chipper*," Ward said when I called with an idea for *Miami Vice*, where I already had a writing credit. The first time I had written for the show it had been producer Michael Mann's idea and I was still drawing a *Newsweek* paycheck. Now I was pitching for real, and Bob and I had reversed roles.

I launched into something about the show's heroes, Crockett and Tubbs, coming across a clandestine group of vigilante cops. The setup was fine, but I had no story. Ward gave me the assignment anyway and we fixed the story by letting the bad guys win, thus giving Crockett existential doubts about what it meant to be a good cop— the soul of every story line *Miami Vice* ever ran.

The episode was called "Over the Line," and Ward and I shared a story credit. Sonny Crockett learned the lesson of Red Baker. There was redemption in simply understanding where you stood and squaring up against it.

The next time I heard from Ward, he had a story for me. I had launched *Smart* by then and he was executive-producing TV shows, but he had looked at the new magazine and "knocked something out" for me.

"I never told you much about my father, did I," he said.

"A little," I said. "That he could be tough on you."

"He was hard to know."

I thought about what Ward had written about Lee Marvin and his father beating him and what had come out of that. Ward's new piece was a short story called "Scouts," about working-class fathers and sons falling away from each other: *Troop 99 in Baltimore was in a bad part of town—and very different from what you'd find in the official handbook.*

The pain in that sentence was ominous. The best writers all knew how to do that. You didn't edit it into their pieces any more than you edited their sensibilities. What you did was ask for more detail.

-ENDIT-

Editcraft (262)

AVOID CLICHÉS LIKE THE PLAGUE, and no matter how amazing or incredible or unbelievable anything is, know how challenging it can be to raise the bar—even when you are writing about icons living in La La Land or Tinseltown or on the Left Coast.

Likewise it is prudent to take Kurt Vonnegut's advice: "Do not use semicolons. They are transvestite hermaphrodites representing absolutely nothing. All they do is show you've been to college."

Think like Mark Twain: "When you catch an adjective, kill it."

"Kill your darlings" means cut anything precious, overly clever or self-indulgent. It is a stark, brilliant prohibition attributed most often to William Faulkner but also to Allen Ginsberg, Oscar Wilde, Eudora Welty, G. K. Chesterton, Anton Chekhov and Stephen King, who used the phrase in his effusive *On Writing: A Memoir of the Craft:* "Kill your darlings, kill your darlings, even when it breaks your egocentric little scribbler's heart, kill your darlings."

When the 2013 biopic of Allen Ginsberg, *Kill Your Darlings,* came out, Forrest Wickman on *Slate* tracked what is probably the best attribution to Arthur Quiller-Couch in his 1914 Cambridge lecture "On Style." The prolific poet, novelist and critic railed against "extraneous Ornament" and emphasized, "If you here require a practical rule of me, I will present you with this: 'Whenever you feel an impulse to perpetrate a piece of exceptionally fine writing, obey it—wholeheartedly—and delete it before sending your manuscript to press. *Murder your darlings.*'"

Wickman's research also brought him to an even more important rule for journalists: "Check your sources."

-ENDIT-

Kurt Vonnegut (1,072)

I WAS ON THE CORNER of Third Avenue and Forty-eighth Street, and Kurt Vonnegut was coming toward me, walking his big, loose-boned walk. It was fall and turning cold and he looked a little unbalanced in his overcoat, handsome but tousled, with long curly hair and a heavy mustache that sometimes hid his grin. I could tell he saw me by his shrug, which he sometimes used as a greeting.

I was on my way to buy dinner for some *Newsweek* writers who were suspicious of me as their new assistant managing editor. I had been brought in from *Rolling Stone,* and no one at *Newsweek* had heard of me. I didn't know them either, but I knew Kurt, who was one of the first people I met when I moved to New York. We were neighbors on Forty-eighth Street, where he lived in a big townhouse in the middle of the block, and he'd invite me over for drinks. I had gotten him to contribute to *Rolling Stone* by keeping an eye out for his speeches and radio appearances and then suggesting ways they could be retooled as essays.

"Come have dinner," I said. "I've got some *Newsweek* writers who would love to meet you."

"Not in the mood," Kurt said.

"They're fans," I said. "It's part of your job."

Kurt lit a Pall Mall and gave me a look, one of his favorites, amused but somehow saddened by the situation. He could act, Kurt.

"Think of it as a favor to me," I said. "They're not sure about me, and I've edited you."

"Sort of," he said, and I knew he had already had a couple drinks. He never got mean, but he got honest.

"What else are you doing for dinner?" I said, knowing he seldom made plans.

"The last thing I need is ass kissing," Kurt said.

"That's what I'm doing right now."

"They'll want to know which novel I like best."

"*Cat's Cradle*," I said.

"Wrong." He flipped the Pall Mall into Forty-eighth Street, and we started walking together toward the restaurant.

The writers were already at the table, drinks in front of them. They looked up when we came in, surprised to see Kurt with me. There were six or eight of them, including the columnist Pete Axthelm, who was my only ally going into *Newsweek* because I knew him from Runyon's, a bar in our neighborhood where everyone called him Ax.

I introduced Kurt around.

"Honored," Ax said, or something like that, and the ass kissing began.

The social dynamic of any table of writers, I had already learned, was dependent on the charity of the dominant writer, in this case clearly Kurt, who was both self-deprecating and blunt. The waiter came but no one ordered food. The empty Scotch glasses were backing up. The writers asked Kurt about his work habits, his hours, stuff like that. When did he write?

"All the time," Kurt said. "That's all I do." He let that settle, stirred his drink with a long finger and added, "You could say I'm writing now."

That last sentence had an edge but it was intimate too, almost generous, the way Kurt said it. Everyone nodded, and some loose talk followed about deadlines and guys who had trouble meeting them. Axthelm, who had started as a sportswriter, said he'd heard a story about how Kurt had worked briefly at *Sports Illustrated* before it launched, when the editors were going through the exercise of putting an issue together every week, practicing to go live. Part of the story was that the managing editor, Sidney James, had hired a collection of established sportswriters from around the country, but they couldn't write well enough. So then he hired a few pros living in New York City, but these guys didn't know sports. That was Kurt's group, and Kurt cocked his head: yes, he had needed the money.

The heart of the story was that Kurt was assigned a short piece about a racehorse that had jumped the fence in mid-race and attempted to escape the track. Ax stopped there to note that it was obviously not much of a story and the details were sketchy—a stupid nothing of a piece, the kind editors were always dialing up hoping to get a little humor into the mix. Someone asked if Kurt had had reporter files to write from, had anyone been on the scene to report back with some detail for him to use? Kurt didn't remember. Ax shrugged. The waiter was back, also listening to the story.

"So Kurt sits there at his desk all morning in the Time and Life Building," Ax went on, his punch line in sight. "He's thinking, and he's thinking about what he's doing and finally he types one sentence and leaves. That's it, and he's not coming back. One sentence on an otherwise blank page still in the typewriter: 'The horse jumped over the *fucking* fence.'"

It was a story about Kurt, but it was also about what Ax called "newsweekly fuckedupedness," by which he meant contempt for writers by silly editors who didn't know what they wanted. More drinks were ordered. Ax said Kurt was the inspiration for how he was going to quit, too, when it came time, which would be soon because of the even worse and increasing *fuckedupedness* at *Newsweek*.

Kurt got that and smiled but there was something in the way he looked at the faces around the table, something now not quite right about his place at that table. Maybe Kurt had heard the story too many times. Or maybe he just didn't like the idea that Ax knew the story. Ax picked up on this too and as the waiter was now, finally, taking food orders, he started talking about how much he loved all of Kurt's novels and could recite from them and wanted to ask Kurt a really lame question that he knew was lame but that we would all want to know the answer to.

"Of all your work, everything you've done, what's your favorite novel, or maybe just which one do you like best now?"

"Good," Kurt said, and stood up from the table. "*Cat's Cradle.*"

He lifted his glass of Scotch as if in a toast but wouldn't look down at me, sitting to his right. "I think you're all moderately gifted."

And he left.

–ENDIT–

Writer's Block (157)

I WANT TO MAKE QUICK WORK of this. As an editor I insisted there is no such thing. Writers could fight through it if they just kept working. If they complained, I'd quote Gloria Steinem: "I do not like to write—I like to have written."

This does not mean editors should be unsympathetic. No one likes to be called "the Stonecutter," as the excellent writer-editor David Felton was by his colleagues at *Rolling Stone,* which was a tough place that way. Besides, careful writers were always worth waiting for, and speed often rode with carelessness. Writing well was just hard, and every good writer or editor I ever knew could empathize with that.

For years there was no finer writer at *Rolling Stone* than Kurt Loder, who wrote very slowly but with great facility before moving on to anchor *MTV News.* When I asked him if he missed writing he said, "You have to be kidding."

-ENDIT-

Steve Jobs (1,167)

NEWSWEEK WAS REELING AFTER ATTEMPTING to buy the bogus Hitler Diaries and then shamefully trying to cover the bad judgment by writing in a cover story full of cloying language, "Genuine or not, it almost doesn't matter in the end." The top editors, we "Wallendas"—a self-important reference to the aerial circus act—brooded about the process that had led us to such a monumental mistake, and thus we became less enterprising.

This was the context in early 1984 when Steve Jobs came to *Newsweek* wearing a sharp suit and a tiny bow tie. He was twenty-eight years old. He met with the Wallendas and our owner, Kay Graham, up from Washington for her weekly visit. For two hours Steve showed off the first Macintosh computer, flirting with Kay and teaching us how to manipulate the mouse and switch disks to launch applications and save work. I remember someone asking, "Why call it a mouse?"

Not long after, I had dinner with Jobs and *Washington Post* writer Tom Zito at Tiro a Segno, a private club in the West Village that had a shooting gallery in the basement. Zito's father was the club president and Tom showed us around. The rifles in the basement were very old, the targets elegant. There were murals of Capri in the handsome dining room and the maître d' looked like the dapper Argentine actor Fernando Lamas. Zito and I had dates, but Steve came alone.

When we sat down, Zito ordered a round of Negronis. It was a long way from Steve's hometown of Cupertino, and he was circumspect, but Zito put him at ease with leading questions that let him show off without seeming arrogant. Dinner became an interview as Zito drew Steve out, and everyone's enthusiasm mounted for his many ideas. He didn't seem to notice, but I could see that the women found him attractive, even though he was at least ten years younger than they were. In fact, they were very interested. Maybe they would even buy one of his intriguing new computers. That, he noticed.

"What are they called?" one of the women asked.

"Macintosh," Steve said.

"Like the apple?"

Steve said his dream was that every person in the world would have his or her own Apple computer.

"That's going to be all about marketing," Zito said.

"I know," Steve said. "But I'm talking about the greatest tool ever." He went on about how people were going to shop on his computers, and keep their own libraries, and even send messages to each other.

"What a great *appliance*," I said. He was just so serious.

"Yes, but don't call it that," he said. "Bad marketing."

We all nodded and Steve said he had to stay focused and pay attention to everything, marketing of course, and all the other details beyond the engineering, even the typography. The design had to have *soul*. If you got it right, a personal computer could be not only the best tool ever but fun, "like a bicycle for your mind" — he had come up with this after reading a *Scientific American* article on locomotion efficiency and was beginning to use it with reporters.

"That's good marketing," Zito said.

I told Steve that maybe *Newsweek* could do a special issue about everything he was talking about—how computers were going to change the way we lived. It couldn't be just about him and his Macintosh, but he would be a big part of it.

"Okay," he said, but then explained that he didn't have much confidence in journalists getting his story right. I said I could understand that, even before he mentioned the Hitler Diaries.

Newsweek Access: The Magazine of Life and Technology came out of that dinner as a one-shot that I hoped would turn into a quarterly. I put Steve on the cover in a tiny blue-and-white bow tie. Zito did the interview:

ZITO

Is the computer business as ruthless as it appears to be?

JOBS

No, not at this point. To me, the situation is like a river. When the river is moving swiftly there isn't a lot of moss and algae in it, but when it slows down it becomes stagnant, a lot of stuff grows in the river and it gets very murky. I view the cutthroat political nature of things very much like that. And right now our business is moving very swiftly. The water's pretty clear and there's not a lot of ruthlessness. There's a lot of room for innovation.

ZITO

Do you consider yourself the new astronaut, the new American hero?

JOBS

No, no, no. I'm just a guy who probably should have been a semi-talented poet on the Left Bank. I got sort of sidetracked here. The space guys, the astronauts, were techies to start with. John Glenn didn't read Rimbaud, you know; but you talk to some of the people in the computer business now and they're very well grounded in the philosophical traditions of the last 100 years and the sociological traditions of the '60s. There's something going on [in Silicon Valley], there's something that's changing the world and this is the epicenter.

ZITO

Do you think it's unfair that people out here in Silicon Valley are generally labeled nerds?

JOBS

Of course. I think it's an antiquated notion. There were people in the '60s who were like that and even in the early '70s, but now they are not that way. Now they're the people who would have been poets had they lived in the '60s. And they're looking at computers as their medium of expression rather than language, rather than being a mathematician and using mathematics, rather than, you know, writing social theories.

ZITO

What do people do for fun out here? I've noticed that an awful lot of those who work for you either play music or are extremely interested in it.

JOBS

Oh yes. And most of them are also left-handed, whatever that means. Almost all of the really great technical people in computers that I've known are left-handed. Isn't that odd?

ZITO

Are you left-handed?

JOBS

I'm ambidextrous.

THE REACTION TO *ACCESS* was mixed. It was a handsome publication, but what was it about? Wasn't it really kind of a cross between *Popular Mechanics* and *Esquire*? And how relevant was that? But Steve liked it—especially the cover shot, which made him look princely and brooding, even with that little bow tie.

Apple loaned me a Macintosh 128K and I took it on vacation to Florida, where I wrote my first business plan for *Smart* magazine on it. When *Smart* launched, it depended on the new desktop publishing technology available to me as a beta site for Apple and Adobe. By then Zito had moved to Silicon Valley to write a book about the early digital startups, but he became an entrepreneur himself. He was living in the best neighborhood in Palo Alto and said he couldn't make any real money as a writer.

–ENDIT–

More Money (1,429)

I₆ you're a writer, you've got plenty of time to think about what you're doing, and eventually you have to confront the question of why you're doing it—writing in the first place. And then come the practical questions. And they keep coming around, like the rent.

"I'm not rich enough to be a writer" was a freelancer homily I heard sometimes, and it would always make me think of Taki (Panagiotis Theodoracopulos), the son of a Greek shipping tycoon with houses in New York, London and Gstaad and a sleek black-and-teak sailboat called *Bushido*. At one of his Christmas parties he pointed to a photo of the yacht on the mantel and said that was where my wife would be when he stole her away from me. *Bushido*, of course, is a Japanese word for the way of the samurai, loosely analogous to the concept of chivalry. We first worked together in 1984 when Taki was serving time in North London's Pentonville Prison for possession of cocaine.

He got away with much as a traditional playboy, and his columns were laced with astonishing ethnic slurs. Lehman Brothers CEO Richard Fuld was "a very homely, simian-looking Jew who couldn't punch his way out of a nursery." Russian manners were a "grotesque deformity." The Puerto Rican Day Parade was a "hoedown for slobs." But now bankrolling *Taki's Magazine* (a libertarian webzine of "politics and culture"), Taki wears the cape of the lovable old rogue. I had to insist on paying him, and he never cashed the checks. But like I said, he was in prison for cocaine possession then.

On the other side of that coin, Rian Malan was down to his last few dollars in L.A., with no car. When I tried to advance him money on a contract for several pieces, he said he couldn't take it because he wasn't sure he could do the work. That he was broke was inexplicable. His searing autobiographical take on South Africa, *My Traitor's Heart*, was a *New York Times* best seller and had already been translated into eleven languages. That didn't mean unlimited cash, but it meant he could get an assignment anytime he wanted one. But the assignment had to be right and he wouldn't take money he hadn't already earned. He seemed haunted by fairness, going back to his childhood in Johannesburg in an Afrikaner clan led by his great-uncle Daniel François Malan, who as prime minister was the ideological force behind apartheid.

Rian was singular. But I had to insist on paying him, too.

THE BEST WRITERS were usually the best negotiators, especially when it came to leveraging where they stood among other writers. Why wouldn't they be—they had the throw weight. Good editors paid close attention to this.

I wrote in the introduction to the 1993 *Lust, Violence, Sin, Magic: Sixty Years of* Esquire *Fiction* that when Arnold Gingrich was thirty years old and launching *Esquire* in 1933, he approached Ernest Hemingway in a New York City bookstore that dealt in first editions. Gingrich had arrived to pick up a copy of Hemingway's *Three Stories and Ten Poems*—one of 350 copies printed in Paris in 1923. Hemingway was just leaving when Gingrich came in, and the young editor went right at him, reminding Hemingway that he was a collector of his work (they had been corresponding in this regard for some months) and pleading with him to contribute to the new magazine.

Hemingway agreed to Gingrich's suggestion that he write "some kind of sporting letter" covering his outdoor activities in the course of his travels. When it came to payment, Gingrich said that he hoped to "make up in promptness of payment what it would lack in size" but that he was going to be forced to start rather low, even if it was "as much as I could to start and going up as fast as we make it, if we make it."

"I don't care how much you pay," Hemingway told him, then reconsidered immediately. "Hell, yes, I do care, but the big stuff I can always get by selling stories and you and I are just talking about journalism. Let's say if you pay fifty bucks or whatever you pay, you pay me double."

Gingrich said he was planning to pay $100.

"Fine," said Hemingway. "That means I get two hundred, and if you find as you go along that you can do better than that, then I get that much more, too, only doubled, and right away, without making me sit up and beg for it."

They shook hands. That was the only deal Hemingway ever had with *Esquire*, and as he conscientiously met deadlines over the next couple of years from wherever he happened to be, the magazine's rate more than doubled. By the late spring of 1936, Hemingway was making $500 per contribution and enjoying his relationship with Gingrich. When he saw he couldn't meet an upcoming deadline for his standard "Letter From . . ." Hemingway sent Gingrich a story he had been working on instead.

It was called "The Snows of Kilimanjaro," and Gingrich paid Hemingway $1,000, double his standard "double rate." It was the most the magazine had paid for any single contribution up to that time, and as Gingrich pointed out in his memoir *Nothing but People*, it was less than a fourth of what big magazines like the *Saturday Evening Post* were paying Hemingway for stories.

Editors today who hear this story are struck by the haphazardness by which that great story came to *Esquire*, not to mention the deal-making eccentricities of its author and the charming opportunism of editor Gingrich. More interesting to me when I edited *Esquire* was Hemingway's willingness to do the work offered by Gingrich for next to nothing because they were "just talking about journalism."

Journalism as Hemingway was referring to it was as greatly undervalued compared to fiction back then as it became overvalued later. In the thirties, the short story ruled, and as the decades moved on, journalists began to adopt the techniques of fiction. Narrative and scene became more important, as did believable dialogue and even speculation about what was going on inside a subject's head. (Thanks, Tom!)

And journalists started making more money. (Thanks again, Tom!!). For almost twenty years it was not crazy to think you could make an interesting living as a magazine freelancer, but that changed when the decline of traditional print economics and the rise of the cheap-skate Internet resulted in what politicians now call an income equity gap. If you're writing short fiction, you've probably got a teaching job.

I ALWAYS PAID MUCH LESS for fiction, and when I went to novelists with an idea for a nonfiction piece, they were surprised by how much more the journalism paid—usually at least double.

"What the fuck have I been doing?" is how Bill Kittredge put it when I called him in Missoula to talk him into what became a widely admired essay called "Redneck Secrets" that ran in the premier issue of *Rocky Mountain Magazine.* He had written mostly short fiction, which is what he taught at the University of Montana, but after that the personal essay was his strongest form and he also became a fine editor, putting together *The Last Best Place,* an anthology with astonishing range about Montana, with the filmmaker and writer Annick Smith.

Writers *have* to be opportunistic. Even if they don't recycle their pieces, exactly, they return to themes they have made their own and rework the language for different magazines. You can't blame them. It's survival instinct. So, too, is writing an online column for little or no money just for the exposure so you can charge more for speaking engagements. But over the years it was especially good news for writers whenever a new print magazine was launching (*Egg, Spy, Outside, Spin, Condé Nast Traveler, Manhattan, Inc.,* all the way up through more recent business failures like *Portfolio* and *Play*). And it was even better if the rates were bouncing up, like when *Vanity Fair* relaunched in 1982, and then when Tina Brown began her luminous run there in 1984, and again when she took over the *New Yorker* in 1992. Condé Nast always paid the most and mounted the last of the big, extravagant magazine launches. Mark Golin, a colleague of mine at Time Inc., explained the writer economics of the $120 million *Portfolio* start-up in 2007 as "like when dogs find a tipped-over dumpster behind the Whole Foods."

Jimmy Buffett (1,201)

JIMMY BUFFETT'S LIFE WAS RICH and open to anyone who knew his lyrics, and he had whiplash intelligence about his own best interests. He never wrote for money, only because it was good for Jimmy Buffett.

We met in San Francisco, where I was editing *Outside*. Jimmy was in a leg cast from a softball injury in Aspen, where he lived then. We went to Vanessi's, in North Beach, where Joe DiMaggio ate sometimes. Jimmy said he appreciated both the baseball and the fishing nuance, and sat with his broken leg propped on a chair. The waiter recognized something about him but couldn't find his name so I said, "Jimmy Buffett, 'Margaritaville' . . ."

The waiter said, "'Wasting away . . .'"

"Not tonight," Jimmy said, and asked for the wine list. "We're working."

His new album, *Changes in Latitudes*, was moving up the charts, and my idea was that Jimmy would write something about . . . I wasn't sure. Jimmy said Antigua Sailing Week might be interesting, "sort of a cross between America's Cup and Mardi Gras. A drunken riot with boats."

"So we're talking serious journalism," I said.

"So you want me to make fun of myself."

"With a straight face."

"Like what?"

"Like 'Why Don't We Get Drunk and Screw.'" Jimmy had written that one as a country-love-song parody under the pseudonym "Marvin Gardens." It was still topping jukebox plays after five years.

"I can do that," Jimmy said.

EDITING JIMMY WAS LIKE HAVING a business partner. His real business partners became his friends, or at least thought of themselves as his friends, and everybody made money. You didn't have to be a Parrothead as long as you respected what his music meant to the millions of them and you worked as hard as Jimmy did on whatever you were doing together. Editing him went the same way.

Starting with that cover story for *Outside*, Jimmy beat whatever deadline I gave him and never objected to any editing moves I made on his copy. There were plenty and he thanked me for every one of them, said he was grateful even, with almost no ego, which I took as confidence in his talent. He had started out thinking he would be a journalist, and told me once almost shyly that he thought maybe he had some books in him if he worked at it. His songwriting was loaded with literary references — Twain, Hemingway, James Jones, Herman Wouk, Pat Conroy, a long list — and he was friends with several writers I was working with, and his lyric *Made enough money to buy Miami but I pissed it away so fast* spoke to every hipster of the moment who could roll a tight joint.

The road was always the best place to reach him. He said he wanted his privacy when he wasn't working. But then again, he was always working:

Hey,

I am going to Cuba next week to reconnect with friends and I need a letter validating my journalistic credentials. I will write you something you can use. I am actually going in search of a Cuban surf club and the secret JB copy band that is reported to exist in some dingy club in old Havana. My friend Patrick Oppmann is now the CNN bureau chief there and I am on the board of the Hemingway Restoration Foundation, but going in on a Sport's Illustrated credential tops the list. I get the feeling things are about to start popping down there, and it might be time to see it again before it becomes a cruise ship stop.

JB

That was the way most of his assignments started—with Jimmy assigning himself. As I moved from job to job, Jimmy would write another piece for me. There were perks for me too, like a quail-hunting trip to Thomasville to take pictures for *Esquire*. It was work but it was fun too and beyond a simple idea of a good time. We walked into a pine grove so I could see the grave of his bird dog Spring. He said he thought that losing a beloved pet helped prepare us for greater loss, a cliché maybe but he meant it and I knew his father was not well.

In New Orleans, after we donated $60,000 from auctioning a guitar that he and all the *Sports Illustrated* swimsuit models had signed, he said onstage that it had been my idea. "God bless you," those Katrina victims told me afterward, but it had been his idea. He also got me great seats at his Detroit shows for the Chevy executives that *SI* advertising revenue depended on, and would even say hello to them backstage just before he went on.

I'd e-mail him that I was in Sicily and had just heard "Fins" in a bar full of anchovy fisherman. He'd send me pictures of a striped bass he had caught on a fly. Wherever I was, if I was looking for a place to eat or whatever, he'd come right back. One spring in Paris I got this:

> *First—you have to do lunch at L'Avenue on Montparnasse just for the scenery. Bellota-Bellota in the 9th is all and only hams, mainly pata negras from Spain and the Pyrenees but it is amazing. . . . Lac Hong—amazing Vietnamese. Out of the way place that reminds you of Viet Nam or Paris forty years ago. They even have Export 33 beer. . . . Marius et Janette for seafood. It is on George V near the river. Very funky but the best plat du jour in Paris is Le Forum in the 8th. That should hold you.*

Jimmy had decided early that knowing the world would be part of his job and he kept working it, writing, touring, making shrewd deals and uncanny marketing decisions. His rise as an entrepreneur was stealth until suddenly it wasn't. He and Warren Buffett had their DNA tested to see if they were related. "Well, we do have certain things in common," said Warren, that old Parrothead.

Jimmy's music and books, restaurants, stores, casino, real estate, labels and licensing put him well over $500 million, worth more than any living musician except Paul McCartney and Bono, depending on which list you look at. And while his writer friends shook their heads, he had three No. 1 *New York Times* best sellers in a row: *Tales from Margaritaville,* a collection of short stories; the novel *Where Is Joe Merchant?*; and *A Pirate Looks at Fifty,* the memoir which made him only the sixth author ever to top both the fiction and nonfiction lists. It would be hard to argue that there was a more successful writer, and certainly none on the *Forbes* list of richest people.

The last time I saw Jimmy, he came up behind me at a crowded party at a house on the water in Sag Harbor. It was a warm spring evening and everyone seemed to be talking about their upcoming vacations, maybe even taking the summer off.

"Hey, old man," he said. "We need to get back to work . . ."

-ENDIT-

Richard Price (2,933)

Wʜᴇɴ ɪ ᴡᴀs ʟᴏᴏᴋɪɴɢ ꜰᴏʀ ᴍᴏɴᴇʏ to launch *Smart,* Richard and I came up with a TV series idea called *Night,* each episode playing out between sundown and sunrise—all very noir. Richard's screenplays for *The Color of Money* and *Sea of Love* were both big movie credits, and I had gotten some slight attention for an episode of *Miami Vice* I had written. Both of our agents had encouraged us to come up with a show to pitch. It was what we did all the time anyway, have some drinks and maybe do a couple of lines and riff on "what if" story ideas: What if there was a nightclub called Night?

Night was about two guys and a girl who owned a club together in Tribeca, an exotic location in 1985, especially if you didn't live in New York. The girl was rich and a smart-ass. One of the guys was a wry police detective, and the other was a hipster journalist. But they were really Becky Thatcher, Tom Sawyer and Huckleberry Finn. And they were all in love with each other. We cracked ourselves up.

Pitch meetings got set up in L.A. right away. On the seven a.m. American flight from JFK to LAX, I pulled out some notes I'd made on the characters. Richard was fidgety, didn't want look at them.

"If we practice," he said, "we'll blow it."

I said that was annoying . . . and if it was true, we should rearrange the meetings to pitch first to whoever we wanted to work with most.

Richard told me about going with Martin Scorsese to pitch Paul Newman *The Color of Money* on Paul's deck in Malibu. "Two ghost-white, asthmatic New Yorkers sucking on inhalers," as he put it, both sweating in the sun as Paul lathered up with the Sea & Ski and they raced through the plot points. "And we almost blew it because I was too locked down."

"You mean Marty had to step in?" I was worried about my part.

"It's a process," Richard said. I'd heard that said before, but never without a smirk.

. . .

WE WERE SHARP in our first meeting, finding our rhythm (shtick?) right away. I would open with how nobody in L.A. knew what was going on in Tribeca, and Richard would break in with whatever story occurred to him about getting in and out of trouble downtown. I might say something about coming of age down there, and Richard would tell another story, and then another and find a bridge to what it was like working with *Marty* and *Paul* and how they'd both love to do something like *Night* but they didn't normally do television.

Then we'd both stop talking, allowing everyone in the room to reflect on the implications of doing or not doing TV, which was Pavlovian for the executives who were in those kinds of meetings and always self-conscious and defensive about not working in film. That's when we'd agree that you could blow out some ambitious work on TV if you were willing to take a chance on quality writing. And, of course, that's what everyone in the room was all about, and someone said that in every meeting, smiling at Richard each time.

"Solid," I think Richard even said once.

I would finish with something about how, obviously, Richard and I lived in New York and knew the scene and in fact we knew people like Tom and Becky and Huck. You could tell by our outfits, especially Richard's black T-shirt. It was also effective in an uncomfortable way that Richard couldn't shake hands when he met you because his right arm had been withered by polio when he was a child in the projects—which I would explain with Dickensian nuance later in private when they'd get me aside to ask about it. This would be after we ended our pitch with how they should come to New York soon, so we could all hang out.

We had two meetings in the morning, a lunch with some network people, and two more meetings in the afternoon before we got to Aaron Spelling, who at the time was building a 56,500-square-foot French château-style mansion in Holmby Hills called Spelling Manor. His numerous hit shows, including *Charlie's Angels, The*

Love Boat, The Mod Squad, Fantasy Island and *Dynasty*, had ruled prime time since the late 1960s.

Aaron was wearing a powder-blue jumpsuit and seemed a little shy, if you can be shy in a powder-blue jumpsuit. He sat in what I thought was a Mies van der Rohe chair and we sank low into a plush couch across from him. It was a bigger room than the conference rooms used for our previous meetings but it was Aaron's office. And there was good art on the walls instead of movie posters.

We tried to make small talk while we waited for Aaron's partner, Doug Cramer, who as an executive at one studio or another had been responsible for *Star Trek, The Odd Couple, The Brady Bunch* and *Mission: Impossible*. Cramer was also a serious art collector, with pieces by Jim Dine, Jasper Johns, Roy Lichtenstein and Ellsworth Kelly, all friends of his, and people said he was the only openly gay player in Hollywood. Richard and I were both very curious, but there was no small talk about Doug or the art as we waited for him.

"We both like art" was all Aaron said, and then "Let's just go," and I said something like "It's an American love triangle," and Richard jumped ahead with "And nobody has ever done it . . . on television . . . and it's New York . . . and it's sexy . . . and it's dangerous . . . and it's very, very hip, you can trust me on that."

Those were not Richard's actual words, but that's what I was thinking he sounded like to Aaron, who was nodding and nodding and after about a minute told us to hold up.

"Just find Doug," he said to an assistant taking notes. "He's got to hear this!"

When Cramer arrived we started over or, rather, Richard did and it was like stand-up when stand-up isn't just funny but serious and soulful, too. Now it wasn't just Tom and Huck and Becky, it was also Butch and Sundance and Etta, and maybe even a little *Casablanca*, but slick and modern, like Aaron's office. Aaron and Doug kept stopping us to call more people into the room to hear the pitch and take more notes and Richard kept starting over, building on himself like Coltrane or Bird or Lenny Bruce or Lord Buckley and the rest of the pantheon of ancient hipsters. I think he even mentioned Bongo Wolf, as in "If Bongo Wolf lived in New York, he'd hang out at this club." And on to the Mudd Club, and Indochine, Odeon—noir heaven, with slick night streets and warehouse fronts and we would all be there and be cool together and . . .

We were in Aaron's office for ninety minutes.

On the way out, Aaron and Doug asked me if Richard was always like this, so creative, so *on!* I said it was most satisfying working with Richard because even as creative as he was, he was very reliable, always on time, always got his work done, never missed deadlines. Aaron and Doug agreed that this was good, and also that Richard could play clubs if he ever felt like it.

It looked like we had a deal but back in New York Richard's phone was ringing with another job. Not television. When he pulled out of *Night* to write *Rocket Boys* for Mick Jagger and David Bowie, our negotiations with Aaron and Doug were over.

RICHARD AND I WERE ORIGINALLY connected in the late 1970s as first novelists and "Write On Guys" in *Playgirl* magazine, along with Winston Groom, Thomas Sanchez, Barry Hannah and some other embarrassed young writers I got to know later, but none as well as I got to know Richard. He was the youngest and his early success with his first novel—*The Wanderers*, written when he was twenty-four—gave his street-kid confidence an efficacy that was attractive, even to other writers.

We started going to the Hamptons at about the same time, Richard because he was seeing Judy Hudson, a painter who looked like Ali McGraw in *Goodbye, Columbus*, except that Judy was a deep WASP with sharp instincts about careers and real estate—the twin obsessions of New York City in the 1980s. Richard got all that, but the Hamptons were not his scene, at least not yet. He had never been tan in his life and hated the beach, and the rounds of parties made us both uneasy—everyone was just too rich. We spent a lot of Saturdays riding around in my old convertible searching for *"Grapes of Wrath* Hamptons."

I'd drive and we'd smoke a joint and sometimes Richard would talk about his work. He was starting a novel about a stand-up comic and would try out monologues—at least it occurred to me that he wasn't just riffing. The Hamptons had a famous Gin Lane, but so did Hogarth—that kind of thing. The closest we got to any *Grapes of Wrath* turned out to be a waterfront strip of shingle houses and fishing shacks called Promised Land, on the shoulder of Napeague Bay, but that punch line ran a little dark and we both knew it.

Promised Land was where a lot of the late-night domestic violence calls to the East Hampton police came from, and the dilapidated houses in the soft, beautiful light, with old boats and pickups in the yards, was material to reference the next time we were eating tiny asparagus spears wrapped in prosciutto on some manicured lawn on Further Lane in East Hampton or wherever we were both feeling uncomfortable.

The new friends who listened to Richard on those lawns and at dinner parties thought he was very entertaining. They told him he could do stand-up if he ever felt like it, and he liked the attention even though there was something about the way they asked him to tell them again about growing up in the Bronx that was starting to piss him off. But he couldn't help himself, couldn't stop inhabiting his characters, with all their street lingo—and rolling out his own deadeye detail and hair-trigger insights. He was so verbally intense, so hilarious, nobody seemed to wonder how he was feeling about what he was saying. When people asked, like they always did, if he'd ever considered doing stand-up, he'd shrug. If he wasn't *on*, he was shy, and I think his shyness used to piss him off, too. There was a lot of coke around, and using and then contending with it got wrapped into his stories in a kind of cannibalization of his own life. We talked about this sometimes, but usually when we were high.

The novel he was writing about the stand-up comic was called *The Breaks,* and when it went a little cold on him it tipped him further into the movie business. He started pitching his ass off—cashing in on his deep homeboy credentials. If you wanted *street,* Richard was your guy. Everybody on both coasts got that. He was approaching forty by this time, and never again had to mention growing up in a housing project. I remember Richard Gere arriving with a "Yo, Richie!" at a surprise birthday party for him at the loft he bought with Judy in the East Village, and I think I remember Robert De Niro arriving at another party with the same greeting.

Richard had a good time with it, but instead of just polishing the image he took it deeper, embedding (a word we never used then) with police units around New York and in Jersey City. Some weeks he'd ride with them every night. He saw everything the cops saw and had after-hours drinks in their bars. Detectives became his friends and they'd come to dinner and to Judy's parties, some with bulges on their ankles if you looked. It was research for the next novel, Richard said, but it informed his movie work, which just kept coming. His collaborations with Scorsese were big-budget hip: *The Color of Money* (a sequel to *The Hustler*) and *Life Lessons* (a segment for *New York Stories*). "I do the words, Marty does the music," Richard said, embarrassingly, more than once. He didn't talk that way about the remakes of *Night and the City* and *Kiss of Death,* but they were good, too. Richard even got hired to conceptualize and write the eighteen-minute video for Michael Jackson's "Bad."

THERE WERE NINE YEARS BETWEEN *The Breaks* and Richard's next novel, *Clockers,* which I excerpted in *Esquire* in 1992. It was set around the workings of a crack cocaine gang in Jersey City and the dynamics among the dealers, the police and the community. Critics loved it. According to the *New York Times,* it came across "as both clear-eyed and big-hearted, able to illuminate and celebrate, in the midst of the most unpromising circumstances imaginable, a cop's heroism and a small-time drug dealer's stubborn resilience, without overly sentimentalizing either." That review described Richard as much as his novel.

Clockers was nominated for the National Book Critics Circle Award and became hugely influential. (TV writer-producer David Simon credited it years later as an inspiration for *The Wire* and hired Richard to write for the show.) What Richard liked best, though, was that he was a novelist again. "No more scripts," he told me. But that was right after he found out that the studio had signed Spike Lee to direct from Spike's own screenplay of *Clockers*.

Richard followed *Clockers* with three novels — *Freedomland* (1998), *Samaritan* (2003) and *Lush Life* (2008) — but his most reliable pay-days kept coming from screenwriting and movie rights. The difference was that now it wasn't the easy money it had been in the 1980s and '90s, when they were still making $40 million movies. He told the *New York Times* that he had found himself "pitching to get jobs on movies based on Marvel heroes, and I said: 'What am I, in a play-pen?' There's no dignity to it."

So with the help of De Niro and Scorsese, Richard sold CBS a TV series, *NYC 22*, about a group of rookie cops. The "22" was for the station's precinct number in Harlem, where Richard had moved into a big solid brownstone. When he told me about the show, he also mentioned that he had been signed to write a series of detective novels for Henry Holt under the pen name "Jay Morris." And he had a Harlem novel going.

Exhausting, I thought. His marriage to Judy Hudson was over. His two daughters were grown. His marriage to the writer Lorraine Adams was beginning. With Judy, he had lived through more than two decades of the New York art scene, building his career while blowing away dinner parties with his stories. Judy painted, and they collected art. Eric Fischl and April Gornik, Robert Longo, name an artist — you met them all at Richard and Judy's various houses — Great Jones Street, Gramercy Park, Shelter Island, Georgica, Amagansett. That was all over now, way over, with much pain all around. But

Richard seemed happy, and grateful for the work in a way I had not seen before, or perhaps had just not noticed.

One night he and Lorraine came down to dinner in the East Village, just a couple blocks from his old loft. NYC 22 had suffered a short run in a bad time slot and had not been renewed, which seemed a relief to him. They were just back from St. Petersburg, where Richard had picked up more research on his way home from a week of work on the set of a new Ridley Scott picture in Prague—*Child 44*, based on the Tom Rob Smith novel about a disgraced member of the Soviet military police investigating a series of child murders connected to leaders of the Communist Party during the Stalin era. Richard had written the screenplay way back, maybe seven years earlier. Now it was finally a go, with big stars and a big budget and that meant principal photography money.

"Ka-ching!" Richard said, but as always when it came to his movie work, he was much more interested in talking about something else. Like St. Petersburg and its deep Russian weirdness for a kid from the northeast Bronx. It was one of his fish-out-of-water riffs, with echoes of our search for the *Grapes of Wrath* Hamptons, except he was in St. Petersburg looking for *Grapes of Wrath* Dostoyevsky. We ordered more wine.

After the next bottle, we talked about our weddings. I was at both of his, and Richard's speech at my second went over like our pitch to Aaron Spelling, especially the part about how he had shown up at my office at *Rolling Stone* way past his deadline to turn in his Richard Gere profile "red-eyed and looking like I'd spent the last seventy-two hours bobbing for apples in a vat of Gold Medal flour."

Several other guests took me aside later and asked about Richard. Did he ever play clubs? He could do stand-up if he ever felt like it. I told them Richard had heard that before.

-ENDIT-

The Hallmarkcardian Wars (1,754)

WHAT WAS FUNNY TO P. J. O'Rourke was never slapstick or absurd, and he loved language, which made editing him joyous — not a word often associated with the editorial process. Sometimes all we did was laugh, although actually *laughing* is something P.J. never did. Our first piece together, "Cocaine Etiquette," was one of the first I assigned at *Rolling Stone*. P.J. wrote: *Cocaine and etiquette are inseparable, they go together like cocaine and, well, more cocaine.*

Our joke was that all we really did was *not* work, but maybe we were working from the inside out, like happy anthropologists comparing field notes. We had another joke about deadlines being our friends, and P.J. always met his with clean copy. He was a tight grammarian; the structural rules governing composition reflected his improbable love of logic. He could talk about *morphology* and *pragmatics* — both words he taught me. Copy editors loved him. One of his girlfriends, a graduate student in biology, told me she thought P.J. was an "explosive thinker." I figured she meant what I thought of as a "dangerous thinker" but had come up with a better adjective. I had just edited this:

Q. What should be served with cocaine?

A. Most people enjoy a couple thousand cigarettes with their "face Drano." Others mix "indoor Aspen Lift lines" with multiple sedatives that achieve that marvelous feeling so similar to not having taken drugs at all. But everyone, whether he wants to or not, should drink plenty of whiskey or gin. If you smell strongly of alcohol, people may think you are drunk instead of stupid.

The explosiveness came with the pop — an obvious truth at the end of the point he was making. It worked with his funny stuff, and more powerfully when his irony turned hard. P.J. on Somalia: *Before the*

marines came, the children were dying like . . . "Dying like flies" is not
a simile you'd use in Somalia. The flies wax prosperous and lead full
lives. Before the marines came, the children were dying like children.

That Somalia piece, "All Guns, No Butter," was for *Rolling Stone*
after P.J. went on contract and was listed on the masthead as the
"Foreign Affairs Desk." What he did mostly in that job was travel
the world from war zone to war zone, shit hole to shit hole, filling
his notebooks with concise if sometimes absurdist reporting, which
he ran through an IBM Selectric back home in New Hampshire or
Washington, D.C.—where he had taken an apartment to be close to
what was becoming his default target, big government. His first book
about politics was *Parliament of Whores* and you could see he was
building on his pants-down Republican conceit. *Giving money and*
power to government is like giving whiskey and car keys to teenage boys.

Beyond his one-liners, P.J.'s basic construct was to take familiar
concepts like, say, God and Santa Claus, push them to their logical extreme with a coating of his seemingly good-natured biases, and
end with a hilarious (and logical) kicker. So God was a Republican
and Santa Claus was a Democrat. God was a stern old guy with a lot
of rules who held everybody accountable, with little apparent con-
cern for the disadvantaged. God was difficult, unsentimental, politically connected and held the mortgage on everything in the world.
Santa Claus was cute, always cheerful and loved animals. He knew
who'd been naughty and who'd been nice, but he never did anything
about it and gave everyone everything they wanted. For his kicker P.J.
wrote, *Santa Claus is preferable to God in every way but one: There is*
no such thing as Santa Claus.

When he branched out from *Rolling Stone,* it was to the *Atlantic*
Monthly, the *American Spectator,* the *Weekly Standard,* and the Cato
Institute. You could see his interests shifting toward policy, which
may or may not have had something to do with P.J. settling in to raise
a family, albeit as the kind of dad who teaches his young daughter
not to use dirty words like *junior senator from New York.* His writing
on child rearing had been percolating since he'd noted that nearly

everything about Hillary Clinton's *It Takes a Village* was objection-able, *from the title—an ancient African proverb which seems to have its origins in the ancient African kingdom of Hallmarkcardia—to the acknowledgments page, where Mrs. Clinton fails to acknowledge that some poor journalism professor named Barbara Feinman did most of the work.*

Anything *Hallmarkcardian* was in for it, and he was especially interested in Hillary, beginning when she was First Lady and P.J. gave the keynote at the opening of the Cato Institute's headquarters in Washington, D.C. *Health care is too expensive, so the Clinton administration is putting Hillary in charge of making it cheaper. (This is what I always do when I want to spend less money—hire a lawyer from Yale.) If you think health care is expensive now, wait until you see what it costs when it's free.*

By the time Hillary was running for president the first time, P.J. had turned her into a cartoon archetype: *Hillary Clinton is Lucy holding the football for Charlie Brown. Hillary Clinton is "America's ex-wife."* Obama supporters couldn't wipe the smiles off their faces. Then, of course . . . *according to the Obama administration, the rich will pay for everything. The bad news is that, according to the Obama administration, you're rich.*

When *Don't Vote, It Just Encourages the Bastards* came out in 2010, the *Guardian* said that P.J.'s wit had won him friends on both sides of the political divide and made him the world's most important living humorist. An earlier *60 Minutes* profile had said almost the same thing—that he was the most quoted living man (according to *The Penguin Dictionary of Modern Humorous Quotations*).

The best sellers had started when he walked away from *Easy Money*, and they kept coming. P.J. quotes got passed around like, well, P.J. quotes. Before the Internet, I kept a file of them, includ-ing some long paragraphs. I used short ones to spice my letters and sent long ones to writers whenever they seemed frozen or blocked, as unsubtle suggestions to take some chances. As P.J. liked to put it, *safety has no place anywhere.*

This sampling of favorites is not just a stunt to get more of his quotes into the book, although P.J. always liked stunts. If this were a magazine, it would be a sidebar.

THE BACHELOR HOME COMPANION:
A PRACTICAL GUIDE TO KEEPING
HOUSE LIKE A PIG (1987)

The only really good vegetable is Tabasco sauce. Put Tabasco sauce in everything. Tabasco sauce is to bachelor cooking what forgiveness is to sin.

REPUBLICAN PARTY REPTILE:
THE CONFESSIONS, ADVENTURES,
ESSAYS, AND (OTHER) OUTRAGES
OF . . . P. J. O'ROURKE (1987)

Some people say a front-engine car handles best. Some people say a rear-engine car handles best. I say a rented car handles best.

HOLIDAYS IN HELL: IN WHICH OUR
INTREPID REPORTER TRAVELS TO THE
WORLD'S WORST PLACES AND ASKS,
"WHAT'S FUNNY ABOUT THIS?" (1988)

Each American embassy comes with two permanent features—a giant anti-American demonstration and a giant line for American visas. Most demonstrators spend half their time burning Old Glory and the other half waiting for green cards.

PARLIAMENT OF WHORES: A LONE
HUMORIST ATTEMPTS TO EXPLAIN THE
ENTIRE U.S. GOVERNMENT (1991)

The Democrats are the party . . . that says government can make you richer, smarter, taller and get the chickweed out of your lawn. Republicans are the party that says government doesn't work, and then they get elected and prove it.

99

GIVE WAR A CHANCE: EYEWITNESS ACCOUNTS OF MANKIND'S STRUGGLE AGAINST TYRANNY, INJUSTICE AND ALCOHOL-FREE BEER (1992)

It's impossible to get decent Chinese takeout in China, Cuban cigars are rationed in Cuba, and that's all you need to know about communism.

ALL THE TROUBLE IN THE WORLD: THE LIGHTER SIDE OF OVERPOPULATION, FAMINE, ECOLOGICAL DISASTER, ETHNIC HATRED, PLAGUE, AND POVERTY (1994)

Traffic [in Vietnam] was like a bad dog. It wasn't important to look both ways when crossing the street; it was important to not show fear.

THE CEO OF THE SOFA (2001)

If you're gay, Al Gore will let you get into the military. George Bush will let you get out. You choose.

PEACE KILLS: AMERICA'S FUN NEW IMPERIALISM (2004)

The idea of a news broadcast once was to find someone with information and broadcast it. The idea now is to find someone with ignorance and spread it around.

THE BABY BOOM: HOW IT GOT THAT WAY — AND IT WASN'T MY FAULT — AND I'LL NEVER DO IT AGAIN (2014)

Board games and card games were for rainy days, and if it looked like the rain was never going to stop we'd get out Monopoly. Despairing of its page upon page of rules, we'd make our own. This is how both Wall Street investment strategy and Washington economic policy were invented by our generation. We also invented selling "Get Out of Jail Free" cards to the highest bid-der. And we made deals with each other that were so complex that by the time six hotels had been placed on Baltic Avenue none of us had any idea what we were doing. This is the origin of the derivatives market and the real estate bubble.

YEARS AFTER P. J. O'ROURKE and I had worked together, we had dinner at a midtown steak house not far from where he had lived in that ship's bow of an apartment. He was on the road to promote his new book, *Baby Boom*, and we saw each other whenever he was in New York. When it came to our politics, we had started in the same place, apolitical kids radicalized by the Vietnam War. As I settled into adulthood thinking of myself as a liberal, P.J. went from pants-down Republican to libertarian philosopher with a mean streak: *At the core of liberalism is the spoiled child—miserable, as all spoiled children are, unsatisfied, demanding, ill-disciplined, despotic and useless. Liberalism is a philosophy of sniveling brats.*

But there we were, both of us wearing ties and ordering Caesar salads. I told P.J. I was writing about the writers I had edited and that while going through my files I had found that our correspondence was a little thin.

"That's because we always talked on the phone when we were working," P.J. said. "Or maybe we went out."

"We never talked politics."

"We were working."

-ENDIT-

Discouragement (386)

EDITORS WORK WITHOUT APPLAUSE, except perhaps from a few of their writers and sometimes just for offering up assignments. You can't trust that, and good editors learn quickly. Still, discouragement comes from being too hopeful, which I sometimes was. Michael Herr's writing and reporting for *Esquire* in Vietnam from 1967 to 1969 was the best I had ever read. His 1977 book *Dispatches* was reviewed as an instant classic of war literature. So as soon as I got to *Rolling Stone* in 1981 I went after him, asking for whatever he might like to write. I took it as a positive sign that the one piece he had previously published in *RS* had become the last chapter in *Dispatches*. Herr wrote back to say that although the magazine's founder and my boss, Jann Wenner, was *alright* with him, the problem of *Rolling Stone* not paying enough was insurmountable.

Frankly, his next paragraph began, it was impossible for him to imagine his work ever again in *the Stone*, and *even more frankly, provocatively*, that was too bad because readers of the magazine could use a little relief from the *ongoing vulgarity*. True enough, I thought. He ended the paragraph suggesting *you might want to put a match to the corner of this letter around now*.

Rather than lighting a match, I looked for an opening somewhere before the end of the letter. That was always how it went with Hunter and many other writers. But then:

> *I spent too many hours with one of your predecessors while his tears scalded his bourbon not to appreciate the difficulties of your position.*

That stopped me. It was far from my first taste of the journalistic frustrations of working for other people. It had been made obvious to me many other times that I didn't have the last word. But this was humiliating in its kindness and understanding. *The difficulties of your position.* I would never enjoy the power of my decisions until my position changed. Rereading the letter, I knew that I would have to start my own magazine, and I saved it as a kind of totem. Remembering that letter helped me when I was raising money to launch *Smart.* And I hear it still, like a wind blowing through my career, every time I pick up *Dispatches.*

-ENDIT-

Jann Wenner (1,620)

I NEVER KNEW ANYONE to bring out as much bad feeling and envy as quickly as *Rolling Stone*'s founder, Jann Wenner. People said they hated Jann. But they loved him too, and if you worked with him on ideas you knew how smart he was and that went a long way. His passion, too, was obvious and moving, and made him vulnerable.

The close of my first issue as *Rolling Stone*'s managing editor coincided with the assassination of John Lennon, in early December 1980. I was in a bar on Second Avenue when the news broke, and I went immediately into the office. Making calls to writers to organize our coverage, I found that most had already heard from Jann, who'd been working his phones at home. Later that night he walked to the Dakota, where John had lived, and stood across the street until dawn.

In the office that morning we argued about what the magazine should run. Jann wanted to keep the name of the killer, Mark David Chapman, out of it. I wanted to include everything we had, including the specifics of the murder. One of our writers, Gregory Katz, lived in the Dakota and had collected eyewitness accounts, and I described the details: Chapman had shot Lennon in the back at almost point-blank range, firing five hollow-point bullets from a .38 revolver, and there had been blood everywhere.

"This is too hard," Jann said, turning away. "I'm sorry."

"I'm sorry, too," I said, and told him I understood how he felt about keeping that story out of what he wanted to be a memorial issue, but still . . . Maybe a minute passed before I asked, "Are you going to write something?"

"We just need to get through this," Jann said, turning back to me, tears on his cheeks.

The day before, on the last day of his life, Lennon had posed with Yoko Ono for a planned cover story about their new album, *Double Fantasy*. Annie Leibovitz's photo of him naked in a fetal position, curled around Yoko, became the cover and ran without a headline. No artist was more important to *Rolling Stone*. Jann had put John on the first cover when he'd founded the magazine as a precocious twenty-one-year-old in 1967. The image was a still from the anti-war film *How I Won the War*, which set the tone for the magazine with its mix of music, politics and culture, as well as for Jann's subsequent one-on-one interviews with musicians, which he conducted with directness and, significantly, a lack of the fawning that usually trivialized the coverage of rock stars. This issue about John's murder was a catharsis for Jann. He wrote on the last page that he had loved Lennon, adding, "Something of being young has been ripped out of me—something I thought was far behind me."

After we closed the issue, Jann and I went through it in his office. The piece he liked best was an essay by the novelist Scott Spencer, which I had assigned with a twenty-four-hour deadline that first night. It ended with "It's hard to believe our luck has gotten this bad." The piece from inside the Dakota that we had argued about was also included. Jann had a small number of issues bound and numbered for some of us who had worked on it.

JANN WAS A RESOLUTE EDITOR, and his eye for talent was irrefutable. When he locked onto a writer—Tom Wolfe, say—he went after him hard and got him into *Rolling Stone* and the work was always superior. Tom said that *The Bonfire of the Vanities* would not have been written without Jann and the deadline pressure of publishing it serially, with a new chapter in every issue. They had agreed that writing a novel on deadline, the way Charles Dickens used to do it, would give Tom the motivation he needed. Tom said Jann was the best editor he ever worked with and that *Rolling Stone* was his home from 1972, when Jann assigned him to cover the launch of NASA's last moon mission, *Apollo 17*. A four-part series, "Post-Orbital Remorse," ran in the magazine, and led to his book *The Right Stuff* in 1979.

Jann never got much credit for his actual editor-to-writer editing work, however, or what he called his "Buddha-like" levels of patience as deadlines approached for Tom (or, in the beginning, for Hunter — who would not finish a piece without him). As with the best and most productive editor-writer relationships, Jann and Tom became true friends. When he presented Tom with the Creative Excellence Award from the American Society of Magazine Editors in 2011, Jann changed into a white suit before going onstage.

As much as he loved his relationship with Tom, Jann was wary of bad work by famous writers he hadn't recruited himself. An editor would wrangle for months to bring in a piece and Jann would call bullshit on it. Which it sometimes was, but not always because Jann carried grudges, which is what the spiked editor would leave his office muttering. Mostly, though, Jann busted pieces for negligible reporting or self-promotion or recycling. Writers feared this from him, but those who stuck respected him for it too, especially when they understood that he really did care about the words. Jann nurtured writers as much as any editor I ever knew, although I doubt *nurture* was a word that came to mind when writers thought about him, and it was one he never would have used. "Buddha-like" was just funny.

Jann himself was easy to edit, a clear writer who always knew what he wanted to say. Although he was never interested in line editing, he knew what a story was and was as good at recognizing a lede as anyone I worked with at *Newsweek* or, later, at Time Inc. When his news judgment lined up with his commercial instincts, he was ferocious.

Arguing once about why I had not put the Rolling Stones (or some configuration of them) on the cover four issues in a row, I said I didn't think that would have been very smart.

"I think being rich is smart," Jann said.

Our numbers were up, and I bristled.

"Don't get woolly on me," he said. "The Stones always outsell everybody."

It was late 1981 and the band was winding up an American tour, playing almost straight through from September to Christmas, making a fortune behind their new hits "Start Me Up" and "Waiting for a

Friend." The tour was important for *Rolling Stone* because elsewhere in rock and roll, both the music and the business seemed stuck. MTV was still in its embryo stage and music felt less important than it had for almost two decades. Even Jann had been a bit disengaged. His interests had drifted into the movie business, and at the same time, his gun-control work after John Lennon was killed was both relentless and frustrating. It was a tricky time to work for him. Chris Connelly (the future editor and ESPN correspondent), who manned the front switchboard then, told me that judging by our body language, "You and Jann don't meet, you collide."

Shortly after I arrived at *Rolling Stone*, Jann moved out of his townhouse on East Sixty-sixth Street and began living in Richard Gere's apartment downtown. He was heavy then, which made him look puffy, and most days he came to work a little ragged, rolling into the office for a call or two before a one o'clock lunch at Harry Cipriani in the Sherry-Netherland Hotel, across Fifty-ninth Street. He made a show about being very busy and was irritable to the point of barking at assistants with messy desks. The joke in the office was that Jann's secret to getting what he wanted from people was that he "had the Polaroids." This implied a sexual friskiness at *Rolling Stone* that didn't exist beyond the usual office promiscuity, and Jann never hit on anyone. His private life was very private.

I was running the magazine day-to-day, and we had seen a surprising (to Jann, at first) success on the newsstand with box-office actors like Jack Nicholson and Goldie Hawn. I had moved the music coverage to the back of the magazine and *Rolling Stone* now led with an "Art & Politics" rubric. New writers included Larry McMurtry, P. J. O'Rourke, Bill Greider (hired away from the *Washington Post*), and even Jayne Anne Phillips with an early short story titled "How Mickey Made It"—a rockspeak monologue about sex. It was a bigger deal around the office that Hunter was back, not in the magazine yet but on an assignment to cover the Roxanne Pulitzer divorce trial in Palm Beach. The magazine seemed to be growing stronger and Jann and I were getting along. We snorted coke in the bathroom at the

RS Christmas party, and I gave him a stuffed piranha as a present—which he bragged about and displayed on his desk for as long as I was working there.

When I told him I was leaving for *Newsweek,* he asked me what my title was going to be. I remember we were both wearing ties. When I said, "assistant managing editor," he got up from the big round table that was his desk and looked out the window with his back to me.

"Humiliating," he said. "*Newsweek* isn't even any good."

I couldn't read him; were we both humiliated? I looked at the piranha and waited for his punch line, which surprised me when it came as he turned back to face me.

"You won't get to work with Hunter anymore."

-ENDIT-

Covers, Newsstands, Hits (1,271)

If you were good at writing cover lines, it was like a gift. Some of the best editors I worked with were lousy at it, in the way some people can't tell a joke. The connection is obvious because the best cover language is almost always funny, and writing good headlines on deadline can make you feel like a Looney Toon producing an anvil or stick of dynamite from behind your back. If you could do that you earned a special status among other editors and word got around. Jann was good and so was David "the Stonecutter" Felton, who slapped "The Quitter" on the *Rolling Stone* cover when Nixon resigned—a particular favorite of mine.

Not long after I got to *Rolling Stone*, we had a big success with a Jim Morrison cover, which was surprising at first because he had died ten years earlier in his bathtub in Paris. We had no new information except the sense that the Doors were having a revival among teenagers. My deputy editor, David Rosenthal, spotted it early and assigned Rosemary Breslin (Jimmy's daughter) to talk to some kids, get the recent sales numbers and bang out a piece. We found a head shot with Jim's blue eyes piercing out at you, but what made the cover was the headline:

He's hot,
He's sexy
and He's dead

The cover, especially the headline, got a lot of pickup and we celebrated with some drinks in the office. I thought I had written the line but David corrected me, pointing out that he had said it in my office when we'd first started fooling around. Then Jann took credit for it, saying that David and I had come up with something like "still sexy" and he had fixed it with "he's dead."

It was a brilliant cover whoever wrote the lines, a meld of idea, execution and timing that pulled huge newsstand sales. For any cover to work it has to be surprising, smart in some way that throws attitude and handsome. Check, check and check.

ALL THE CLICHÉS ABOUT COVERS are true and I revisited them often. The cover is the face of your magazine; it should be a poster for what's inside; it should stop people for a second look; it should make them want to *buy* it. Some editors thought a bad cover that sold well was better than a good cover that didn't, but that was only true in terms of their job security. You could humiliate yourself with a bad cover, the way desperate editors still do all the time.

Some editors talked about "building" covers, and that's the right verb to use. The idea comes first, even if it's just "beautiful famous person looking beautiful and famous." Once the art director and I had two or three photos we liked (or were resigned to using the best of what we had), we would sit at a huge screen and start trying different crops, headlines, type sizes and styles. For a while I was prone to adding borders, and I went through two sticker phases—first real stick-ons (*Esquire*) and then fake photoshopped replicas (*Men's Journal*). Some editors were superstitious. Not me, except for no green logos, *ever*. Covers usually took a day or two because you wanted to reflect and tinker, but I've done them in ten minutes.

When I was first thinking about covers, I looked at a lot of album jackets and the best of them were wordless—the Beatles' *Abbey Road* and White Album, Pink Floyd, Led Zeppelin. It's a very long list. The strongest magazine covers don't need language, either. Annie Leibovitz's image of John and Yoko, and later images of 9/11 on *Time* and some other titles, proved that. The devastating torque of the story made any language beyond the date banal. The popularity surge of a dead rock star was, of course, a very different story. And so too was Caitlyn Jenner on the cover of *Vanity Fair* thirty-four years later.

EDITORS KEPT SCORE WITH NEWSSTAND sales. Many had bonuses based on the percentage of sell-through and total copies sold built into their contracts. Richard Stolley, the preeminent Time Inc. editor who bought the Abraham Zapruder footage of the JFK assassination for *Life* and was later the founding managing editor of *People*, had a kind of mantra for what sorts of covers sold best.

> Young is better than old.
> Pretty is better than ugly.
> Rich is better than poor.
> Movies are better than music.
> Music is better than television.
> Television is better than sports.
> . . . and anything is better than politics.

He wrote it for his editors to follow, and it was key to *People*'s success as the most profitable magazine of all time. But he amended it in 1980, following John Lennon's murder, which for many magazines was the best-selling cover until Princess Diana died.

> . . . and nothing beats celebrity death.

Coverage of Diana both before and after she was killed was like an open cash register for the print media. "Lady Di launched at least a thousand covers," wrote *Newsweek* media critic Jonathan Alter, "and hundreds of millions of newspaper and magazine sales." The most uncomfortable irony was that she was being chased by motorcycle paparazzi in Paris when her Mercedes swerved head-on into a pillar in the Pont de l'Alma tunnel at sixty-five miles per hour.

All the newsweeklies scrambled to put her on the cover, and then *Time, Newsweek, People* and *TV Guide* followed up with commemorative editions as well. On newsstands, *Time*'s first issue about Diana's death sold about 850,000—which was 650,000 more than usual. The commemorative edition sold 1.2 million copies. *Time*'s managing editor at the time, Walter Isaacson, announced that they were the two largest sellers in the history of the magazine. *People*'s commemorative issue ran without a headline and sold over 3.1 million, which makes it the second-highest *People* cover of all time, behind 9/11.

IF I'D HAD A NEWSSTAND MANTRA, it would have been that there are no rules. And smart wasn't necessarily better than dumb. By the 1990s celebrity weight loss and TV reality shows sold the best, except, of course, for dead celebrities. Now nothing sells like it used to.

Page views are the new measure, and cute puppies and cheap-trick penis headlines rule the click-bait newsstand. But before you feel too sorry for the old newsstand stars (both the subjects and the editors who put them on their covers), note that in an ever-fractionating media universe of aggregation and crypto-plagiarism it's both easier and more fun to manipulate traffic than it ever was to game the old newsstands. I leave it to someone else to say which turns editors more cynical.

The Big Get is always obvious in retrospect. When *Vanity Fair* put Caitlyn Jenner on the cover in July 2015, its website scored its largest ever single-day audience, with over nine million unique users, and according to a company-wide memo at Condé Nast, more than 46 million people consumed Jenner's cover story–related content on digital outlets like VanityFair.com, YouTube, Facebook and Twitter in the first twenty-four hours. But the print newsstand came in at less than 500,000. Gone are the days of a decade ago, when Jennifer Aniston gave *Vanity Fair* a newsstand record with 738,929. What is also obvious is that the newsstand as the anchor of any magazine business model is long dead.

DAVID ROSENTHAL AND JANN each still insist that the Jim Morrison headline was theirs. I'm the only one who can settle that argument. I think of it as mine.

–ENDIT–

Hunter Thompson (1,858)

THERE WAS A PARTY for Hunter upstairs at Pete's Tavern on Irving Place. It was to start early, after Hunter's *Letterman* taping in midtown, and I brought my sons, who were then five and seven. They were promised a burger and a quick exit after we said hello, but both were skeptical, especially Thomas, whose middle name is Hunter. He had heard too much about Hunter promising to bring him "a pony from the swamp," as Hunter had written to him in a note from Palm Beach before he could read.

We passed through the bar and went up a steep, narrow staircase. Hunter was standing at the top of the stairs, looming and vaguely menacing when you looked up at him. As we climbed, the boys scrambling in front of me, I could see that he was smiling.

"Good," Hunter said. "Too much fun, eh . . . ho ho . . ."

As the boys reached the landing, he squatted like a catcher, eye to eye with them, and presented his pack of Dunhill Reds.

"You guys want a smoke?"

THE FIRST TIME I SAW Hunter he was smoking alone, leaning on a terra-cotta urn that held a large palm in the fake-marble lobby of the Century Plaza Hotel in L.A. He was tall and unmissable, with cigarette holder, short-sleeved shirt, high-top Converse sneakers and sunglasses, and had just bellowed some explosive insult at the closed-circuit Nixon speech the media was being served. He was covering the end of the 1972 Nixon-McGovern presidential race, doing the work for *Rolling Stone* that would become *Fear and Loathing on the Campaign Trail '72*, and was already notorious in the press corps as "the Prince of Gonzo . . . the quintessential Outlaw Journalist," according to J. Anthony Lukas. Tim Crouse, who was also covering the campaign for *Rolling Stone*, wrote later in his book *The Boys on the Bus* that Hunter had a "touch of Genet" in him, and that "he

113

wrote to provoke, shock, protest, and annoy." Hunter was, de facto, not on the bus, and his reporting technique was often to hang back, as he was doing that night in L.A.—except for barking at the TV.

Nixon was there for a $1,000-a-plate dinner with his Southern California VIPs. Bob Hope was the master of ceremonies. Outside on the Avenue of the Stars, two thousand demonstrators were taunting the LAPD and reminding each other of 1967, when thirteen hundred club-swinging police tried to control ten thousand anti-war protesters while President Johnson spoke inside at a Democratic fund-raiser. Everyone was older, but the war was still with us.

I walked up to Hunter with the photographer David Strick and asked him if he'd been outside. I was working as a reporter for the Other Bob Sherrill and knew I was going to need a quote from Hunter.

"I'm *working* here," he said, and mumbled something about getting recognized outside. I could see he wasn't interested in explaining. "Fuck it," he added. I nodded, and Strick ran some frames through his motor drive as we left.

"If you see Kovic, tell him hello," Hunter said after us, jamming another Dunhill into his cigarette holder as we headed for the door. He was talking about Ron Kovic, the activist ex-marine who had been paralyzed from the waist down in Vietnam and years later would write *Born on the Fourth of July*, which Oliver Stone turned into the film with Tom Cruise playing Kovic. If you knew anything about Kovic, you knew he was a hero way before that movie came out, and *Rolling Stone* readers already knew because of what Hunter had written about him.

Outside, it was now very loud. Police lines had been set up on both sides of the avenue, creating a no-man's-land in the middle, where the TV crews were operating. Crossing the first line was easy. As I was crossing the second, a handsome young LAPD officer told me it might not be as easy getting back. I pointed to the credential around my neck and he shrugged, saying, "Like we're gonna care if they start throwing shit."

Most of the demonstrators were UCLA students, but some serious SNCC organizers and other anti-war leaders were there, too. I saw the guys from the L.A. chapter of the Vietnam Veterans Against the War, maybe forty of them in their battle vests and field hats, about to raise their upside-down American flag. I knew some of them from a piece I had recently done.

The double police lines were keeping the vets too far from the hotel facade, hung with Nixon banners, to make for good pictures. Everybody who was ever in what they called "the Nam" was hip to the value of the right image. The year before, a thousand vets had stepped forward one by one to hurl their medals at the Capitol Building in Washington, D.C. Kovic and many of these guys had been there, throwing away Purple Hearts and Bronze Stars on the steps of the Capitol with a big "Fuck you!" The pictures were devastating.

Hunter had been there; and he'd been with Kovic again in Miami at the Republican National Convention for the vets' "Last Patrol":

Not the kind of procession you just walked up and "joined." Not without paying some very heavy dues: an arm gone here, a leg there, paralysis, a face full of lumpy scar tissue . . . all staring straight ahead as the long silent column moved between rows of hotel porches full of tight lipped Senior Citizens, through the heart of Miami Beach.

. . . The only Vet speaker who managed to make himself plainly understood above the chopper noise was an ex-Marine Sergeant from San Diego named Ron Kovic, who spoke from a wheelchair because his legs are permanently paralyzed.

I would like to have a transcript or at least a tape of what Kovic said that day, because his words lashed the crowd like a wire whip. If Kovic had been allowed to speak from the convention hall podium, in front of network TV cameras, Nixon wouldn't have had the balls to show up and accept the nomination.

Writing like that rattled you awake, especially now that Nixon had a lock on the election. I found Kovic and delivered Hunter's greeting.

"He should be out here with us," Kovic said.

Meanwhile, Nixon's photo op was inside the hotel with several hundred Youth for Nixon bussed in from his hometown of Yorba Linda and other conservative spots around Orange County. They were fresh-faced kids, as was reported by the pool reporters allowed into the ballroom. Nixon smiling with those kids was going to be the front-page photo in the morning and the demonstration was going to be a sentence or two buried in the jump. Standing with the vets and Kovic in his wheelchair, you knew they knew all about that. Their frustration with journalism was another layer of their hatred of the war.

Back inside the Century Plaza, Hunter was still smoking next to the palm tree and watching the press corps milling around in the lobby, complaining about the lack of access. That was their story. My story was going to be a ground-level look at the way the Nixon campaign stage-managed the event inside and neutered the demonstration outside. I would skip all of the beside-the-point argument that the anti-war movement was dead and go with the obviousness of the in-your-face efficiency of the Nixonians. I figured Hunter would agree.

"Fucking sheep," he said when I walked up to him.

"Sheep?"

"Those kids downstairs . . ." he said, with deadpan emphasis. I nodded. He rolled the cigarette holder to the other side of his mouth, leaned his head toward me. "We're all sheep."

I had my quote. I studied him closely for detail to set it up, to describe what the Prince of Gonzo looked like talking about sheep. Even behind those dark glasses, he looked sad.

COVERING THE ANTI-WAR MOVEMENT always felt a little uncomfortable if you had not been to Vietnam yourself, and when Hunter finally went, he said he had no choice. In 1975, he had talked Jann Wenner into sending him to cover the fall of Saigon for *Rolling*

Stone, but when the assignment blew up, he quit the magazine cold. It was one of those apocryphal, myth-building stories about Jann that Hunter banged like a tambourine. The details, according to Hunter, had him arriving in Saigon (without a promised $75,000 advance) to find the country in chaos and other journalists scrambling to get out before the city fell. Hunter's plan had been to ride into the capital on an NVA tank but Jann had not wired the money and had canceled Hunter's company life insurance.

"Fucking Jann . . ."

My first move as managing editor at *Rolling Stone* was to try to get Hunter back in the magazine. He had remained on the masthead (his piece on the fall of Saigon wouldn't run until ten years after the city fell), and what *Rolling Stone* staffers called his "goat dance" with Jann was bumping along with predictable skirmishes. I called Hunter and suggested that he write about Roxanne "Foxy Roxy" Pulitzer and the mischief around her divorce from her significantly older newspaper-heir husband in Palm Beach. Both claimed the other had wrecked their marriage with drugs and adultery with more or less the same people, including the wife of the heir to the Kleenex fortune.

It was, as I explained to Hunter, a media story and a chance to write about tabloid journalism—which I suggested was as much a part of the American Dream as Las Vegas. And, of course, he would have to stay at the Breakers, the historic luxury hotel, to get the true feel of Palm Beach.

When I told Jann I wanted to send Hunter, he said sure, go ahead, try, but it would never happen. The next day I got a memo from him about how I was wasting my time. "Hunter won't do the work," Jann wrote. "You'll see!"

I sent Hunter a copy of Jann's memo.

The piece ran after I left for *Newsweek*, shepherded by David Rosenthal, who replaced me (and would later support Hunter with book advances many times when he was running Simon & Schuster). The headline was "A Dog Took My Place" and eight thousand words later the epilogue was as high-riding as anything Hunter ever wrote:

I am living the Palm Beach life now, trying to get the feel of it: royal palms and raw silk, cruising the beach at dawn in a red Chrysler convertible with George Shearing on the radio and a head full of bogus cocaine and two beautiful lesbians in the front seat beside me, telling jokes to each other in French . . .

We are on our way to an orgy.

When I called Hunter to congratulate him on the piece, he sounded strong and strangely sober. "I sent that fucking memo back to Jann with my expenses," he said.

–ENDIT–

Gonzo (455)

THERE ARE CONFLICTING STORIES about the first use of the word *gonzo* to describe Hunter's journalism but all credit Bill Cardoso. Maybe it was on the press bus during the 1968 New Hampshire primaries, maybe it was in a letter praising Hunter's 1970 Kentucky Derby piece, maybe it was just one night in a bar, but it was definitely Cardoso who used *gonzo* first, and he and Hunter agreed on that. It came to mean more than the lack of objectivity in the amped-up first-person voice that Hunter's work personified, but Cardoso would say only that he meant the word *scatologically*—as in crazy shit—and that he had used it many times before he applied it to Hunter's journalism.

Cardoso worked for the Other Bob Sherrill during the last two months *LA* was alive. He was getting back into journalism after owning a jazz club in the Canary Islands but was already famously the most *unfamous* practitioner of the New Journalism, among the New Journalists. I wish that sentence was as sharp as it is true in the way Cardoso wrote that the Tournament of Roses Parade was "the meeting ground of Babbitt and Costello."

Cardoso and the journalist and promoter Harold Conrad painted layers of polish on the word *hipster*—or, as Cardoso sometimes put it when describing himself, *wordhipster*. Conrad was less unfamous, since his friend Budd Schulberg had based the cynical fight press agent in *The Harder They Fall* on him, and Humphrey Bogart had played him in the movie. Harold wrote what used to be called a "Broadway column" for the *New York Mirror*, and the masters of the form, Damon Runyon and Walter Winchell, both wrote about Harold—mostly about his nights out with the gangster Bugsy Siegel. Conrad introduced Cardoso, Thompson, George Plimpton and Norman Mailer to Muhammad Ali, and put them in ringside seats. His idea was that if you get important journalists to cover the fights, the rest takes care of itself—especially after a toke or two.

You could ask Cardoso about that if he were still around, calling Conrad his main man for supplying all the bangi-bangi at the Muhammad Ali–George Foreman fight in 1974 in Zaire. *Bangi*, of course, translating from the Swahili as weed, or marijuana. With Cardoso gone since 2006, Bill Murray is probably the best authority left on Conrad. I assigned Conrad a cover story on Murray for *Rolling Stone* and they got to know each other. Bill's still got the classic bar furniture from Harold's place on West Seventy-second Street in his house at Snedens Landing. "I used to think I was sort of hip before I met this Harold Conrad" is what he said at Conrad's wake.

-ENDIT-

Dark Nights (1,223)

SNEDENS LANDING, SOME TWELVE MILES UP the Hudson River from Manhattan, is rich and discreet, with beautiful old trees. Celebrities and publishers and some writers lived there, but not writers I knew. The *New Yorker* writer Calvin Tomkins lived there and had written *Living Well Is the Best Revenge*, about the expatriate glamour couple of the 1920s, Gerald and Sara Murphy, who had made their home there into the 1960s. Over the years other "colonists" included Noël Coward and Ethel Barrymore, and later Orson Welles and Vivien Leigh and on and on. Many of the houses in Snedens had names like the Red Barn, Pirate's Lair and, my favorite, Ding Dong—suggesting a wild-ass Brigadoon. The Ding Dong House belonged to Margot Kidder after she moved from Montana via L.A., when she was burning through what she called her "Lois Lane money."

Margot loved writers and writing and politics and had started her memoir. Bill Murray was a neighbor. So was Mikhail Baryshnikov, whom her Montana friends called "that toe dancer." Her best friend, Rosie Shuster, who had launched *Saturday Night Live* with her first husband, Lorne Michaels, married the painter John Alexander on Margot's sloping lawn with summer light bouncing off the Hudson. It was Brigadoon with CAA on hold on Line 2. But there were dark times, too.

ONE WINTER NIGHT I was seated across from a former lover of Margot's, the ex–Canadian prime minister Pierre Trudeau, whom she had just started seeing again. William and Rose Styron were on either side of Pierre. *Nation* editor Victor Navasky was there too, with his wife, Annie. I met them all for the first time that night. Margot looked fresh and happy, eager as always for her friends to like one another. She knew more people from different directions than you'd expect from a movie star—a circumstance she mocked the more complicated her celebrity got for her. "Real life is more important" is what she would say when fans asked her what it was like to kiss Superman.

That night at the Ding Dong House, she started the dinner with a toast to Pierre and the declaration that the night would be "all politics and books, no show business." Everyone seemed to have a lot to say about both, except Styron, who said he was only allowed to drink wine these days, no more of the hard stuff, and then glanced from face to face around the table. He was handsome still, and thought by many to be America's greatest working writer. But that night, at that table, he seemed to smolder. This was five years before he wrote about his crippling depression in his "Darkness Visible" piece for *Vanity Fair.*

It was a long drive down from Roxbury, Connecticut, for the Styrons, and I wondered about that as the conversation rolled around the table, mostly about politics, but also some jokes about the cravat Pierre was wearing. At one point Pierre got up and played the sommelier, complete with towel over his forearm. Margot's various ex-boyfriends and husbands were also discussed, with Tom McGuane as the narcissistic but brilliant centerpiece. I knew Styron had helped McGuane when he was first trying to get published and that McGuane loved Styron's work, and I said that. Styron didn't seem to hear and I went on to say something flattering about Styron's first novel, *Lie Down in Darkness,* being important to McGuane. No response.

Margot and Rose were doing most of the talking, anyway. I kept glancing at Styron, who wouldn't look directly at any of us. At some point Pierre must have decided to take charge and, after answering Rose's question about the poetry of politics or some such, he turned to speak directly to Bill. I never saw anyone ask a more poorly timed question with better intentions.

"Can you tell us, Bill, about what you're working on? How is it going?"

"I want to leave," Styron said. "I'm sorry."

The Styrons left right away. It was a long drive home, Rose explained. Margot took this hard, and her mood dropped. The plan must have been for the Styrons to spend the night, but there was something more. The rest of us, except Pierre, left shortly after, saying good-bye to Margot shivering on her cold porch.

MARGOT HAD BEEN RICHARD BRAUTIGAN'S Montana neighbor when he killed himself with his .44 Magnum back in California in the large, old house he had bought in Bolinas before he started spending time in Livingston. His body was not discovered for a month. I had run a short piece of Richard's in the first issue of *Outside* and knew him well enough in Livingston to hear the story circulated among his friends that he'd left a suicide note that read, "Messy, isn't it?"

The story was apocryphal, and not funny when you thought about it. *Not discovered for a month.* Drinking and loneliness were the mix of Richard's depression, as they were for many writers, but until Styron's *Darkness Visible,* few wrote about it. Styron called alcohol *an invaluable senior partner of my intellect, besides being a friend whose ministrations I sought daily—sought also, I now see, as a means to calm the anxiety and incipient dread that I had hidden away for so long somewhere in the dungeons of my spirit.*

Maybe it is in those dungeons that creativity rages. Maybe we all catch glimpses of it many times without recognizing what we are seeing.

I HADN'T SEEN MARGOT in years when, at a stoplight in Livingston on a trip back to Montana, she pulled up next to me in an old SUV. It was the Fourth of July and a parade was planned for later that day. She had moved back to be near her daughter and grandchildren, and bought a big, solid house in town. She had climbed out of her own bipolar hell after landing, disoriented and terrified, in a stranger's backyard in L.A. Now she was getting acting jobs again and devoting herself to politics, which explained, sort of, why she was made up in a strange oxidized green color and had an oversized tiara on her head. I didn't recognize her.

"It's me—Margie," she said, leaning out her window.

"Who are you supposed to be?" I asked, when I saw that it was her.

"The Statue of Liberty."

She was on her way to a political rally she had organized, where thirty-five other women in similar costume were waiting for her to lead them in the parade—replete with suffragette banners that read "Montana Women for Peace," "Montana Women for Gay Rights," "Montana Women for the Environment," "Montana Women for Equal Pay for Women," "Montana Women for . . . ," etc., etc., etc. Life was good, she said, and that I should come over to her house later, which I did.

We sat in her backyard talking about old friends, writers most of them, crazy times—one insane night in Key West with McGuane and Hunter competing to take the most drugs. Crazier times. We knew who was already dead, suicide an answer to questions suffered in what Styron had called *depression's dark wood*. At one point we were almost making a list . . .

"Everyone we knew then had that in them," she said.

-ENDIT-

Bibliomemoir (338)

A NOTHER EDITOR, A RIVAL OF MINE with a fondness for hypocrisy, once said there was nothing worse than a truthless writer, but I didn't know any. I knew some whose writing had too much style and not enough story, but their lives were never like that. The writers I knew made their lives more interesting just by being writers—which is not the same as writing, but that divergence leads to nasty distinctions good writers never care about anyway. Let's just acknowledge that writing is hard so it is okay to be a little tortured, and some writers are. It can all go very dark, but there is no sweeter validation than getting published for the first time. I sometimes reminded writers of that.

Good editors, like doctors, develop a bedside manner. My editing was full of questions— all the same question, really. What *is* the story? What's the point of it? What do these sentences mean? Do they mean what you want them to mean? What if I told you they read like walk-ons in a Pirandello play?

To diagnose is an excellent verb for editors to keep in mind. *But what are you trying to say?* is not always an easy question, and the story isn't always what the writer says it is. I thought often about what it was like to read the writers I knew best, how direct their prose seemed and how the work spoke for itself, yet that made them even more mysterious. It was that way with all of the writers whose work I loved.

Bibliomemoir is a word I never used, never wrote until this sentence. It was defined beautifully by Joyce Carol Oates as "a subspecies of literature combining criticism and biography with the intimate, confessional tone of autobiography." Put another way, it is defining or giving meaning to a life through reading, and then writing about that reading. There is probably a seam between the reading and the living, but as an editor I could never find it.

–ENDIT–

II

One of the basic rules of *Esquire* was, if you're
going to write about a bear, bring on the bear!

— BYRON DOBELL,
Esquire EDITOR

Ambition (977)

WHEN I DIDN'T STAY OUT LATE I went to bed early but would wake in the middle of the night thinking about my next issue. It wasn't dread, but the ideas seemed relentless and exhausting. This was a problem until I forced myself to make notes.

There is science related to this, with studies supporting a theory of creative insomnia. I have no problem correlating creativity with sleep disturbance, but for editors I think the insomnia is a marker for ambition. They need to succeed so badly that all they can think about are ways to make their magazines better or at least fuck over a rival or two. I told myself that while timid editors would be seeing their lack of confidence blooming into futility in the glow of their digital alarms, I would get up and write something down, working simultaneously with the exhilaration of being too early and the fear of being too late. No wonder I couldn't sleep.

If I woke at three a.m. with a fresh thought about the lede of a problematic story, it might lead me to the layout or how that story fit into a package that hadn't occurred to me, or a sidebar or a cover line or whatever. Maybe that troublesome piece was really a sidebar to another piece if I just cut it by two-thirds.

I kept a notepad on the night table, but that wasn't as good as getting up and going to the typewriter or, by the mid-'80s, the computer. (Only now, with an iPhone, do I write in bed.)

In the beginning my notes sometimes went unread, but they cemented this or that idea in my head as I wrote them down. I tried to work in complete sentences. *Rank journalists by audience, best sellers and income* is more valuable the next morning than *journo power list*. But lists were also good, especially of calls to make. I never made lists like that during the day, when it would not occur to me to stop what I was doing and cold-call Robert Stone to ask him to write for *Rolling Stone*. But he got on my list one night when I woke up thinking about how much I liked the *New American Review* and remembered that my favorite story in all of the issues had been his "Porque No Tiene, Porque Le Falta" and that for the title he had used lyrics from "La Cucaracha" about not being able to get anywhere without marijuana . . . And that's how I met Bob Stone.

EDITORS ARE EXPECTED TO WORK all the time, which is no problem for highly motivated and ambitious people, but their ambitions vary. Some want the fame and power that comes with editing a prestigious title. The freedom to do what you want, and the expense-account hedonism that can come with that, is another road. So is knowledge, etc. The one thing I am sure of is that ambition and creativity do not always go together, or we would have much better journalism.

Some editors have egos bigger, even, than those of their star writers. You would think the most confident editors would have the biggest egos but they are usually the most reflective and accessible. They also keep the most complicated appointment calendars but are usually on time. The most effective media executives are like this too, but that doesn't mean editors are media executives—certainly not in the way Rupert Murdoch thinks of himself, although Rupert can write headlines and certainly knows his way around a newsroom.

As much as egos are reflected in the personalities of editors, specific magazines take on the personalities of their editors like owners coming to resemble their dogs. Put another way, a magazine always reflects the editor's ego, and the various personas of that editor follow along behind like parade floats. The more ambitious the editor, the more obvious what the parade is celebrating and where it is going. The biggest parade for the last three decades marched behind Anna Wintour at *Vogue*, but Tina Brown's parties celebrating *Vanity Fair* and Graydon Carter's *VF* Oscar parties were bold and effective bandwagons for the journalistic Big Life as well.

Until quite recently, many top editors had lavish offices with private bathrooms, kitchens and personal conference rooms. My first office at *Esquire* was like that, and I was self-conscious about it. But two floors above me, the editor of *Town and Country*, the sophisticated innovator Frank Zachary, had a suite of five rooms, including a sitting area with a view of Columbus Circle and a fireplace. He said it was designed to be comfortably intimidating. Top editors hate going to another top editor's office, however faint the whiff of subservience.

Calling people to your office might be good for your ego, but it will never build loyalty unless you sometimes insist on going to the office of whomever you want to see. And having an assistant place calls is both a sign of efficiency and a badge of arrogance. To show respect, I always placed my own calls to writers unless I was under deadline pressure or trying to make a point. Sometimes they'd tell me how annoying it was to pick up and hear "Please hold for . . ."

That annoyed me too, but I was not afflicted by the sense of being disrespected that I figured for many writers was related to their suspicion that nobody was reading them. Many said that that was what kept them awake at night. My job was to be encouraging, to keep them working. I suggested they try taking advantage of their insomnia: the middle of the night was a fertile time for thinking about difficult work. Many said they already had a similar routine but would rather just get some rest. Not me.

-ENDIT-

Shooters (1,093)

I DON'T REMEMBER THE EXACT YEAR, but it was before we worked together at *Esquire* that I was in a cab going down Fifth Avenue on my way to the office earlier than usual one morning when I saw the photographer Peter Beard emerging from Central Park with a beautiful woman, a model I recognized but couldn't name. They were both barefoot and laughing.

A journalist I knew told me later that Peter often insisted on taking new women friends on predawn walks through the park and that it was part of his charm. She knew about this firsthand.

"Photographers," she said. "You know . . ."

I did know. But the glamour of being a photographer was misplaced. Peter's sybaritic reputation (Bob Colacello famously described him as "half Tarzan, half Byron" in *Holy Terror,* his book about Andy Warhol) masked the meticulous nature of his work. Peter always prepared for shoots, sometimes compulsively, submitted budgets and all the rest that it took to keep working, and then obsessed over what he brought back before distressing and drawing on his prints (sometimes with his own blood) to turn them into *documentation* in the way that art critics use the word. He wasn't vain about his images, but you could tell he loved some of them more than he could articulate. He'd tap at a print with one of his crooked fingers and nod to himself.

Most of the photographers I knew were like that: not especially good at explaining themselves but loving what they did more than writers loved writing. And they all guarded their work, but in very different ways. Annie Leibovitz never wanted to show you any but what she thought were her best two or three frames. Neil Leifer loved his pictures so much he wanted to show you everything, and would talk about how you had to "prepare your own luck." Walter Iooss said he sometimes had trouble recognizing his best shots but was so calm about it he almost always got his way when he said he preferred one image over another. David Strick described a "sense of confused awe" that came with the surreal movie-set shots he was known for, but he usually knew what he had before he looked at his contact sheets. To work with any of them you had to remember that their talent spooked them a little, and you had to respect the larger *idea* of photography as the soul-stealing juju it is.

As an editor I favored large, type-free, full-frame images—a photographer's sensibility which, I was told, was obvious in my assignments and photo selection. I positioned myself as a purist and talked about knowing the great Eddie Adams at the Associated Press, which was true, although I am sure his awareness of me then did not go deep. But I studied his work, how he caught the off moment as well as the explosive image. It wasn't just his Pulitzer Prize–winning 1968 picture of the street execution of a Viet Cong prisoner, it was his portraits of West Virginia coal miners and Anwar Sadat looking out a window and Louis Armstrong cleaning his trumpet in Las Vegas. I told photographers that I wasn't interested in the obvious picture, and beyond that they were on their own.

That changed when I couldn't get what I wanted. Over the years, I occasionally said I would look only at images for a particular assignment that were framed horizontally if I already had such a layout in mind. I threatened to make photographers use lens filters with our cover's dimensions and logo to frame their cover tries. I even refused to sign off on expense accounts if there was not an admission or catalog receipt proving attendance at a gallery show I wanted a particular photographer or photo editor to see. And there was always someone new to work with.

There were many, many good "shooters," as some liked to be called, and an entire school of smart, artful celebrity photography was fanning out behind Annie. Plus, the great lions of fashion from the 1950s and '60s were still hungry for work. The suave and eminent Norman Parkinson, who shot several stories for *Smart* after he stopped working for *Vogue* and *Harper's Bazaar*, told me that if he didn't work he didn't have any fun. "Parks," as he was known to his many friends, had had plenty of fun reinventing his style decade by decade since the late 1930s—always with what appeared to be spontaneous images. Most charmingly, he insisted that he was a craftsman, not an artist, and also said, "A photographer without a magazine behind him is like a farmer without fields." I loved that.

The obvious implication was that magazine editors wielded almost feudal power. I kept that in mind when I was making assignments but never used the quote on photographers. "Surprise me," I'd say, falling back to my little speech about not being interested in the obvious. "Of course you're not" was Peter Beard's response. He said otherwise we wouldn't even know each other.

He was taking two assignments for *Esquire Gentleman*—standalone special issues timed to the spring and fall fashion collections in 1993. Fifteen years earlier, I'd edited the text when *Outside* had run images from *The End of the Game*, the first collection of Peter's documentation of the destruction of African wildlife, even though, as Peter said, it probably "wouldn't save a single fucking elephant." His next project, *Eyelids of Morning*, was about the crocodiles of what was then called Lake Rudolf (now Lake Turkana), and was my favorite photo book. But then his images for the first of these assignments—an "existential safari" to Miami Beach with the novelist (*Candy*), screenwriter (*Dr. Strangelove*) and *Esquire* vet Terry Southern—were obvious. We dressed them up with language about taking the obligatory swimsuit piece to a "harrowing, hallucinogenic new level" and called Miami "a place where nature's spectacle is overwhelmed by stress and density," but all we really had were good-looking models almost naked on a beach. I told Peter I thought the pictures were obvious.

For the second assignment, he chartered small planes to Kenya's northwestern frontier and hired hundreds of Turkana tribesmen as extras to surround his mostly naked white models as background and shot tribal elders at the center of the story in Armani blankets, Dolce & Gabbana patchwork sweaters, Byblos scarfs and Norma Kamali leopard-print coats. The elders all looked great and kept the clothes.

That's where the glamour was.

-ENDIT-

Slide Culture (1,135)

IT HAD OCCURRED TO ME in the summer of 1987 that I needed my own light box. Launching *Smart* out of Jean Pagliuso's photo studio on West Sixteenth Street, that simple plastic-and-metal box, with its translucent top and the light shining up from inside, was crucial throwback technology, even as we were "desktop-publishing" a national magazine for the first time. To see an Alvin Satin-Glow light box sitting on a worktable next to a Mac II was to see the past and future prankishly paired.

I already had my own loupe (magnifying hand lens), which I had taken to wearing around my neck as an unconscious if unsubtle signal that I was spending much of my time looking at pictures — which, because of the great photographic work being done seemingly everywhere then, was the right thing to be doing if you were a magazine editor. That was my message. I had already been acting like a photo editor, calling in submissions and looking at so many pictures I'd come to realize I was spending much too much time walking between my desk and the light table in the art department, way at the other end of the studio.

For those of you born after 1990, a "slide" was a positive photographic image recorded on 35mm film — usually either Kodachrome or Ektachrome, which were the best when it came to color accuracy, tonal range and sharpness. Kodachromes actually exhibited a visible "relief" image on the emulsion side. It was beautiful. Ditto Fujichrome when it came a little later and could also be processed a little faster, which was good for news and sports action. One or the other was what all the pros used, but everybody else could use them, too — typically Kodachrome. Every serious shooter I ever knew swore by this film. You could get technical and explain that a 35mm Kodachrome slide held detail equivalent to twenty-five or more megapixels of image data, but you didn't need to know that to be blown away by what you saw through your loupe on your new light box.

The two-by-two-inch cardboard or plastic mounts on the slides both framed and protected the images when photo editors dropped them into plastic carousels. The ensuing slide shows brought together various editors, researchers and designers working on a particular story. These shows could be shocking and disturbing, with thick silence in the room as you clicked through Jim Nachtwey's combat images. You could also be moved while viewing an old slide of a teenage Marvin Gaye when you were looking for an obit picture after the singer had been shot dead by his father in 1984. It felt like theater in those so-called color rooms.

Depending on the time of day and the proximity of the deadline, the shows could also turn suddenly into boisterous, impromptu captioning sessions, like one I remember at *Newsweek*, when an image was shown of vice presidential candidate Dan Quayle holding up a golf club with a particularly stupid look on his face: *Tennis, anyone?* Sometimes it also felt important.

I remember one Sunday night at *Newsweek*, sitting in that cool, dark color room on the nineteenth floor at 444 Madison Avenue drinking lukewarm coffee and looking at academic slides of Paleolithic cave paintings for a back-of-the-book piece about a discovery in southern France, when I made the connection between what I was doing and the thirty-thousand-year-old art I was looking at. It went beyond that art history experience we have all had sitting in a college lecture hall looking at Gothic cathedrals. It was tribal. It was what we did in my tribe. Prehistoric hunters squinted in the firelight at shamans' paintings of game on cave walls; editors like me looked at slides.

Slides had a physical reality that you could play with, move around and sequence and move around again on that light box. A short stack of slides felt good in your hand, like poker chips. Some editors held slides up to overhead lights and blew on them, as if that was a smart way to get rid of dust. Others wore thin white editing gloves all the time. The big light tables at magazines like *Rolling Stone* and *Esquire* became editorial watering holes where people would meet to socialize, and the translucent surfaces got smudged with Brie and spilled wine, some of which dried in the lines scratched from chopping cocaine with an X-Acto blade—a standard art department tool. Slide culture threw good parties.

PAUL SIMON WILL TELL YOU that he came up with his song "Kodachrome" while trying to rhyme "going home" into a melody he already had. But "going home" was much too square, and he already had those wonderfully defiant first lines, the true ones:

When I think back on all the crap I learned in high school
It's a wonder I can think at all

So he kept working, letting his mind wander until it slipped into something less familiar, and his cultural pitch was perfect. It (both the song and the film) was just so *not* full of crap. Nikons were cool; so were the growing number of hard-core professional and semi-outlaw freelance photographers roaming the world. When you were working at a light table in those days with a spread of images glowing up at you under your loupe, the film was so rich and sharp that those slides could, in fact, make you think all the world was a sunny day— especially for the photographers out there in it.

Making a deal to run William Wegman's photos of his Weimaraners Man Ray and Fay Ray, it struck me, strangely, that all the new creative photography had the feel of something coming and going very fast. That felt good and I even mentioned it to other editors, who agreed. But the changing technology rather than the art was the metaphor—a theme that would repeat with paper and ink. What we didn't understand was that the slides themselves would be disappearing, and fondness for our unnamed slide culture would look increasingly sentimental in the rearview mirror.

138   It was all over by the mid-1990s, when Kodak abandoned Koda-

chrome and digital photography came of age with the refinement of Adobe's Photoshop. A refrigerator full of the film still lingers as status among the most veteran pro shooters, but everyone knows that digital allows higher resolution at faster speeds. The only problem is almost academic: the concept of photograph as document is lost. Altering images with no record or verification turns everything into photo illustration as memory cards are wiped over and tricked out. Forget Peter Beard distressing and drawing on his prints with blood. Think instead of ISIS manipulating propaganda images and the betrayal of photography as witness.

-ENDIT-

Collaboration (with Rust Hills) (2,590)

Rust hills was a clever, precise writer known instead for his work as the fiction editor of *Esquire*, where he discovered, edited, championed, befriended and drove crazy generations of literary talent, including many of the writers in this book. By the time I got to work with Rust, he had published three books of personal essays, known as the Fussy Man Trilogy. Their titles were straightforward, their subtitles long winks at the reader:

- *How to Do Things Right: The Revelations of a Fussy Man*
- *How to Retire at 41; or, Dropping Out of the Rat Race Without Going Down the Drain*
- *How to Be Good; or, The Somewhat Tricky Business of Attaining Moral Virtue in a Society That's Not Just Corrupt but Corrupting, Without Being Completely Out-of-It*

I loved them all. When they were collected into a single volume, Rust wrote in an introduction that his mission was to create order out of chaos, but by then I knew he more often accomplished the opposite.

I arrived at *Esquire* in the late fall of 1989, and that July, in its annual "Summer Reading" issue, the magazine had run a "Tree of Fame." This was, more exactly, a "Pyramid of Shame," made of perhaps three hundred small yellow Post-its with the name of a writer carefully hand-printed on each and arranged on a bulletin board. The Post-it on top had Saul Bellow's name on it. Tom Wolfe was three rows down. (!!!) Cormac McCarthy was in the middle (suggesting that the idea was to move an author up and down as his reputation waxed and waned). The bottom row had twenty-seven names: Jennifer Allen, James Kaplan, Lionel Shriver. . . .

This was humiliating, and in that way "despicable," as the editors themselves pointed out in the issue. It was not really about writing talent and quality, of course, but about fame. What decent writer could be proud to be on it and yet, as it said in the caption, *no writer would want to be left off, either. Our hope is that, like Dracula when exposed to the sunlight, the tree will now die.*

It was brilliant, and everyone who followed literary politics knew it was Rust's work. As a younger editor, he had come up with the equally abhorrent "American Literary Establishment," which the magazine had published in July 1963. Early that year, Rust had taped a large sheet of white cardboard to his office door, with handwritten categories (publishing houses, magazines, agents, college MFA programs, etc.), and asked everyone on the staff to help him develop lists of the most important authors and influential literary forces on the scene. Rust then massaged the lists into what would become a map of the literary world in 1963, with a section in the middle called and colored the "Red-Hot Center," where the most worthy (Styron, Kerouac, Matthiessen, et al.) were proclaimed, to the subsequent horror of those placed elsewhere (the *New York Times Book Review* was in a section tagged "Squaresville") or not at all.

This was Rust at his best: not yet forty, chain-smoking and smiling his handsome, golden-retriever smile and quickly becoming as big a factor as anyone on his chart not just by creating it but by leading a renewed charge for literary fiction; he recruited Mailer, Nabokov, Heller, Malamud, Vonnegut, Styron, Updike, Bellow and Pynchon to write for him when they were still emerging. All white men, which today seems as distant as looking through the wrong end of a telescope, but Rust was a brilliant line editor and clever with titles, and he had a gift for pulling chapters from novels and making them read like short stories.

Walking into *Esquire* I knew all this about Rust, but I had never met him. We shared many writers, if "shared" is the right word, which it probably is not. (Rust would always catch that kind of thing.) But I too had edited Harrison and McGuane and James Salter and so on. And I was sure Rust and I were looking for the same charged mixture of passion and action, emotion and intellect, drama and melodrama, and sublime sentimentality. In other words, the kind of great fiction Rust had put in his Red-Hot Center.

I had gotten the job without having to tell anyone about my plans for fiction in the magazine and it felt like having a secret crush in high school. I remember that on my first day I was way too enthusiastic with everyone I met, and my exhilaration peaked when my new deputy, David Hirshey, said, "Rust is going to call you."

"Good!" I said. "What's his number? I'll call him!"

"Oh, don't call him," Hirshey said quickly.

I didn't know what that meant, but I let it go and continued down the hall to introduce myself to various editors in their offices. I didn't ask about the "Tree of Fame" that first day, but I was very interested in seeing it, as it was something I wanted to talk about with Rust. It had to be somewhere in the *Esquire* offices, maybe just propped up in a cubicle in a remote corner of the floor, as far as you could get from my new office, which is where I learned Rust sat, but I had not met him yet and he wasn't in his office and he didn't call.

WHEN I GOT HIM on the phone the next day, we both seemed to be talking very quickly, as if on our own deadlines, and Rust said, "You know, we have to talk," and I said, "Well, you're right." He said, "But I have some things we need to talk about." I said, "Well, what might they be?" This is where the conversation slowed down. I thought I heard him lighting a cigarette.

"Well, you know," he answered finally, "I have a certain . . . at *Esquire* I enjoy a certain . . . I have a kind of autonomy here when it comes to fiction and I need to talk to you about my autonomy."

"Well, you know," I echoed, and told him there was nothing I liked better than a good chat about autonomy. I couldn't help it. I heard his Zippo open and close again.

"Why don't you come on down to my office," I said.

"Well, you know, I'd like to . . ." But he couldn't because he was in Florida, where he lived with Joy Williams, who was a favorite writer of mine—but Rust didn't know that. What he knew and what he wanted me to know was that the reason he was in Florida was that his expense account had been cut back so drastically that *in fact* he could afford only a certain number of trips a year up to the New York office, and although my arrival was very important it was also a surprise, and so we were going to have to put off this very, very important conversation about autonomy, unless of course there was some way that a plane ticket could be purchased and he could *in fact* come sooner than he had planned out of fiscal responsibility.

And I thought, *Nah.*

Rust came quickly enough, though, and we were going to meet in my office and then go to lunch. I prepared for this because I wanted to disarm him. I had been listening to stories in the office about his passive-aggressiveness, and the deadline misunderstandings that grew out of the fussiness that lurked within his brilliance. When he walked in, I said, "You know, Rust, that Fussy Man material of yours is some of the best stuff I've ever read."

He cocked his head, as if he had heard but maybe not really heard, or certainly not accepted, a word of the compliment. This was too bad, because I'd meant it.

"Well, you know," he said, "I've been doing a lot of thinking about the fiction at *Esquire* and what you might be thinking that you want to do with the fiction at *Esquire,* and I must tell you I have no idea what you're thinking, but I am almost certain that I disagree with it."

"Well," I said, "I do have some ideas." I went on to explain that I loved fiction and fiction writers and always brought them in wherever I was working, sometimes persuading them to write nonfiction with a kind of literary rope-a-dope that had worked on a number of high-end fiction writers, who'd enjoyed the turn and had great success with it. I mentioned McGuane, for one, and Harrison, Jay McInerney and some others.

"All fine, fine writers," Rust said. "And you know, all friends of yours, too."

"Well, I know they're friends of yours, too. Let's talk about collaboration."

"No one knows who I am," Rust said, which I think meant he didn't get sufficient credit for editing the fiction because he wasn't a self-promoter. The implication, of course, was that collaborating with a shameless self-promoter like me would guarantee his obscurity.

"Everyone knows who you are," I said. "Plus, everyone says you always want to spread the credit around."

"Well, that's true," he said, frowning. "But you know, there's another thing. I have to buy lunch for every writer we want whenever they come through and . . ." And on he went about his expense account.

It turned out okay between us, though. We published some writing that we were proud of, and we, you know . . . well, some things happened that we both enjoyed . . . but then again, Rust never did get as much credit for *Esquire*'s fiction as he deserved and I feel bad about that still.

I HAD ARRIVED AT *ESQUIRE* just when the National Magazine Award nominations came out for that year. The magazine was up in five categories and, as usual, there was a nomination for fiction. My predecessor, Lee Eisenberg, had been responsible for these nominations, and it would not be the most comfortable of career moves for me to accept any of the awards at the banquet if *Esquire* won, but that's the way it worked and still works. Whoever is the sitting editor in chief goes to the podium with remarks and thanks from the magazine, no matter how tenuous his or her connection to the work being honored.

So when the day came, off I went with the other *Esquire* editors to the ballroom at the Waldorf Astoria Hotel. We had a good table near the front and *Esquire* won for fiction. I was determined to be gracious and had prepared a short observation about the importance of the short story in American culture. There was some applause when I got to the stage and was handed the Calder stabile, known as an "Ellie," for elephant, which it resembles abstractly.

"Thank you," I said. "Fiction has always been important to everyone at *Esquire* . . ." I looked out over the room and then down at the table where my colleagues were sitting, and there was Rust waving at me. I had been planning to get on and off fast, but Rust kept waving.

"Never mind the rest of us," I went on. "If there's anyone who deserves this award, it's Rust Hills, because Rust has been the fiction editor at *Esquire* since . . ." I believe I said "1936," as a joke (he had come to the magazine in 1957). I mentioned the "Red-Hot Center" and the "Tree of Fame" and called Rust to the stage—a dubious move that in the interest of time is never done. The room went very quiet. But then, as Rust's name registered and the room broke into enthusiastic applause, I thought, *Aha, the collaboration begins now.*

"See," I said into his ear when he got to the stage, "everyone knows who you are."

He looked at me stunned, maybe even angry, for what seemed like a long time, at least until the applause began to die. I pushed the Ellie at him, and he took it and gazed out over the tables and said, "Thank you." That was it and off we went.

We returned to our table, and as it was the custom at those luncheons to put the Ellie in the center of the table, that's what I made Rust do. He kept staring at it, and I could see that he was thinking hard, perhaps about the speech he hadn't made, perhaps about collaboration. Finally, when the last award was announced and *Esquire* didn't win it, Rust leaned forward, grabbed the Ellie and, pulling it toward himself, said, "I really can keep this, can't I, Terry?"

"Of course you can't keep it," I said. "The magazine won it and, more importantly, the Hearst Corporation likes to show them off in the lobby. We have a lot of them. And that's where they all live, in that big glass case. Editors don't get to keep them."

This made Rust sad, as if I had said that everything we did was collaborative and there was no autonomy. This is not what I meant, and when I think back, it makes me sad, too.

• • •

RUST DIED IN THE SUMMER of 2008 and that fall a group of us who had worked with him over the years at *Esquire*—Will Blythe, Byron Dobell, Lee Eisenberg—or been edited by him there—Richard Ford, Jim Salter, Beverly Lowry—spoke about Rust to a small audience in the Trustees Room of the New York Public Library.

To prepare, I asked several writers, including Jim Harrison, what it had been like working with Rust. Rust had engineered *Esquire*'s publication of Jim's novella *Legends of the Fall*, which had been a very important moment for the magazine and, of course, for Jim. Jim sent me a short note and I read it at the library: "I knew Rust Hills since the seventies. Like all true lovers of literature, he was a remarkably cranky man. I was thrilled when he got my *Legends of the Fall* into *Esquire*. I visited he and Joy on their lagoon in Sarasota and it took us four liquid-filled days to edit seven pages out of 'Revenge.' We always had a fine argumentative time together. Jim Harrison."

That's the way it had been with Rust and me, too. And I said that, and told the story about Rust wanting to keep the Ellie. I also said how it had bothered me more and more as Rust and I became friends and, you know, friendship can be a bumpy road, but the one I traveled with Rust still makes me smile because the truest thing I can write about Rust is that no one I ever worked with cared more about writers and writing and the writing life and how it worked, and living that life and editing and all of that in some swirl that once in a while would lead to something like the friendship we had in the end and maybe even a National Magazine Award or two.

"Shit yes, Rust, take it!" is what I should have said and handed it to him and told him to put it in his solarium in Sarasota or wherever that lagoon of his was.

Years later when I told him that, it was not long before he died and he had grinned and lit a cigarette.

"Well, you know," he said, "maybe it's not too late."

-ENDIT-

Assignments (1,339)

*Once upon a time a journalist and a photographer
set out to whore their way across Asia. They got a
New York magazine to pay for it by claiming they
were going to do a story about the Khmer Rouge.*

— WILLIAM T. VOLLMANN

THE NEW YORK MAGAZINE WAS *Esquire*. The assignment was
mine. I had made it thinking I knew the promise of Vollmann's work
and I was looking for something surprising. On George Plimpton's
suggestion a year earlier, I had assigned Vollmann a vaguely defined
"travel" piece and paid his expenses to an abandoned research station at the magnetic North Pole, where he spent two weeks alone
almost freezing to death. He wrote a slapstick but harrowing essay
that told of accidentally setting the place on fire and waking up with
his sleeping bag in flames—permanently singeing off his eyebrows.
There were also hallucinations involved.

It was all research for his novel *The Rifles*, partly about Sir John
Franklin's doomed 1845 expedition to the Arctic. Vollmann was up
front about his research motive, so that was fine, and he was an interesting new-writer experiment that had paid off.

The Khmer Rouge piece started with his idea that he could track
down the infamous Pol Pot, who had been responsible for the deaths
of three million Cambodians during his four years as prime minister
and was now supposedly hiding out at a secret ruby mine on the
Cambodia-Thai border. I had no illusions about Vollmann finding
Pol Pot, but as another off-beat travel piece maybe it could turn into
something.

About two months later, Will Blythe, who was *Esquire's* literary editor and often handled difficult pieces, told me Vollmann had filed almost one hundred pages—apparently planning to publish them intact as part of his next book. Blythe said that it was brilliant but *problematic.* "It could get you fired" is how he explained what he meant by that. He also mentioned that Vollmann had been meticulous with his expense account, although most of his receipts were from prostitutes. "At least you'd go out with a bang," Blythe said.

Vollmann was calling it "More Benadryl, Whined the Journalist," and Blythe seemed surprised, and then delighted, when I said we should start cutting and see where it got us. We worked on it for two weeks, trimming and framing it into shorter sections, until it was down to nine thousand words. But we didn't touch the "Once upon a time" lede quoted above. Running the piece with that first graph intact may have been self-conscious and offensive for many reasons, but it signaled Literature, which got us off the hook a little as pornographers.

Perhaps pressing our luck, we called Vollmann a "postcolonial Henry Miller" in the Contents and a "libidinal Joseph Conrad" in the "Backstage with *Esquire*" notes about contributors: "As his hellish journey into the sexual Heart of Darkness attests ('De Sade's Last Stand,' page 161), Vollmann confronts all the preconceived notions about sex and death in Southeast Asia and remains utterly undaunted."

You have to take literature where you find it.

THE PERFECT STORY IDEA, the winning query you get from a writer trying to sell you a piece, is not the same as a movie or TV pitch. It has to go deeper, not like the one-hundred-page book proposals that are now common, but it has to have more to it than some snappy patter about Huckleberry Finn owning a nightclub. I also insisted that my editors get pitches in writing from writers, or write them down themselves to distribute at idea meetings.

Many writers sent clips of their published stories, but when I took the time to read them I always imagined how much better the pieces might have been. This was not healthy and I knew it, so I occasionally asked for writing samples of stories before they were edited. The Other Bob Sherrill had taught me that, although he'd hinted that it sometimes made writers uncomfortable once they thought about it and got over their enthusiasm for the lack of solidarity among editors.

Graydon Carter, who cofounded the brilliant *Spy* and has edited *Vanity Fair* now for almost twenty-five years and counting, says the best stories are a combination of access, narrative and disclosure, which is very smart and explains why editors always look for those possibilities in a query. They also look for texture and depth even if what they're reading is only a one-page letter.

The pieces to bet on from new writers, the ones that seldom fail, are stories the writer had been living with or at least thinking about for years, if not their entire life. I'm not talking about a memoir but, rather, a writer dropping in somewhere where something is going on with their own rich memories of the place. This is the way John Kaye, the best writer at *LA*, explained why he was qualified to write about Ryan O'Neal.

> In high school Ryan was noisy, unpredictable, and sometimes violent. We partied and surfed together, along with Jan and Dean, future Beach Boy Bruce Johnston, and two of the guys who kidnapped Frank Sinatra Jr. My brother dated Frank Jr.'s sister Nancy while he was at U.S.C. In 1969, my wife, Harriet, and Ryan's first wife, Joanna Moore (Tatum O'Neal's mother) were roommates in the same mental hospital, and both died as a result of alcohol abuse and mental illness. Two years ago, while I was directing my first film, Ryan's second wife, Leigh Taylor-Young, auditioned for a featured role. She was a lovely woman and a fine actress, but she didn't get the part.

There is at least one good assignment per sentence in that paragraph.

ESQUIRE RAN A SERIES OF "Why I Live Where I Live" pieces in the 1960s that worked on the same principle: reporting by osmosis. At *Sports Illustrated*, I sent Francisco Goldman to the final Yankee vs. Red Sox play-off game in 2004 knowing that he had grown up a Boston fan and that loyalty to the team was the strongest bond he had with his father. Frank wanted the assignment so bad he said he'd write it in exchange for a ticket: *Most Red Sox fans are the offspring of Red Sox fans, and every one of them has a father whose story is longer and more painful than his own.* No amount of reporting will give you that.

Most stories that get better as they get longer are charmed like that from the beginning. When I read in a bound galley of Rick Bass's *Oil Notes* that just by the way the corporate guy "put his hands on the table you knew they were going to make a deal," I knew that Bass was the real deal himself. Of course Bass had worked as a geologist. Like his father.

Sometimes I saw talent everywhere, in everything I read. Other times I thought there was no such thing as a bad idea, just bad execution. This sounds self-serving, but being interested in everything makes you a more effective opportunist—and that's what an editor has to be, a student of unintended consequences.

That issue of *Esquire* with the Vollmann piece had Winona Ryder on the cover in a black slip (the piece by Michael Hirschorn: "Winona Among the Grown-ups") and a literary and journalistic lineup that featured Ken Auletta on the presidential press corps ("The Boys on the Bus Are Dead"), Jim Harrison with "Outlaw Cook," Jacob Weisberg with "The Devil in John McLaughlin," Stanley Bing offering advice to "Fail Big. Win Big Bucks," Kurt Loder with "Honky-Tonk Heaven," David Owen with a "Letter from Golf Camp," Ivan Solotaroff on crack in the NBA ("Swee'pea and the Shark"), and a "Best New Restaurants of 1992" package by John Mariani. It was a good issue, even without Vollmann, but it needed something more. Something nobody had ever before thought to write or assign.

Even if it all came together with the fortuity of drawing to an inside straight.

–ENDIT–

Little Jimmy (1,471)

JIM HARRISON LIVED ON A FARM in Lake Leelanau, Michigan, fifty miles from where he was born. There was also a cabin on sixty acres off a two-track road five hours north by car, beyond Grand Marais on the Upper Peninsula, where he sometimes retreated to write. But Jim could write anywhere, and he did.

Some writers set themselves up so they could work with a view — the mountains, the sea, a river, perhaps an interesting cityscape. Others worked closed in, with no distractions, just their desk and whatever they had on the wall in front of them. Jim was like that, working best from two to four in the afternoon in tight places like the one-room ranch cabin with small windows and a calendar twenty years out of date on the back of the door. This was the winter place in Patagonia, Arizona, that Jim's early screenwriting money had paid for. A journalist sent from New York to interview him had walked with Jim the half mile from the main house to his writing cabin and asked if it was a movie set. This turned into a story Jim would tell about what he saw as the double misunderstanding about his work because no, he wasn't in the movie business. Not really, anyway.

The stories about Jim's adventures writing for film began when Jack Nicholson loaned him $30,000 to live on for the time it would take to write three novellas that might make good movies. They could also be published together as a book, which was more important to Jim. He had a draft of *Legends of the Fall* in ten days and was done with the second, *Revenge,* in another two weeks. *The Man Who Gave Up His Name* came a little slower and was the only one that didn't become a film. It was about a just-retired midwestern CEO named Nordstrom who visits Manhattan to see his betrothed daughter, does battle with coke dealers and moves on to the Florida Keys, where he finds work as a chef and dances all night with the waitresses.

Jim kicked off all three novellas with great show, but the lede of *The Man Who Gave Up His Name* was my favorite:

Nordstrom had taken to dancing alone. He considered his sanity to be unblemished and his nightly dances an alternative to the torpor of calisthenics. He had chided himself of late for so perfectly living out all of his mediocre assumptions about life.

But it was the title novella, *Legends of the Fall*, the one Jim said he wrote in ten days, that became his big ticket. It was a triumph when then editor Clay Felker ran it in *Esquire* at twenty-three thousand words in 1979, followed by *Revenge* at a thundering thirty thousand. The magazine appeared bolder than it had been in years, and Jim seemed to have invigorated American fiction. The traditional four-thousand-word short story, the meat of MFA programs and the staple of all the major magazines, looked claustrophobic in comparison. Jim's vocabulary was not tricky. Although his sentences ran long and were compound, it was a surprising style, fast and clear, that suggested moving water that one reviewer said "you could see through down to the bottom of his meaning." Other reviewers mentioned Hemingway's "iceberg," with its unstated currents beneath the surface, and for years after, the prominent blurb on the paperback editions of all of Jim's books was from Bernard Levin in the London *Sunday Times* about the *Legends of the Fall* collection: "Jim Harrison is a writer with immortality in him."

Immortality is a big word, but Jim's friends, his rivals even, just nodded and looked forward to the next book. The novellas were heroic, in what Jim later called "an oracular style." That's what sold to the movies—or, rather, to the specific people in the movie business who wanted to work with Jim. Not just Jack Nicholson but producers and directors like John Huston and Mike Nichols. The list was long and Jim was proud of it, and he liked being friendly with movie stars. I think everyone Jim knew in the movie business got something memorable from him, something personal, a little bit of poetry like the story he sometimes told over steak dinners about the most devout girl in his youth Bible group having "the feral odor of a butcher shop to go with her great beauty."

Jim became more self-referential as you got to know him. Some people were put off by this, but I liked it because the stories would tumble out. My mention of the documentary *The Kid Stays in the Picture* prompted a story about going to the director Bob Evans's house with Jack to screen movies and play tennis. Or about how Jack bought Bob's house when it was in foreclosure and then gave it back to him. Or how Nicholson's business manager said that Jim was the only guy who ever paid Jack back.

JIM WAS INTERESTED IN VISITING the graves of writers and sometimes traveled for that purpose. Out of that came the idea (mine) of a literary travel column (mine), which became "The Raw and the Cooked" when Jim turned it toward food (his idea). It was also Jim's idea to borrow the title from the French anthropologist Claude Lévi-Strauss, following Lévi-Strauss's idea that "opposites drawn from everyday experience with the most basic sorts of things—e.g. 'raw' and 'cooked,' 'fresh' and 'rotten,' 'moist' and 'parched,' and others—can serve a people as conceptual tools." Heavy lifting, but then suddenly on the nose and droll when applied to, say, *cuisine minceur*, which Jim wrote was *the moral equivalent of the fox-trot*. After a massive lunch at Ma Maison, in West Hollywood, with Orson Welles, Jim wrote that he had to *brace his boot on the limo's doorsill to hoist the great director to the curb.*

Food—cooking it and eating it—had always been central to Jim's writing in that it offered *a commensurate and restorative joy.* A large portion of his days fishing and hunting, especially with close friends, were, as Jim Fergus described it in his introduction to his "Art of Fiction" interview with Jim for the *Paris Review,* "devoted to planning, shopping for, preparing, discussing, and finally eating one breathtaking meal after another, at the end of which preliminary discussions and preparations for the next meal begin almost immediately." Jim's e-mails often noted cooking truths, such as the impossibility of finding Gambel's quail or antelope in the supermarket—or that *in my youth there were so few presents that I liked, mostly a jar of herring or a small orange.*

"The Raw and the Cooked" began in *Smart* in late 1988, moved with me to *Esquire* in 1990 and ran up twenty-nine columns there— all of them about joy, obsession, love, sex, family, landscape, life, death and all of the confusing reasons why there is nothing better than having something good to eat. I bragged that Jim was giving America its appetite back.

Most publicly ambitious of all Jim's meals was a thirty-seven-course lunch prepared by French chef Marc Meneau from recipes drawn from seventeen cookbooks published between 1654 and 1823. Jim wrote that the meal lasted *the same amount of time as the Varig flight from New York to Sao Paulo.* The piece ran in the *New Yorker* in 2004, and gourmands still talk about it. Chefs loved him too, because he cooked himself, with great attention to detail and respect for the most normal foods.

Eventually, Jim wore some of this on his face, and with the blind eye from a childhood accident and the disappearing teeth that he refused to replace, he could look a bit weathered, but he was still handsome in the manner of a mahogany stump. He also put on some weight, which annoyed him, and he watched it in his own way, explaining that a two-hour walk in the woods earned him a thirty-two-ounce rib eye. Tom McGuane said that if he added up all the weight Jim had mentioned losing over their years of correspondence, it would top two thousand pounds.

Jim's seventieth birthday dinner was private, except for the e-mails that went to friends who would not be in attendance but needed to know that Mario Batali would be flying out to Patagonia loaded with food and wine to prepare an appropriate meal. I noted that Mario had made sure the Sauternes and the Madeira were from Jim's birth year, 1937. When Jim sent the menu, he explained that it was for "Little Jimmy's" birthday dinner. You could almost see him cocking his head like he did sometimes to emphasize a childlike joy that I figured went back to that *jar of herring or a small orange.*

–ENDIT–

Display (511)

I<small>F THE EDITOR IS GOOD</small>, you can understand every story in his or her magazine just by reading the display copy—which is what a lot of readers do, no matter what the research says. Display copy includes headlines (or "heds"), subheds (or "decks"), pull quotes and captions; and it is usually finished last, on deadline. Tone lives in display copy, and so does credibility.

Even short captions have to add facts and narrative; you can't just drop "Lake Tahoe" under a photo of Lake Tahoe. Depending on what the story is about, Lake Tahoe has to be polluted or mysteriously deep or perhaps where Michael has Fredo killed by Al Neri in *The Godfather: Part II*.

My rule about profanity was that it was allowed in body text, never in display copy. But there were fine lines there, too. I cost *Rolling Stone* $500,000 in automotive advertising when I ran the phrase "Mexican hum-job" in a pull quote from a Richard Price short story called "Walk on It." The client was offended. At least that's how the agency guy explained it, even though the client was infamous in the Detroit advertising community for making sales reps pay for many drinks and tip wildly at his favorite topless bars on Big Beaver Road. It didn't matter that "Walk on It" was nominated for a National Magazine Award.

The best headlines are witty and a little self-mocking, like the all-time great "Headless Body in Topless Bar," from the *New York Post* in 1983 or, more recently in the *Sun*, the playful "Obama Lama Ding Dong" over a photo of the president and the Dalai Lama meeting in the White House.

You can kill a great story with a bad headline. But writing heds can be the most fun part of editing if you're good at it. If you're not, collecting howlingly bad ones makes you a better editor. I am thinking here of "Federal Agents Raid Gun Shop, Find Weapons" and "Statistics Show That Teen Pregnancy Drops off Significantly After Age 25" and "Missippi's Literacy Program Shows Improvement." Bigger mistakes are never that kind of funny.

When his film *Malcolm X* came out, I put Spike Lee on the cover of *Esquire* with his arms crossed in an X. It was a strong cover. But the headline inside the magazine on the story by Barbara Grizzuti Harrison was a big, smart-assed mistake: "Spike Lee Hates Your Cracker Ass." I knew it was all wrong the moment I saw it in print, which was, of course, too late. It was so simple in retrospect, like all stupid mistakes. I thought about blaming my staff of editors for not talking me out of it. None of them had tried. Naturally, Spike called to tell me with measured politeness what a cheap shot it was.

That headline was hate-mongering and I'm still ashamed of it. But it wouldn't have been, and it would have been so easy to make it a much better headline, by changing just one word: "Spike Lee *Loves* Your Cracker Ass."

-ENDIT-

The Older Bob Sherrill (885)

Eᴅɪᴛᴏʀs ᴀʀᴇ ᴜsᴜᴀʟʟʏ ᴏʟᴅᴇʀ than the writers they edit, but I was younger than most until I was over forty and editing *Rolling Stone*. By the time I got to *Esquire*, ten years later, I was interested in what it—growing up? growing old?—was like, but I wasn't sure how to frame it as a piece. I wanted something amusing and smart, targeted toward *Esquire*'s aging male demo. My young editors thought it would be a downer however I framed it. They said the *Esquire* I was editing was too serious. Floundering, I gave up on the feature but wrote to Sherrill with the vaguely related suggestion that he write an advice column for the magazine. That's all I said, on a postcard with the image of a crazy-looking Albert Einstein on the front—the one with him sticking out his tongue. I figured Bob would come up with something.

Dear Terror:

Mr. Lonelyhearts? You are serious, aren't you. Good boy! I am, too, but we better get even more serious. Certainly I am interested in giving advice to anyone who will listen. Let's start with you. I am old, and time's winged chariot doesn't seem to be just flubbing around. Sooooo . . .

I have been filing stuff for, maybe, a book, In Praise of the Accidental Life, *a title that you will recognize as more than a little ironic. It's about letting life happen to you, regardless of the pain and so on but with its soaring joy. I think I could draw a good bit of stuff from those files, and my experience . . . love, rich, poor, trouble, horror, panic, deep mystery, love . . . lying a lot and narrow-eyed chronic suspicion (both rife in that reality of mine) . . . you can only get into trouble, get hurt, feel fine, exhilarated, get sick, die etc. How about we try for something about that . . . But funny.*

Behave,

BS

"The Truth About Growing Old" by Robert Sherrill ran in *Esquire* in July 1992. It was a wry masterpiece. He was sixty-seven, which doesn't play as old in 2016 but did then, and if he were writing now, at ninety, maybe that would be the new sixty-seven.

In one section, Bob responded to an editorial in the *Greensboro News and Record* that had pissed him off. "Retirees now are basically a gender-role traditional group," the writer claimed. "They are the baby-boom parents. For this cohort to have house-husbands just doesn't work very well. It might change once you get the more so-called gender-role-modern generations retiring. . . . There needs to be a dialogue when they're forty-five or fifty." Editor that he was, Bob couldn't help attacking the jargon inherent in his subject matter. *Hey, you old basically gender-role cohorts, let's dialogue!*

From there on, he blasted away at platitudes and stereotypes, *the Gospel of the Golden Years*, which he called *The Big Fib*:

> . . . *nouveau fogies in expensive sweat suits (sweats to hip ancients) . . . AND NOW FOR THE FUN YEARS. . . . Alzheimer's (a word that once specifically meant premature senility but now means any senility or senile dementia. I prefer dementia or senility, thank you), and on and on and on. . . . But whatever, death does not interest me. Fuck death.*

The photo I ran with the piece was of Bob standing on the hood of his car—that sky-blue *sixty-fo fo'd*. He was not pissing into the wind like he was in the image he had conspired with the photographer to make, but it was from the same roll. When I told him I couldn't use the pissing shot, he asked me who had made me an editor, anyway. And when we were closing the piece, he edited me editing him, not my line work on his copy but my thinking about how to kick the magazine in the ass. He said something about "finding another pony at the bottom of the box." Push it, maybe with another piece or two. That's how good editors were thinking back when he was at *Esquire*.

I came up with a series of "The American Male at Age . . ." pieces—starting in childhood and hitting milestones as a man grows older.

For age ten, I assigned Susan Orlean, who spent time with a fifth grader in suburban Glen Ridge, New Jersey. Her lede was "If Colin Duffy and I were to get married, we would . . ." followed by a run of details she pulled from inside Colin's head, including "be good at Nintendo Street Fighter II" and ending with "For fun, we would load a slingshot with dog food and shoot it at my butt. We would have a very good life."

That's the way editing could go sometimes—from marginal idea (Mr. Lonelyhearts) to good idea (Bob on getting old) to good execution (his piece) to bigger idea (the series about men aging) to great work (Susan's piece). But I also knew that the adjective for editors who got to enjoy that kind of editorial progression was *lucky*. Sherrill had two things to say about that: Susan's piece kicked his piece's ass; and luck didn't have anything to do with it.

-ENDIT-

Women's Magazines (1,840)

Besides the top job — editor in chief, it was usually called — there were five key masthead positions on every magazine: art director, managing editor, copy chief, research editor and photo editor. At every place I worked except *Sports Illustrated*, at least three (and often four) of those five jobs were done by women. At *Rolling Stone*, the three editors directly below me, the art director and the photo editor were all women—and they were not "the kind of girls who get high with their cats," as I once heard female staffers at *RS* described.

It might sound condescending, sexist even, to write that those women were all creative and tough and thoughtful beyond any cliché about making the trains run on time (although they did that too), but that's the way I remember them. "She's a great number two" was what you heard about strong women editors, which was usually true, but at the same time there was nothing more patronizing. Tellingly, applying the same praise to a man would have been devastating— which underlines a lack of fairness when it came to moving to the top of the masthead.

Magazine mastheads have always reflected the lack of equality in the separate-but-never-equalness of the men's and women's magazines themselves. You could define the difference by the amount of so-called *service* they ran. Women's magazines were full of advice and how-to pieces, many written by women who would have preferred covering politics to comparison-shopping for panty hose. Men's magazines were understood to be more serious and ran journalism and important fiction. Perhaps men didn't need any advice.

Until the 1960s, most of the women's magazines were even edited by men, most notably John Mack Carter, a diminutive Kentuckian and "bluegrass evangelist" for women's magazines, according to *Advertising Age*. John Mack, as he was known, arrived at work one morning in 1970 to find his office at the *Ladies' Home Journal* occupied by dozens of feminists demanding his resignation, as well as services like day care for staffers' children. Some were sitting on his desk smoking cigars. He wasn't about to give up his job, but he listened for eleven hours. "There was more discrimination than I thought," he said later.

John Mack also edited *McCall's* and, ultimately, *Good Housekeeping*—the other top women's titles in the "Big Three"—making him theoretically the most important shaper of women's magazines from the 1960s into the '90s, when he stepped down. They were "badly behind the times," he told the *New York Times* in an interview in 1963. "They were using baby talk to communicate with their readers." But the earth had already moved, so to speak, in 1962 when Helen Gurley Brown, a forty-year-old advertising copywriter and self-described "mouseburger," published *Sex and the Single Girl*.

It was an immediate best seller, although, preposterously, Helen was barred from saying "sex" during her afternoon television appearances, which made it impossible for her to mention the book's title. She was soon a favorite on *The Tonight Show*, where she told Johnny Carson, "Good girls go to heaven. Bad girls go everywhere." And maybe Natalie Wood, playing Helen, even slept with Tony Curtis's character in the movie—which contributed further to what Helen called "the hullabaloo."

It was a moment. Helen worked up a prototype of a women's magazine and started showing it around. Gone were the etiquette tips and recipes. Her frank and hilarious observations about young women were both shocking and obvious. Of course they liked sex, and wasn't it more interesting than the search for the perfect Jell-O salad? These women needed a magazine, and Helen became editor in chief of *Cosmopolitan* in 1965 with no editing experience. In its initial incarnation, in 1886, *Cosmo* was a "first-class family magazine"; it later became literary, publishing writers like George Bernard Shaw and Sinclair Lewis. But by the 1960s it was in economic free fall. Helen's prototype and energy made her new *Cosmo* an immediate success. Her first issue sold out, featuring an article on the (then-new) birth

163

control pill. She said her readers were single career women, and she was the first magazine editor to suggest having it all: "love, sex, and money."

Helen's *Cosmo* was famously ridiculed to be about orgasms but it was also about health, careers, self-improvement, celebrities, fashion and beauty, and about being clear about what you wanted. Running pieces about orgasms was just smart editing: take something that is true but not talked about (premarital sex) and blow it out: *Sleep with the boss? Why not?!* Feminists branded her as anti-feminist at first but most came around: *Don't use men to get what you want in life. Get it yourself.* If P. J. O'Rourke was a pants-down Republican, Helen was a feminist in a minidress and fishnet stockings.

WHEN I ARRIVED AT HEARST to edit *Esquire,* Helen was the star of the company. In the late sixties and early seventies, Helen's *Cosmo* made greater profits than all the dozen or so other Hearst titles combined. That year, 1990, her newsstand sales averaged over two million copies and total ad revenue was over $150 million, not counting the twenty-seven foreign editions. She asked me *to take her* to lunch (an important distinction for *Cosmo* girls), and told me over her salad that the most important attribute for an editor was confidence. I wasn't to let our adorable Hearst executives *buffalo* me. And I should stay close to my readers. One way Helen stayed close to hers was by riding the M10 bus down Central Park West to work every morning. And you know what? Those readers liked it when she got a little outrageous. And liked it best when they got real information.

Helen never carried cash, at least not when we went to publishing receptions, as we did sometimes. At some point during what were always cocktail events, she'd ask for "a fin for the ladies' room." The next morning there would arrive by messenger a crisp five-dollar bill and a short thank-you in her beautiful hand. Before she died in 2012, she and her husband, film producer David Brown, had donated $30 million to establish the Brown Institute for Media Innovation as a joint venture between Columbia University Graduate School of Journalism and the Stanford University School of Engineering. When I heard about that, I thought of Helen riding the M10 to work while black radio cars were dropping the other editors in chief in front of the Hearst building. And I doubt it still shocks, but when I read a recent *Cosmo* headline about penis size, I noted that the piece also included real information, the kind Helen always insisted on: "[Ed. note: the average penis size is 3.61 inches flaccid and 5.16 inches erect.]"

THE WOMEN I WORKED WITH when I was a young editor didn't read *Cosmo* or any other women's magazines except *Ms.* and the fashion titles—and I looked at those, too. They read what I read: the *New Yorker, Esquire, Harper's,* the *Atlantic, Rolling Stone, Mother Jones,* the *Face,* the *New York Review of Books,* the *Paris Review, New York,* the *Village Voice,* the *New American Review* and the newspapers. Most of those magazines are still around and if you look at the mastheads you will find many women executive editors, deputy editors, managing editors, Web editors, mobile editors, art directors, copy chiefs, research editors, photo editors . . . Too bad only two of those magazines are edited by women (*Harper's* editor Ellen Rosenbush; *Mother Jones* editor in chief Clara Jeffery).

But before we put another nail in the self-carved coffins of the magazine business, note that two warhorse legacy titles now have women running the edit: Susan Goldberg at *National Geographic* and, at *Time,* the exquisite writer Nancy Gibbs, who was hired there as a part-time fact-checker in 1985. *Vice* magazine's editor in chief is former intern Ellis Jones, who when she got the job in 2015 said, "Expect writing by even more female correspondents; expect new fiction and photojournalism and columns by big-name writers; and expect even more in-depth reports from global hot spots." That same year the *Guardian* got its first female editor in chief, Katharine Viner. Marcia McNutt became the first female editor in chief of *Science Magazine* in 2013.

If you look at digital-first operations, you see more women: Yahoo

News (Megan Liberman, editor in chief); *Slate* (Julia Turner, editor in chief); CNN Digital (Meredith Artley, editor in chief); Politico (Susan Glasser, editor); and Refinery29 (Christene Barberich, founding editor in chief). And forget not Arianna Huffington, on top of her eponymous website that for the second year in a row (2015 and 2014, according to the Women's Media Center) had the highest percentage of female bylines: 53 percent of contributors were women. Those same years, the awarding of bachelor's degrees in communications (where journalism usually lives) was even more lopsided: men 37.5 percent, women 62.5 percent; master's degrees: men 32.4 percent, women 67.6 percent.

These are all rosy developments but other appallingly less optimistic research (by the Nieman Foundation) shows that back in 1998, 36.9 percent of journalists were women; that figure was 37.2 percent in 2013. Two years later, the Women's Media Center analyzed 27,758 pieces of news content (TV, print, Internet, wires) and found that 62.1 percent was produced by men. As *Ms. Magazine* cofounder Gloria Steinem said, "The truth will set you free, but first it will piss you off."

WOMEN'S MAGAZINES HAVE BEEN COVERING so-called women's issues—abortion, sexual health, domestic violence—for a long time, and often out in front of newsweeklies and newspapers run by men and subject to both gender-driven cluelessness and editorial arbitrariness. At the same time, it is very hard to find female journalists who buy into the idea of women's issues in the first place. That these issues are only for women because they are covered more aggressively in magazines like *Marie Claire* or *Elle* is a distinction as absurd as the idea that nobody reads them. But then . . .

Robbie Myers, editor in chief of American *Elle* since 2000, has a story about giving a Delacorte Lecture at the Columbia University Graduate School of Journalism in 2008. She talked about the mix of stories and fine writing that gives her magazine its distinctive voice. During the requisite Q&A, a guy raised his hand. "I had no idea that you did ten thousand words on Senator Obama," he said. "How do you feel about the fact that nobody reads it?"

Myers pointed out that she had an audience of twenty million across print and digital in the United States alone and that American *Elle* was the largest syndicator of content in the *Elle* network of forty-five editions. "We have hundreds of millions of women around the world," she said. "I'm sorry that you think we're nobody." The last time Myers told this story, it was for a 2015 piece about her in *Women's Wear Daily*, so "nobody" probably read that, either.

-ENDIT-

Men's Fashion (526)

THE EDITORS WHO REPORT ON, curate and manipulate men's fashion are tribal. The fashion week shows in Milan, Paris and New York are like Tlingit potlatches, where gift giving is the economic system and personal style is the currency. What's on the runways isn't the attraction. That's just the business; the most interesting anthropology is in the eccentricity of the editors and stylists—not just what they wear but what they care about and how hard they work.

The first fashion editor I worked with was Tony Melillo, who dressed like a European playboy and gave *Smart* a presence in Milan, Paris and London, as well as New York, with almost no budget—an impossibility without great charm, which he had enough of to talk Norman Parkinson and Horst P. Horst into shooting more or less for fun. When Tony brought "Parks" into the office so I could meet him, they were both wearing ascots.

Another time he left for Europe with four trunks of conservative business suits and returned three week later with fashion shots by Alfa Castaldi of the wildest of the avant-garde elite in five Eastern-bloc cities—they all wanted to be in an American magazine. He also introduced me and the magazine to Alfa's wife, fashion conceptualist Anna Piaggi, who reminded me of Pinkie Black except that her clothing collection included 2,865 dresses and 265 pairs of shoes. Anna was known as a "walking museum" and a muse to many designers, most famously Karl Lagerfeld. Then there was the stylist Vern Lambert, who always hung out with Alfa and Anna, and who had dressed Keith Richards in snakeskin boots and feathers when the rest of the Stones were wearing suits.

"Fashion is all politics," Vern said when we met. This was something he said often.

. . .

AT *ESQUIRE*, MELILLO AND I worked with Bob Beauchamp, the smoothly wry and established fashion director with wonderful taste who schooled me in the importance of fabric and detail; and the fashion editor, John Mather, who drank twenty espressos a day, made all the shoots happen, and was effectively antisocial when we all traveled to the shows in Milan. Perhaps most eccentric was the gifted writer Woody Hochswender, a tall, suave, masculine guy with orange-red hair, who gave up his popular fashion column in the *New York Times* to edit *Esquire Gentleman*. Woody also happened to be a Buddhist, a very tough Buddhist.

They all warned me individually that working together would be impossible because of the deadliness of fashion politics, but the first issue of *Gentleman* was called a breakthrough by the important designers. When it launched, during the '92 spring shows in Milan, Alfa and Anna came to our party—Anna making an entrance in a combination of vintage haute couture and what either Hochswender or Melillo identified as "maybe pieces from her collection of fast-food uniforms." Vern Lambert came too, wearing candy-cane-striped silk pajama bottoms and a rainbow Aborigine jacket, his gray goatee styled under his chin with a child's plastic barrette and a black ribbon.

"Fashion is all politics," he said. "But I didn't feel like it tonight, so I didn't dress."

-ENDIT-

Liz Tilberis (2,862)

In the spring of 1992, Liz Tilberis came to visit in the Hamptons, in Wainscott, where I had a place. It was Easter weekend and that Sunday we went to a lawn party at Jann Wenner's house. It was to be relaxed, but with an elaborate egg hunt for the children, and Jann's guest list included a range of people from the media, show business and publishing. Turning into the long driveway, Liz joked that she was nervous, that this was going to be her first important party since moving to America from London and she wouldn't know anyone.

I told her she didn't look nervous.

"Of course not," she said. "Can't let it show, can we?"

I said most of the guests already knew about her, knew she had come to New York to rejuvenate *Harper's Bazaar.*

"Do not abandon me," she said, widening her green eyes, a look I came to know as a kind of ironic kabuki. She wasn't nervous at all. She was going to work that party.

I remember watching her, vivid with her shining white hair, from across the lawn. Driving home, she told me she had received six invitations for weekends over the summer.

"Imagine," she said. "They were all very nice, but they don't know me at all."

OUR PACT WAS that she would help me with *Esquire*'s fashion and I would help her with "getting on in America." We joked about it as she got on fine on her own, not just staffing her magazine and settling her sons in private school but becoming a Knicks fan. Her "field study" took her to gardens and museums, but also to Q-Zar, a laser-tag arena in New Jersey, for a "jolly riot." Within less than a year, she and her husband, Andrew, had slept in the Lincoln Bedroom as guests of the Clintons. "My team," she called Andrew and the boys, but it wasn't sappy. What worried her, she said, was being too English: "Mustn't ever use that word *jolly*."

For my fashion education, we traveled together to Milan, flying overnight from JFK to Malpensa, eating caviar and drinking vodka. On that flight I learned that she had refused to be confirmed at her all-girls boarding school ("I didn't believe in God") and had been expelled from art school for entertaining a man in her room. I also learned that she had almost moved to New York five years earlier to head Ralph Lauren's design team. She had decided to stay in London when, two days after she'd given notice, Anna Wintour, who was then the editor in chief, told her that *she* was moving to New York—to become the editor of *House & Garden* (ten months later, she would be running American *Vogue*). Liz could have British *Vogue* if she wanted it.

Of course, topping British *Vogue* had been another *jolly riot*. Bruce Weber's first *Vogue* cover shoot was for Liz—a laughing model wearing minimal makeup. Pure Liz, her colleagues said. And it became an even better story when the proofs came back touched up with lipstick red because the printers were sure there had been a mistake. "They actually made it better," Liz said. When she persuaded the Princess of Wales to pose for a British *Vogue* cover, the image was clean and simple—the look Diana made her own from then on. "It just made sense for her as a modern princess," Liz said. "And I'm a little like Machiavelli."

Our first day in Milan was to end with a benefit in the courtyard of an old castle that had been tented with an enormous tarp against the forecast showers. It began to rain hard in the afternoon, and by evening the waiters were poking up at huge puddles on the sagging canvas with long poles. Sting was on the program and waved to Liz as we entered. She looked from the candle-set tables to the dripping canvas and announced that we were going immediately to Bice.

We couldn't find our car and started walking toward the restaurant in the downpour, getting soaked. Within a block, a limo driver—not ours—pulled over. He knew Liz and liked her, thought she might want a ride.

"Fashion," she said, climbing in, "is about long black cars when you need them." The driver told us the tent had collapsed.

Walking into Bice, we saw Valentino and his inner circle at the large round table in the back corner—like a tableau I had seen before but couldn't place. The women, all in red gowns, were exquisite, the men handsome in black suits, but their frowns gave the scene a starkness. Valentino made a slight nod in our direction, and when we walked over he asked if the collapsed tent would reflect badly on the fashion houses. (Armani and Versace, both based in Milan, and Valentino, from Rome, had organized the event.)

"Not on those from Rome," Liz told him, and she went around the table complimenting everyone on how chic they looked. "Totally Valentino," she said, and when the great designer smiled slightly the mood changed and we were invited to join them for dinner.

"I wish we could have shot that table just exactly as it was when we walked in," Liz told me as we left Bice after midnight. "The cold power of it, like those Bronzinos of the Medici."

Early the next morning, we began a round of appointments at designer showrooms. All went more or less the same way: Liz explaining to me (so the designer could hear) how brilliant the new line was, and then whispering to the designer what a formidable editor I was. We had a simple lunch in the backyard of the Armani palazzo with Giorgio and his top aide at the time, Gabriella Forte, while his Persian cat, Hannibal, hunted through the garden. Giorgio, too, was concerned about the collapsed tent, but he and Liz talked mostly about the distinctive cuts he was showing that season, and the importance of fine tailoring.

Our week in Milan paid off in many new advertising pages for *Esquire*, but when it was over Liz thanked me for helping her get through it. Her advice was to bring presents the next time I visited, something personal that this or that designer could relate to, perhaps a cat toy for Hannibal.

I thought hard about this and, since Armani was the most important advertiser for *Esquire*, I asked Gay Talese to sign a copy of his new book, *Unto the Sons*, to Giorgio. *Esquire* had excerpted Gay's history of his family's immigration to America from Italy. The book's most intimate passages were about Gay's father, who was a tailor. I had the book with me when I saw Armani the following spring at the men's shows in Milan. Without Liz beside me, there would be no lunch, but we had coffee in his office. Giorgio opened the book, saw that it was signed, passed it over his shoulder to an assistant without reading the inscription, and asked me about Liz. When was she coming next to Milan?

I saw that same copy of *Unto the Sons* a year later on a bookshelf in Gabriella Forte's apartment in New York.

LOOKING FOR FASHION MATERIAL for my "Editor's Notes" column in *Esquire*, I asked Liz what it was she noticed first when she met someone—expecting, I suppose, something smart about shoes or haircuts. Instead she paraphrased a line from a Katharine Hepburn film: "I notice whether the person is a man or a woman."

Very sexy, when she said it—and direct, like her taste as an editor. She had a clear eye for the sociology of fashion that could capture (or shred) any look she saw on any runway or street. "Downtown Marie Antoinette" was the look her friend Jean Paul Gaultier was showing that year. "Blind Anchorwoman," which she pointed out to me one day when we were walking across Central Park South, was maybe a bit of a reach but I knew what she meant. Our boss was "Black Paw" because of his fingernails. "Being wicked," she called it and we did a lot of it. Her only insecurity as an editor was dealing with writers.

In England she had been a celebrity as a fashion editor, even appearing on the sides of double-decker buses with her oldest son in an adoption-awareness campaign; but there was a disconnect with journalists, because she was *just* a fashion editor. She was worried that New York would be like London, where the literary scene was closed to her. This could be problematic if she couldn't get interesting writing (part of *Vogue*'s mix) into *Bazaar*. I said I could introduce her to writers if she was feeling pressed. 173

"What about you," she said. "I wouldn't be afraid of editing you."

"You wouldn't be doing the editing anyway," I said. "What's your idea? You have to give your writers an idea first."

"Oh, yes, I know that," she said. "Write fashion and rock and roll. You edited *Rolling Stone*, or so you say."

"What's the piece again?"

"Roll over, Beethoven," she said. "Tell Balenciaga the news."

When I finally wrote that piece for her, it was called "Not Fade Away: Mingling Destinies of Rock and Roll and Fashion." I was all over the map—her map—when it came to which designer went with which rocker. I had the obvious: Giorgio Armani with Eric Clapton, and Calvin Klein as a Mudd Club vet. Liz explained that fifteen years previous, Richard Tyler had dressed Rod Stewart in glitter and spandex for his *Blondes Have More Fun* tour, and last year he had fitted himself with the Council of Fashion Designers of America's most prestigious award as Womenswear Designer of the Year. "That has to mean something," she said.

Voguette that she was, having begun as an unpaid intern in the late '60s, Liz was amused by my characterizations of the period. "All that hard-rocking creative sexuality and open rebellion, come on . . ." Where was my nuance? She told me about Pop and Op Art overpowering textile design, and Twiggy flirting around London in little gym slips. She told me not to ignore Dr. John because his gris-gris was about voodoo *accessories*, and that Carnaby Street had a men's shop named I Was Lord Kitchener's Valet; it sold used military uniforms, and she had slapped several into her "More Dash Than Cash" pages as soon as she saw them.

She insisted she was not about language ("My mind is too full of pictures, not enough room then for words") except she was as hungry for specific details as any line editor I ever worked with.

WHEN SHE TOOK OVER at *Harper's Bazaar* in 1992, Elizabeth Jane Kelly Tilberis was a size 12, which she said was "practically illegal in our business." One gossip column applied the word *bovine*. She laughed that off and lost weight as her *Bazaar* came together, dropping to a size 8. She said her "slinky" staff helped her look the part but added, with a green-eyed wink, that "fashion editors should never look better than their models."

Liz knew every fashion trick, every cliché, but she didn't pander. Instead of snapping at the heels of the flush and splashy *Vogue*, she decided to simplify. Her relaunch of *Bazaar* (September 1992) was quieter than expected. The cover was a very graphic Patrick Demarchelier shot of Linda Evangelista looking smart and confident with a small cover line: "Enter the Era of Elegance." It was cool, but there was no snobby chill. Even cooler, the logo was unbalanced, an act of innovation that winked with subliminal ink. By comparison, *Vogue*'s grunged-up models covered with type looked sloppy. Downtown suddenly seemed almost quaint. Liz's inside pages too were sleek and inviting, with understated glamour in the white space and more of creative director Fabien Baron's innovative typography. It was practical, democratic fashion, elegant in its execution.

In a little over a year, *Bazaar* was back as one of the world's preeminent fashion magazines, challenging Anna Wintour's *Vogue*. The paparazzi loved Liz, and she dazzled them with her bob of white hair, which looked silver in photos. She was having another *jolly riot. Bazaar*'s circulation climbed as she nurtured her photographers, swapped risqué stories with models, complimented stylists and charmed advertisers. With readers, she stressed building personal style with common sense. One of her "Editor's Letter" columns celebrated the humble sweater. By then she was a size 6.

THAT DECEMBER, some 250 fashion and publishing people were invited to the brownstone in the East Eighties she and Andrew had rented from director Mike Nichols. There was a huge Christmas tree in the living room and white flowers everywhere, and the townhouse was packed with her New York friends—Calvin Klein, Ralph Lauren, Donna Karan, Leonard and Evelyn Lauder, Barbara Walters, Jann Wenner, people named Trump. The party was to celebrate her triumphant first year and *Bazaar's* many honors, which included two National Magazine Awards. Hearst had taken out a full-page congratulatory ad in the *New York Times*. The columnist Billy Norwich wrote that it was the kind of soigné party he used to read about in urbane novels.

When Liz walked me to the bar, I said, "The gang's apparently all here."

"Someone named Jerome just whispered to me, 'There are people in this room who should not be here,'" Liz said. "I don't know what that means exactly."

"Yes, you do," I said, figuring it had to have been the notorious "social moth" Jerome Zipkin. "You want me to kick his ass?"

"Oh yes, please."

She made a very short speech that night. "A magazine is only people," she said. "It walks in the door in the morning, and out the door at night. Please let's never forget that."

None of us knew she had been diagnosed with stage III ovarian cancer and had a procedure scheduled for the next morning.

WHEN HER CANCER WAS REPORTED in the media, she came forward with some of what she had been going through, first on the "Editor's Letter" page: *I never wanted to be a poster girl for cancer. But cancer has become part of who I am, along with my big feet and my English accent. I have greenish eyes, I was born on Sept. 7 (the same day as Queen Elizabeth), and I have ovarian cancer. So do almost 175,000 other women in the United States.*

Privately she joked that she had arrived hungover for her procedure, the day after her Christmas party. For the next seven years she would balance treatments and operations with her work at *Bazaar*. She wore catheters under evening dresses. She escorted Princess Diana on one of her visits to New York, even though she was in chemotherapy. Diana had been one of the first people on the telephone when Liz emerged from her first major operation.

"Diana who?" said Andrew.

"Diana Windsor."

Sometimes Liz didn't feel like talking to anyone, but the depression that must have come with the cancer otherwise never showed. "My cancer diet" she said of her slender figure. There were sores in her mouth and her appetite was gone. Then her mouth dried out and her fingernails splintered. Growing weaker, she would tell a story about Andrew having to get her tights on for her in the morning, and somehow make it funny.

One morning in her office, when I said something about how good her hair looked despite chemotherapy, she laughed. "It's a wig," she whispered. Her sons called it "Larry," for the way Laurence Olivier looked in *Henry V.*

By then she was a size 4.

Her memoir was called *No Time to Die.* In it she wrote about the place she and Andrew had found on the bay in East Hampton: *I'd go down to the narrow strip of beach at the back of our house each morning and sit on my favorite rock with a cup of tea, often so weak that he'd have to carry me back. In what was a real family tragedy, Sophie, one of our Labradors, had recently died.*

I knew that dog. That house was where Liz and Andrew had sheltered me during the summer when my marriage was ending. Too soon after, I got a call from Andrew.

"She's gone," he told me. "There's nothing left to say."

THE BARE STAGE WAS EDGED by pots of her favorite white orchids, and overhead was a large black-and-white Patrick Demarchelier photo of Liz, smiling out at the more than a thousand people filling Lincoln Center's Avery Fisher Hall. Every important designer was there, along with top editors and Hearst executives. Si Newhouse and Anna Wintour came together. Hillary Clinton sent a statement. Bruce Weber, Trudie Styler and Calvin Klein were on the program, along with Liz's doctor, and her brother, Grant, also a doctor. I spoke, too. I said Elizabeth Jane Kelly Tilberis was a caviar hound and a rocker. Last on the program was Dr. John. He played "My Buddy."

-ENDIT-

Cowboy-Hippie-Poet Weird (459)

*In the Pitt Rivers Museum at Oxford there is a
display called "Treatment of Dead Enemies." Behind
some very old glass, you can see shrunken heads,
ear awls and change purses made out of scrotums.*

WRITERS CAME AND WENT, usually moving on to other
magazines or writing books or for television or films. (*Eureka!*) Most
were careful to avoid any bridge burning. Editors tended to stick
where they were and found it in their competitive interest to mock
other editors.

Art Cooper, the shrewd and affable editor of GQ, once called me
"Montana-cowboy-hippie-poet weird," a phrase that my publishing
colleagues at *Esquire* said GQ advertising sales people were using
to illustrate the difference between us (the hillbillies) and them (the
sophisticates). Art lunched in the Grill Room of the Four Seasons
restaurant almost every day, wore black turtlenecks and was famous
for his colognes—which I thought was differentiation enough. But
he was also smart and mockingly funny, hence his description of me.

I didn't hear from Art when I was unexpectedly fired from *Esquire*
(another story), but two years later when I landed back in the men's
category editing *Men's Journal*, Art wrote me a note: "Here we go
again."

When he died in 2003, after announcing his retirement from GQ
after nearly twenty years, his final issue was just hitting the newsstands. We were friends by then and sometimes discussed how our
magazines ran on the same economic formula: the fashion paid for
the literary journalism—which is the only model that still works for
legacy publishing in the men's category. These were helpful conversations and ranged sometimes into where to eat in Milan during

fashion week or if it ever made sense to invite Ralph Lauren to an NBA game (no). Art was competitive, even trying to spin a sports magazine out of *GQ* when I was at *Sports Illustrated*, but I always learned something when we ran into each other.

The bigger lesson is that if you get to the top of a masthead, everyone with an equivalent title will make a good ally, even if they're in direct competition with you. This may be counterintuitive, but if you think of it as making as many friends as you can among equals, it will make more sense. It's like celebrities in television green rooms greeting each other as if they're best friends even though the only place they see each other is in green rooms. It's intimidating if you want it to be. And now, with so many confusing hierarchies across both old and new media companies, you need to look like you have as many friends as possible—especially if your title is now chief content officer instead of editor in chief.

-ENDIT-

Truth(s) (665)

Editors should never preach and that is not my intention, but whether you are a writer of fiction or a journalist or an editor of either one, when you look in the mirror you should think *tireless* or *dogged* or maybe even a stronger word (*indefatigable?*) to describe what you need to be to become successful, and what you should be as you go after the truth—which is your job.

Look for the smoking gun but also for the occasional blip that at first may seem old but then suddenly makes complete sense—like finding out that the Dalai Lama likes to fix wristwatches. This is a small truth, a fact, loaded with implications because of the synchronous orbits it shares with His Holiness's day job. Squint at it. Look closely, too, at the reach between, say, the Ogaden shepherd with his cell phone in Ethiopia and the Seattle software engineer sipping his Ogaden Americano. This is different from the false range that appears so often in flawed journalism about entertainment ("from Brad Pitt to George Clooney"). The Ogaden reach can be a zip line for all the complicated and contradictory ornaments you want to hang on it as a fiction writer or journalist.

Fiction has its own truth in what is made up to help us see what is real. ("One morning, when Gregor Samsa awoke from troubled dreams, he found himself transformed in his bed into a horrible vermin.") But Gregor is not going to sue, and whoever they write about, journalists have to watch out for that—even when their most important job is telling true stories. Here is the definition of "journalistic truth" that comes out of the Journalism and Media division of the Pew Research Center: "a process that begins with the professional discipline of assembling and verifying facts. Then journalists try to convey a fair and reliable account of their meaning, valid for now, subject to further investigation."

This is good thinking but it often gets bumpy in practice.

Objectivity is an illusion. Every writer knows that and makes their own deal. If you're a journalist, this is very big. The unwiped truth is that the so-called journalism of empathy—written with an understanding of the point of view of sources and building a reciprocal relationship with readers—is a convenient escalator to ethical justification. At its best (Sebastian Junger, Gary Smith, Francisco Goldman, Susan Orlean, Jon Krakauer), you get the most powerful nonfiction narratives. At worst, truth never gets in the way.

In her book *I Remember Nothing*, Nora Ephron wrote in a chapter called "Journalism: A Love Story" that there is no such thing as the truth, that people are constantly misquoted, that the media is full of conspiracies "and that, in any case, ineptness is a kind of conspiracy." And then she killed you with "emotional detachment and cynicism get you only so far. But for many years I was in love with journalism."

Loving journalism is usually the beginning of the story. Then, inevitably, you find that some of the best journalists are troubled by what they do. Gore Vidal called source betrayal "the iron law of journalism." With her usual reverberating truth, Joan Didion wrote in her preface to *Slouching Towards Bethlehem*, "Writers are always selling somebody out." You understand, and figure that is never their intention, until you come across an even more disturbing quote, from Janet Malcolm. It is the thesis of her 1990 book *The Journalist and the Murderer*. It is also her lede:

> *Every journalist who is not too stupid or full of himself to notice what is going on knows that what he does is morally indefensible. He is a kind of confidence man, preying on people's vanity, ignorance, or loneliness, gaining their trust and betraying them without remorse.*

The indictment is more powerful because Malcolm never renders herself immune. She is, in this way, *indefatigable*. But so too is the truth, even when there are many truths.

Richard Ford (2,066)

*Nobody gives a damn about a writer and
his problems except another writer.*

— HAROLD ROSS,
FOUNDING EDITOR,
The New Yorker

I LEARNED AN IMPORTANT TRUTH about editing from Richard Ford, although my writing this will probably surprise him.

Richard called himself a white-buck southerner and liked to say he had some arrows in his ass, meaning it had not always been as easy as it looked—handsome novelist, beautiful wife; the Pulitzer and the PEN/Faulkner (an unprecedented double for *Independence Day*); the American Academy of Arts and Letters. As far as I knew, no one believed him about the arrows. He was important and somehow confounding—all that success!—but you wanted to be friends with him. At least I did.

I had admired his writing since discovering A *Piece of My Heart*, an audacious first novel with a fineness of language that caught something violent and unsettling about our generation. We were the same age, and I was in my first editing job at *Outside*. Richard had enlisted in the marines and tried teaching and law school, and picked up an MFA. After A *Piece of My Heart* came *The Ultimate Good Luck* but they were both small novels—"small" as in strong reviews, low sales. He figured there had to be at least some money in journalism and he liked sports, so he got a package of his writing together and sent it to *Sports Illustrated*. Word came back that he should stick to fiction, although when I checked years later, there was no record of this at *SI*, which I think annoyed Richard because the rejection had obviously piqued him.

Richard didn't know what else to do but try another novel—maybe about a guy who's a sportswriter with *a glossy New York sports magazine you have all heard of.* That sportswriter became Frank Bascombe, who says at one point, *I had written all I was going to write . . . and there is nothing wrong with that. If more writers knew that, the world would be saved a lot of bad books.* Amen to that, but not where Richard's breakout 1986 novel, *The Sportswriter,* is concerned. Forget any silliness about Richard being tagged with "neo-Faulknerianism" (an early arrow): Frank Bascombe would evolve into your realtor as Everyman, although Richard doesn't like that characterization.

People who knew Richard thought real estate had always been his context. Over the years he often owned several houses at the same time. He could give you sharp details on every house he'd lived in—in fourteen states, plus France and Mexico. The expatriated life—France, specifically—didn't prove up, although he was sitting in a restaurant in Brittany when he learned that he had won the Pulitzer.

Richard moved so often not just because he could but because he was married to Kristina Hensley Ford, a striking urban planner with a doctorate from Michigan. Her career took them from Princeton to Missoula to New Orleans, where she was director of city planning until she resigned, before Hurricane Katrina, over what Richard described as "issues of conscience" with Mayor Ray Nagin. Kristina was serious business, and graceful and fun. As a couple they scared the hell out of any literary hostess, from Iowa City to Palo Alto.

They would hold hands at dinner parties and tell you they didn't want children because children would interfere with their life as husband and wife. For *Esquire,* Richard wrote a long piece called "Hunting with My Wife . . . and Others." When he filed, he insisted that Kristina get her say in a sidebar we called "Hunting with My Husband . . . and No One Else." They were both honest, shrewd pieces, and as thickly mysterious as other people's sex lives.

The pieces demanded that you look at what Richard wanted you to look at: *Most adults don't want to learn anything; they only want*

*to seem to want to learn, and be diverted a moment from their usual
rounds—which seems no more than normal.*

I thought about these pieces a few years later when I saw Richard
on *Charlie Rose*, quoting Jasper Johns on the New York School of
painting. To paraphrase: "There are many things that are known so
well they're never seen." The directness of that idea was like a spear.
The deeper you took it, the sharper and more cogent it became.

I wrote in a 2006 *Vanity Fair* "Spotlight" that his third Frank Bascombe novel, *The Lay of the Land*, was about "the weirdness of the
ordinary, the intensity of everyday." I quoted Richard's Bascombe
character calling his life a "high-wire act of normalcy." As the kicker
to the piece, Richard said, "In the end, I think I'm just too damned
normal American." That's what he wanted.

WHEN IT WAS TIME to get an advance on his next novel, *Canada*,
Richard left his longtime editor at Knopf, Gary Fisketjon, for what
was reported to be a $3 million, three-book deal at Ecco, a Harper-
Collins imprint. He and Gary had worked together going back to the
publication of *The Sportswriter*, by an imprint Gary had created at
Random House. They had been tight friends, and both of them said
they wouldn't talk about the split, but they talked about it a little and
their friends talked about it all the time.

Maybe it was simple, just about the money. Maybe it wasn't. You
heard people call Richard an arrogant prick or say Gary and the rest
of the people at Knopf were artless, corporate assholes. Everyone who
knew both of them felt lousy.

The irony was that Richard had written so brilliantly about literary friendships in "Good Raymond," his profile of Ray Carver for
the *New Yorker* (1998). Carver had introduced Richard to Gary, who
was Ray's editor and great friend too, which didn't help anyone feel
any better. Richard's piece was concise, and heartbreaking. He wrote
that such friendships would *routinely eventuate in absurd miscalcula-
tions, unwinnowable confusions, and deep rivalries often so at odds
with amity as never to be set right.*

But it was not like that between Richard and Ray. He said that they avoided *hurt feelings . . . hard lessons about trust and rivalrousness (I am trustworthy; I am not rivalrous) learned the hard way, then learned again down through the list of friends, including the ones who remain my friends to this day.*

As an editor, I worked the fringes of some of those literary friendships, editing many of the writers Richard was referring to on his list. My hard-to-swallow realization was that writers made better friends for writers than editors did. They were competitive and could be very petty, but writers were more trustworthy than editors when it came to both writing and the business of writing. Maybe money and the need for it and who paid whom drove some of that, but while a writer would be an advocate for the work, the writing, the editor would be an advocate for his or her magazine or publishing house.

I thought about writers everywhere trying to get their heads, as Richard wrote . . . *up out of the foggy ether young writers live in . . . mostly . . . just beavering away trying to make isolation and persistence into a virtue, and anonymity your sneak attack on public notice.* How could editors understand?

Richard was also clear in saying that Ray simply wrote the truth of his experience, with all its crazy sadness from the drinking, bad-marriage, repo days, but with kindness shining. It was what Jasper Johns had been talking about, identifying the many things that are known so well they're never seen, knowing things in a fresh, unblinking way. This was what it took, Richard explained, *to re-create the condition of not knowing once experience has made so much known . . . a phenomenon writers all puzzle about as we try to make made-up experience seem real.*

As an editor, I could understand that and was struck by it. How difficult it was to write well.

IN THE FALL OF 2011, Richard was in New York on some business to do with both him and Kristina teaching at Columbia, and I got him Yankee tickets at the last minute for a night game with the Red Sox. The seats were good ones but not difficult because of my job. Richard made a big deal out of it anyway. We invited each other to dinner as we always did, and Richard also suggested I join him for quail hunting in Thomasville, Georgia, early the next year.

We had talked about hunting together since that *Esquire* piece. There was never a bad year at this place, he told me, and Kristina would shoot, too. We never made the trip because the logistics broke down, as they always did with all of our plans to have dinner with our wives whenever we were within a hundred miles of each other. But I enjoyed our arm's-length camaraderie, just as I did with many writers I had sought out early in my career but no longer edited—a reality of mine no less sentimental for being so widespread as everyone got older.

The Sportswriter had begun the unexpected (to Richard) trilogy that he intended to finish with the publication of *The Lay of the Land*. But it didn't end there. Frank Bascombe came back in a narrative about an old house on the Jersey Shore destroyed by Hurricane Sandy. The story worked because it had been Frank's house, where he had lived for years but then sold just before the storm to a guy he knew pretty well. The house was a total loss, a situation intensified by Richard's sinewy language, which, again, made you look at something in plain sight that you had not explored before with any honesty.

The first time Richard read the piece to an audience it was at the Kaufman Concert Hall at the 92nd Street Y, in New York, that validating venue for writers on the way up and a place of dignity for writers who had arrived. He read with James Salter, who was glowing with the success of his new novel, *All That Is*. Richard came out first and read his new Frank Bascombe story. He got a big hand when he finished, and again when he returned to the stage after Jim read to lead their conversation—which he did with deference and class.

Salter said he was pleased that *All That Is* seemed to be selling.

Richard said he was happy just to have new work on his desk. That desk was in East Boothbay, Maine, a settled home base for him and Kristina, still going their own way, still together—married forty-five years, no children, all eleven of his books dedicated to her and only her.

The morning after the reading, I e-mailed Richard to say that I had been there and liked his new story and also that I thought he had led the conversation with Jim with grace. I said I was sorry I hadn't been able to stay to say hello. He wrote back complimenting Salter and repeating what he had said from the stage about being happy to have new work on his desk. He also hoped our paths would cross and said I was always invited to come hunting with him at the small place he kept for bird seasons in Havre on the Montana Hi-Line. Again I was pleased to be invited.

In the fall of 2014, Richard published *Let Me Be Frank with You: A Frank Bascombe Book,* four connected novellas that he had started with the story he had read at the 92nd Street Y when he'd said he was happy just to have new work on his desk again. The novellas were all sharp, echoing. It occurred to me that perhaps it is true that for writers nothing ever completely disappears once it has begun. Richard wrote about that in his first novel, *Piece of My Heart,* and it has stayed with me.

Now more time has passed and Richard and I have never been hunting together or had a dinner with our wives. That bothered me for years, but not now. For an editor, being friends with the work should be enough.

-ENDIT-

Fiction, Nonfiction (594)

A YOUNG WOMAN IN A BAR asked me if my novel, which she
had heard about from the bartender, was fiction or nonfiction. The
awesome post-literateness of her question was picked up by most of
the fiction writers I worked with as evidence of the precariousness
of their place in the culture, and they hurled it back and forth as a
kind of crybaby mantra. I was editing *Esquire* and I told them there
would always be a place for fiction in the magazine, but I wondered
sometimes if I was lying.

Esquire was thought of as the most important cradle of New Journalism, if not the actual birthplace. *Esquire* ran the work of Mailer,
Gay Talese, and Tom Wolfe, among many others who locked into the
new form. Those writers have, of course, been claimed by every magazine that ever published their slightest ruminations, but while working primarily for Harold Hayes (at *Esquire*), Clay Felker (the *Herald
Tribune, Esquire,* the *Village Voice, New York*) and Jann Wenner
(*Rolling Stone*), they gave journalism a new position of importance
above the short story—a status that lingers not as the fifty-year literary
hangover still talked about in MFA programs but as a paradigm shift.

Yet even as journalists were making their reputations by using the
techniques of fiction, *Esquire, Harper's* and the *New Yorker* were also
publishing short stories by writers who were rooting their work in a
grittier reality, even if that reality was imagined. Raymond Carver
called it "a bringing of the news from one world to another."

What was unfortunate during all of the ping-ponging of techniques
between fiction and nonfiction is that very little attention was paid to
the fiction side of the game and a most important idea was lost. The
best fiction written since *Esquire* began, in 1933, had almost always
answered the who, what, when, where and why questions associated
with solid journalism but in ways that made it what John Updike
called "the subtlest instrument for self-examination and self-display

189

that mankind has invented yet." Updike wrote this in his introduction to *The* Esquire *Fiction Reader: Volume II* (1986) and went on to explain that fiction "makes sociology look priggish, history problematical, the film media two-dimensional and the *National Enquirer* as silly as last week's cereal box."

How silly, then, not to recognize that questions of what is imagined and what is observed cannot be answered by simply asking what is true and what is not. This is what Tim O'Brien (*Going After Cacciato* and *The Things They Carried*) meant when he wrote about "story truth" being "truer sometimes than happening truth." This is also what Ken Kesey meant when he would say that some things were "true even if they never really happened."

That woman in the bar turned out to be plenty smart, and in another context—the one outlined above by Kesey and O'Brien— her question was a good one. And beyond the tricky jujitsu of journalistic ethics, it can be answered in one word: both. Or maybe with something about two plows in the same field.

If you were keeping score, like I had to be, it was the nonfiction that was pulling readers, but maybe the fiction writers were throwing the longest shadows. The best writers could handle the truth either way. I think this is because of a commitment to revealing the shadings and complexities of the human condition. This sounds ambitious and it is, weaving a safety net for the most difficult truths, catching them as they fall through our lives.

-ENDIT-

James Salter (2,804)

At first you had to find things out about Jim. He never volunteered, never talked about himself, never. If you asked, he would answer questions, and sometimes tell a story if you pushed. But that's not what I mean.

His great confidence had a rightness about it that left him seemingly without vanity. I believe his work gave him that, and so too did the way he lived with his talent. In his "Art of Fiction" interview, he told the *Paris Review* that there was a right way to live and that some values were *untarnishable*.

The immense depth of that was in his descriptions of the intimacies of love and the details of disappointment and loss and regret, and it made reading him an ecstatic experience. You read to see what would happen, sure, but you read every word to savor the meaning and balance of each sentence—it was a way to look at life as it passed.

Maybe that was one of the reasons critics said he was a writer's writer, a label that annoyed him and, I suspect, everyone else. Jim's friend Bruce Jay Friedman told a story about a weekly writers' lunch he was part of in the Hamptons that included Mario Puzo (*The Godfather*), Joe Heller (*Catch-22*) and Mel Brooks (*The Producers*). The group was looking for a new member to liven things up but decided not to ask Salter to join because, as Puzo put it, Jim was "too good of a writer."

If you're an editor there is no such thing, but the implied problem with *being* a writer's writer is that it goes along with semiobscurity and a lack of commercial success. Not that Jim didn't do fine; it was just so obvious that his talent outweighed his notoriety and his paydays. Of course Jim never talked about any of this. Then, finally, with the novel *All That Is*, he was poised for the hit his talent had been promising for so many years.

From the fall of 2012 everyone who knew Jim was optimistic that the momentum was building, and he knew something was happening, too. "Oh, please," he would say dismissively, but you could tell he was hopeful. There was a lot of press about *All That Is*, every piece noting that it had been more than thirty years since his last novel, *Solo Faces*, which Jim had written off of an unproduced screenplay he had done for Robert Redford based on the life of outlaw mountaineer Gary Hemming, who shot himself in Grand Teton National Park in 1969.

I knew a little about Hemming's suicide and the climbing culture from editing *Outside* magazine, and I heard about *Solo Faces* when it was in galleys. Without reading a word of it, I got Jim's number from Aspen information and called to ask about the new novel. We made a deal that afternoon on the phone to excerpt it in *Rocky Mountain Magazine*.

"Don't you want to read it first?" Jim said.

"I don't have to," I said, and I'm sure Jim saw right through that. It would be a big deal for me, landing James Salter for a regional start-up, and I had enough literary pretension to think that I could edit him.

Jim's novel *A Sport and a Pastime* was already considered a classic. I had found it years before when I started following the *Paris Review*, which published books back then. As the story went, Jim's manuscript had made the rounds and been rejected everywhere when he finally sent it to George Plimpton, who read it and told Jim there was a problem. I think now that George was looking for a way to soften the sex in the book, and Jim probably thought that at the time. What George told Jim was that he didn't think the novel worked in the first person but that if Jim would rewrite it in the third person, the *Paris Review* would publish it. Here was Jim's last chance, but he dug in. He would not rewrite. George suggested that successful novels were never in the first person. Jim mentioned *All Quiet on the Western Front*.

"Ah," George said. "Yes."

Jim never talked about that conversation until much later, after it had become a well-known writer-and-editor story because George often told it on himself, explaining that when he had thought about it for a second or two he'd had no choice but to bow to the power of Jim's language. In its review, the *New York Times* agreed: "Arching gracefully, like a glorious 4th of July rocket, it illuminates the dark sky of sex. It's a tour de force in erotic realism, a romantic cliff-hanger, an opaline vision of Americans in France. Fiction survives through minor novels like this one. They assert its power to make us suffer shock, compassion, regret. They bring the private news history never records."

Except for the word "minor," I agreed with every line of that *Times* review when I called Jim in Aspen about *Solo Faces*, but I had no idea about his one hundred combat missions as a fighter pilot or his sixteen screenplays or his photographs of Rauschenberg and other artists or the eclectic mix of people he knew and the glamorous rooms he had moved through. I did not know, as he would write later in *Burning the Days*, his memoir *of London in the evening and girls in Rolls-Royces, faces lit by the dash* . . .

Thinking back, my call seems worse than impertinent, but on the phone that day Jim asked, almost patiently, if I knew anything about climbing. I told him its culture was rich like surfing's but more intellectual, with more interesting new technology. Plus, I knew about the Vulgarians, radical climbers from the late 1950s and 1960s notorious for raucous partying, rich girlfriends and the occasional nude climb. I had an issue of the short-lived *Vulgarian Digest* that featured the Snake River ("Obscenic Float Trips") and the Tetons—where Hemming had killed himself. I went on and, I'm afraid, on . . .

Jim heard me out and then, after a silence I was determined not to break, said he would sell me a piece but he was not remotely interested in being edited. Not even a comma, especially not even a comma, without checking with him. That was fine with me. I already had a hands-off policy when it came to excerpts and wrote thank-you notes suggesting that I was there only to get thorns out of paws. It was always satisfying to see how careful some writers were with pieces from their books. Cormac McCarthy once sent back a galley of my cut from *All the Pretty Horses* with a single comma circled as an intrusion—a copy editor's change that I had not caught. Tom Wolfe would sometimes rewrite entire paragraphs if you asked him to look at one sentence. The best writers, like Jim, were always hard enough on themselves. Here is a paragraph of a letter from Jim to a friend of his, the writer and editor Robert Phelps, when he had finished polishing *Solo Faces*:

> *I mailed off the revised Solo Faces two days ago. Endless fretting and worrying about things that are at their best imperfect anyway. I added a chapter, changed the ending, and did innumerable small things throughout. It's a bit better. It's astonishing how the crossing out of a line, sometimes a phrase, or the substitution of something right for something false can suddenly let light in on an entire chapter. My typist accidentally left out seven lines at the end of Chapter 16 and I said, wonderful, it's much better without them. I'm already ashamed of the first version.*

I had not read that letter, of course, but when I did Jim's characterization of the isometric relationships between the words he chose redefined him for me as a so-called writer's writer. Maybe that's what Mario Puzo meant, too.

IN THE SPRING OF 2013, *All That Is* was published by Knopf, and when Jim appeared with Richard Ford at the 92nd Street Y, the room was buzzing like an opening night of beloved theater. I was in the balcony, first row. After they both read, Richard led a conversation between them. He told me later that he'd been keeping company with Jim both personally and in his books "these past months"—the buildup to the pub date, I assumed. A great, great delight it had been, and Richard wanted the evening to be commensurate with his private experience. They sat center stage, a small table set with water between them. Richard looked lean and handsome as always. Jim looked strong, too. Handsome still, but no longer young, like a man grown comfortably fit into his sixties, when in fact Jim was eighty-seven. "Dashing" was how I'd heard a woman describe his arrival at a book party on Park Avenue a few nights previous.

"I never thought I was very smart," Richard offered, charmingly, at one point and went on to explain that Jim had always known he was smart and the result had been a confidence that was the foundation of Jim's sentences and the ambition he used to put them together. Richard quoted Walter Benjamin's essay "The Storyteller"—which ends on a note that a storyteller "is the man who could let the wick of his life be consumed completely by the gentle flame of his story."

Jim nodded but didn't say anything. They had already agreed that the pages that were the easiest to read were the pages most difficult to write. Jim said the new novel gave him a chance to show himself *in a mature way*. The crowd was riveted by the two of them—Richard so tall and commanding, and Jim still, somehow, a fighter pilot.

I went home hungry for more Salter and opened *Burning the Days*. Two letters from Jim were there in the pages as bookmarks. One had come with the book galleys, thanking me for *Esquire's* support and noting correctly that although I had not been there at the beginning I was there to run pieces of that book at the end. It was written on Gotham Hotel stationery but he had datelined it Bridgehampton, June 9. It was 1997 and the book would be published that fall. Although we had always described the pieces as memoir, I saw on the galley subtitle that Jim had insisted on *Recollection* over *Memoir*. He had signed off hoping that we would see each other over the coming summer.

The second letter was from early that summer, explaining how the *New Yorker* would not also be publishing an excerpt because "they dislike publishing anything another magazine will be publishing." This meant Jim was choosing to publish in *Esquire* instead of the *New Yorker* even though it would be costing him money (at least $10,000) and prestige (not to mention reach). On top of that, he had not yet been published in the *New Yorker*, where his friends and rivals

195

had been running for years. Jim turning away from that was an act of loyalty unmatched in my experience as an editor. I put the letters in a safer place and reread *Burning the Days* into the night.

ALL THAT IS was a compounding critical success and sold very well, especially the foreign rights. It was finally the commercial book everyone who knew Jim had been hoping for, although he didn't talk about success as a matter of principle. His friend and neighbor Peter Matthiessen told me he thought Jim was somehow disappointed by the sales but that, of course, you would not hear that from Jim. That's just the way it was if you were a serious writer . . . it was competitive. He and Jim were almost the same age, and Peter was just completing what would be his last book, the novel *In Paradise*, published three days after Peter died, just a few months later, at eighty-six.

There was a small graveside service when Peter was buried at the tiny cemetery just down the road from where he lived in Sagaponack. I saw Jim that afternoon at Peter's house, where friends gathered to remember him. Jim spoke briefly about the respect Peter had earned among his neighbors, but did not mention his writing.

When the remembrances were finished we talked about how Peter would be missed, but Jim did not say that he had just written 1187 perfect words about their friendship and the writing life they had shared. The piece went up the next day on the *New Yorker*'s website:

> *I was reluctant to give him my work to read. I was afraid of his disapproval and too proud for advice. This may seem funny, considering how much we were with one another and how freely we talked, but there was always that slight competitive element to things. He did give me suggestions about "Burning the Days" that I took.*
>
> *I'm leaving out the trips to Europe and the intimacy that developed between our families. My children felt close to him, especially Theo, my younger son. When you celebrate Christmases together and everyone's birthdays and other events through*

the years, a dense and indestructible fabric is made, really too rich to imitate or describe. We sailed up the Nile. We were in France together, St. Petersburg, Italy. We drank together, sometimes quite a bit. For a few years, in our sixties, we had a ritual of throwing ourselves into the cold sea on November 1st, then having an icy martini with our wives on the beach.

There was more above and below those two paragraphs, all about writing and friendship, all of it *too rich to imitate or describe . . .*

IN LATE 2010 I called Jim and told him that the *Paris Review* would like to give him its highest honor. "Oh no," he said, and tried to talk me out of it. Obviously it would be much better to encourage someone younger. Well, obviously not, because as defined by George Plimpton, the Hadada, as it was called, should go to "a unique commitment to literature" over time. The name came from George's favorite bird, the hadada ibis, which has an extremely loud and distinctive "haa-haa-haa-de-dah" call—hence the name. Jim's story collection, *Last Night*, was dedicated to George with a single word beneath his name: *Hadada*. I pointed this out.

So, well then, yes, maybe for George. Jim would be honored.

Accepting the award, he explained with a straight face that in the African language from which the word comes, *hadada* means "Hail, great father." As in "Hi, Da-da!" So it would be hard to get too serious about a prize with such a silly name. But Jim got very serious about what it meant to him in light of his history with George and the *Review*, which had published *A Sport and a Pastime* and where he had first placed a short story. And then he said, holding up the small statuette of the bird, "This is my Stockholm."

The room went silent—five hundred people frozen in awe of such soulful irony—before exploding into standing ovation.

SOMETIMES WE PLAYED TOUCH FOOTBALL, sometimes we ate oysters and sometimes we just stood together at cocktail parties. I wanted to keep up but hold back at the same time, to soak him in somehow.

My father died as a navy pilot in 1944, just when Jim was leaving West Point for flight school and, ultimately, F-86 fighter jets. I never said anything about that until the night of Taylor Plimpton's wedding. We were standing at the bar with Jim's wife, Kay, watching a storm over Gardiners Bay, and there was something about Jim's posture that reminded me of a line from Tom McGuane, another admirer of Jim's, about a man "putting his drink down behind him on the bar without looking, like a cavalry officer." And I told Jim that line, and then that my father had flown F4 Corsairs in the Pacific.

"Well, you never mentioned that," Jim said. Then that squinty smile. "But of course you didn't," he said. "Of course you didn't."

I was on a plane to California when I learned that Jim had died. It was June of 2015. I looked out the window to see if the sky was one of Jim's skies, *filling with the bright cumulus that comes with fair weather,* as he had written in *Burning the Days.* Or perhaps his *clouds would become dense and towering, their edges struck with light; epic clouds, the last of the sun streaming through.* And then he wrote, *flying itself, the imperishability of it, the brilliance.*

-ENDIT-

Rocks, Feathers, Shells (1,942)

O<small>NE THANKSGIVING NIGHT</small> in a modern, art-filled beach house on Gardiners Bay in Amagansett, several women, some in their early twenties, some much older, put garlands in Peter Matthiessen's hair as we sat around drinking. I lifted my phone to take a picture and he turned away, looking in profile, one of the women said, like Alexander the Great as she had once seen him on a coin in the National Archaeological Museum in Athens, minted in gold when he was still alive.

"Or an old lizard," Peter said, when she showed him the picture I'd snapped. Every woman we both knew found him attractive and commented on it at one time or another—including my wife and ex-wife and my sons' girlfriends.

Peter liked to tease women—from twenty-one-year-old river guides to his old friend Jean Kennedy Smith. She liked to be called "Daphne," a joke I didn't understand, but it was somehow sexy. One night we were pouring wine at Peter's kitchen table in Sagaponack and he was beaming, still handsome many decades beyond when they had met at a long-ago Kennedy family picnic in their teens.

"You are still so full of yourself," Jean said, her eyes sparkling.

"I know, Daphne," Peter said, "I know."

I thought of the story Plimpton told about Peter showing up with a single, perfect peach at the Paris door of the beautiful, ineffable, literary Patsy Southgate, whom he had met at the Sorbonne. This was the early 1950s and they were starting the *Paris Review*; all the men were in love with her, the story went, but she was Peter's from the beginning and he had become engaged to her and then behaved badly in a way that George implied without detail.

"Peter got her back," George would say, sometimes frowning. "That peach was perfect."

When Patsy died, her obit in the *New York Times* noted that "in a city that treasures beauty she was renowned as the most beautiful woman in Paris." It went on to tell Plimpton's story in reverse, with Patsy arriving at Peter's door with an orange and the line "I thought you needed this." Peter told me that both stories were true.

Peter's second wife, the poet and writer Deborah Love, was beautiful too, and interested in LSD and Zen, both of which they explored together—with one evolving into the other for Peter. When she was dying of cancer, his friend Jim Harrison told me, Peter slept in her hospital room for weeks, even though they had been on the verge of divorce. In *The Snow Leopard,* he quoted her beloved Zen expression: "No snowflake ever falls in the wrong place."

For all the years I knew Peter he was with Maria Eckhart, once an advertising executive, born in Tanzania, whom he married in a Zen ceremony at Sagaponack in 1980. With Maria, his creative output increased as she alternatively protected his privacy and turned their home into a kind of intellectual safe house. Maria would joke that Peter "is a lot of trouble." Whatever she meant by that was unknowable beyond the great care she took of him. Writers' romantic lives have always seemed fraught and complicated by success (Hemingway, Mailer, et al.), but that can be an obvious function of fame and money for anyone. More interesting are the exceptions, writers with discretion and wives whose magnetism matched their own, like Peter's.

AT THE END OF 2012, Peter left on his last expedition, to Sagsai, Mongolia, to observe its ancient *eagler* culture, in which, he told me on the phone, men hunt wolves, foxes and deer from horseback using female golden eagles, which they carry on their arms. He had not seen that before, but he didn't sound as enthusiastic as usual about an upcoming trip. He didn't have to go, of course, and friends told him that, but Mongolia was where he had spent months with his beloved cranes for *The Birds of Heaven*—the cranes he loved *not only as magnificent and stirring creatures but as heralds and symbols of all that is being lost.* It was as if he was being called back. He said he had to go and he did, but it was a hard trip. Peter returned exhausted and was diagnosed with acute leukemia.

Just off the kitchen of Peter's house in Sagaponack was a small patio with a wooden table where we sat one Sunday after he had started treatment. He was optimistic about the chemo, although it put him down for one week a month, and said he was looking forward to physical therapy. He was thinner but still looked strong. We talked about the touch football games with Jim Salter and other local writers played in the potato field behind the house, and how he used to sneak onto private golf courses for a quick round now and then and had been caught only once. And we talked too about Leonard Peltier, as we always did.

Lawsuits challenging Peter's insistence on Leonard's innocence had blocked the paperback edition of *In the Spirit of Crazy Horse* for close to ten years, but it became a best seller in 1992, including this passage:

> *Whatever the nature and degree of his participation at Oglala, the ruthless persecution of Leonard Peltier had less to do with his own actions than with underlying issues of history, racism, and economics, in particular Indian sovereignty claims and growing opposition to massive energy development on treaty lands and dwindling reservations.*

The ladder of court rulings highlighted important free-speech issues, but Leonard remained in prison. Peter had never backed down from his story, and he was still outraged at President Clinton's refusal to pardon Peltier after Clinton had met with Peter at the White House but then pardoned the tax cheat Marc Rich, who had fled to Switzerland. Leonard's release date was still 2040 and Peter was still in touch with him. They spoke on the phone on special occasions like Leonard's birthday. Or if Leonard just wanted to talk.

"Does Leonard know about the leukemia?" I asked.

Peter nodded, and smiled slightly.

"Is Leonard a Buddhist now?" I asked.

"In his way."

I learned later that Leonard's last words to Peter were "Don't leave me behind."

PETER AND MARIA LIVED in Peter's low-ceilinged, two-story wooden house separated from the dunes of Sagaponack Beach by a half mile of those potato fields. You could smell the ocean from the patio. He had bought it cheaply in 1961 from the graphic designer Alexey Brodovitch, who, as art director of *Harper's Bazaar*, had developed a signature use of negative space, although he had gone the other way on his country property, planting tree after exotic tree. Peter planted more trees and hedges, until the six acres were so densely protected that you could only guess there was a house inside by noticing the dirt track that led into his bird-thronged sanctuary. No cats allowed because of the songbirds.

On the porch was the huge skull of a finback whale Peter had salvaged from the nearby surf. Peter wrote about it in a way that spoke to his life in that house, walking to the ocean as he did every day.

From the beach landing, in this moody sky and twilight, I saw something awash in the white foam, perhaps a quarter mile down to the eastward. The low heavy thing, curved round upon itself, did not look like driftwood; I thought at first that it must be a human body. Uneasy, I walked east a little way, then hurried ahead; the thing was not driftwood, not a body, but a great clean skull of a finback whale, dark bronze with sea water and minerals. The beautiful form, crouched like some ancient armored creature in the wash, seemed to await me. No one else was on the beach, which was clean of tracks. There was only the last cold fire of dusk, the white birds fleeing toward the darkness, the frosty foam whirling around the skull, seeking to regather it into the deeps.

Inside the house were spears and poison arrows on the walls, along with Michael Rockefeller's photographs of Stone Age war in New Guinea. There were books everywhere, sorted into what seemed like small, discrete libraries of his interests. On a shelf in the small study off an upstairs bedroom was his collection of the *Paris Review*, every issue arranged in order over six decades, from the first issue planned in Paris cafés in 1953, when he was the fiction editor, to the most recent, for which he had judged the year's literary prizes.

Peter's Zendo, where he taught and led services, was in a converted stable with a grassed yard and a centered Japanese maple and a small statue of Buddha. Inside on the floor was a heavy, bowl-shaped gong that a writer who'd once profiled Peter had noted would reverberate for as long as you could hold your breath. A shaded path around the side led to a raked stone garden perfectly in line with the gong and the window of the Zendo.

On the other side of the house, beyond the patio in the direction of the ocean, was his writing "shed," as he called it, where he worked every day he was not on the road. Much bigger than a shed, it was a high-ceilinged cottage with a sleeping loft and a long desk. The work he did there was an extension of his solitary travel and astonishing in its range — from journalism anchored in descriptive naturalism to narrative-driven fiction to personal essays to experimental combinations of all of the above. *The Snow Leopard* won the 1979 National Book Award in the Contemporary Thought category, and then the National Book Award for Nonfiction (Paperback) the next year. In 2008, at age eighty-one, he received an almost unprecedented third National Book Award, for *Shadow Country,* a one-volume 890-page revision of his three novels set in frontier Florida published in the 1990s. His favorite of his books was *Far Tortuga,* an innovative masterwork of simplicity that reflected his experimentation with form and innovation with language. Peter wrote more than thirty books, his last the ambitious novel *In Paradise,* published the week he died.

Above his desk was this from Ikkyu, the iconoclastic Japanese Zen Buddhist priest, poet and calligrapher:

Having no destination,
I am never lost.

PETER WAS BURIED on a clear, sharp day with no clouds and a slight breeze off the ocean. Perhaps a hundred people, almost all of them locals, gathered on that patio off Peter's long living room, many spilling out onto the lawn among the cedar trees and the more than one thousand tulips and daffodils Maria tended each year. I met many more family members than I'd known Peter had, and his sons spoke.

Farmers who had known Peter stood back shyly at first and then delivered simple words with great power about how Peter had loved the land that gave them pride, and about how they loved "Peter's birds," and that best of all Peter had understood the connections that could only come from working the land. One older, very heavy man with an eastern European accent who must have been in his eighties said that he loved the dirt and just looking at the fields early in the morning, and that Peter had loved that too and in the same way.

Before I drove back to the city, I walked to the tiny cemetery on Sagg Main Street where Peter was buried that morning, his grave marked only by rocks and feathers and shells.

-ENDIT-

III

Don't get too annoyed if I say that I write in the
way that I do because I am what I am.

— GRAHAM GREENE

Elaine, Francis and Louie (1,619)

Places to meet writers and talk about story ideas or just talk about writing were important, especially certain bars in San Francisco and New York. For a while you could score coke at some of them, although that didn't matter because the drinking always came first anyway.

Elaine's was the only place where you always had something to eat. Elaine Kaufman made you eat, but that wasn't the only reason Elaine's was different. It was on Manhattan's Upper East Side, and the insouciant glamour of the place was an organizing principle. She really did direct someone to the bathroom once by telling them to "turn right at Michael Caine." When she died, that's what her friends put on her prayer card.

There was a large photo of Hunter Thompson hanging high on a back wall and there was a bust of George Plimpton next to the bar, although most people didn't think it looked much like him. By the time I knew them, George and Elaine didn't talk much—no long conversations, anyway. It was as if they had gotten all they needed to say to each other out of the way. Hunter never talked to Elaine, but that didn't matter because she'd known all about him before they met and that was enough. Plus, Hunter was difficult to understand in bars because he tended to mumble.

Who Elaine liked to talk to the most, except for maybe Yankees owner George Steinbrenner, was Bruce Jay Friedman, and she was quick to tell you that he was the handsomest man who ever came through her front door—along with Frank Sinatra (whom she and Plimpton both called Francis).

With Elaine, you didn't have to talk, and you could definitely talk too much, sometimes disastrously if you were drunk or full of coke or both. Quiet was fine, especially if you stayed late and spent a little money. Elaine's friendship requirements called for dignity, generous tipping and no whining—and she always helped you with the dignity.

A story Bruce told was about one night in the late '70s when Sinatra was eating dinner with Plimpton, and Elaine was sitting with them. Bruce was at the bar, ten feet away, nursing what he still calls the worst hangover of his life, feeling vulnerable. He noticed Elaine whispering something to George, who got up and came to the bar, put an arm around Bruce and said, "Francis would be delighted if you would join us."

Bruce says he barely had the strength to apologize and wave George off, and it troubled him afterward that he didn't stumble over to say hello. "Who knows," he would say later. "I might have been the most sober person *Francis* met all that week."

Bruce felt bad, though, as if he had missed an opportunity that should have been more important to him, and would have been, as he wrote in his autobiography, *Lucky Bruce*, if he didn't drink so much. He had left something on the table without even sitting down. After all, who wouldn't want Francis to know you by name, especially if you were making a living in "the show business"? But if Elaine liked you (and she loved Bruce), she opened possibilities so relentlessly you could take a pass once in a while, even with someone like Francis. Later that night she told Bruce, "When you don't feel like it, you don't feel like it."

I WAS LATE TO THE PARTY, as they say, which meant Elaine introduced me to people I already knew about—not Francis but some movie stars and, more important, people I admired, like Lewis Lapham, the editor of *Harper's*, who was from Northern California, like me. But unlike me, Lewis had come east to prep school, where one of his roommates had been John Knowles, who went on to write the coming-of-age standard *A Separate Peace*, while my high school friends mostly hung around gas stations. I admired Lewis as a superb writer and what a New York *Daily News* sportswriter who was around Elaine's then called "a skyhook of literary sophistication."

The night I met Lapham, Elaine stopped me on my way to turn right at Michael Caine and introduced us with a nod toward me and two words to Lewis: "Help him." When Lewis said he was uncertain of her meaning, Elaine said, "You'll figure it out, *Louie.*"

I never heard anyone else call tall, elegant Lewis Lapham "Louie." It was a wisecrack full of love.

That first night, Lewis asked me if I regretted that I had not gone into banking. This was years before investment banking was interesting to anyone except investment bankers. I had no such regrets. Lewis told me he did, which surprised me. "The numbers, the money," he said, "interest me more and more." I said the "Harper's Index," which he had invented, was interesting to me. He sighed and invited me to sit down.

Once I relaxed at his table with a drink in front of me, I naturally wanted to impress Lewis with some smart talk about his editing and writing, and I had questions about why he seemed to hold the West is such disdain. Instead we talked about the private school our sons attended. I didn't know then that his family had been "in shipping," and that his grandfather had been the mayor of San Francisco, his great-grandfather one of the founders of Texaco. Elaine told me all that later.

"Yeah, that Louie," she said. "Classy as it gets." I wondered if she had introduced *Louie* to *Francis.* Of course she had.

Elaine's was supposed to be a kind of writers' club, with Elaine playing an ironic Wendy to all the Lost Boy writers. But there were often as many cops, lawyers and producers in the place and, as far as the club went, a lot of those writers thought of Elaine's as a place to get work done. "Writer work," that is, which included divulging confidential sources, spitballing story ideas and trolling for book contracts. One evening, for example, the somewhat dubious "Cocaine Etiquette" piece I had assigned to P. J. O'Rourke for *Rolling Stone* evolved into what would be the best seller *Modern Manners,* for P.J. and his editor Morgan Entrekin at Atlantic Monthly Press. We all agreed on how flattering the light was in the men's room. Plus, as P.J.

put it: "It's better to spend money like there's no tomorrow than to spend tonight like there's no money."

Elaine's was a great place to hire someone or assign a piece because nothing was more flattering to a junior editor or out-of-town writer than to be introduced to Elaine and have her say, "Of course," like she already knew who they were. The truth was, she never paid any attention to anyone until they showed up at her place. What she knew was how the world worked, what people wanted to hear.

When I was fired from *Esquire*, I called Elaine. I was ashamed and embarrassed—clueless, really, about why I was suddenly out— but thought I should try to explain what had happened because she had always been so encouraging, helping me find my way when I'd arrived in town to edit *Rolling Stone*, introducing me to important writers and editors, like *Louie*, and sitting with me and whoever I brought with me from *Newsweek* on late closing nights. She had even invested when I was raising money to launch *Smart*, which made enough noise for a year or so to get me considered for the *Esquire* job in the first place.

"I heard," she said.

"Everybody's heard."

"Fuck that!" she said, and asked if she would see me that night. I said no.

"Whenever you're ready," she said, and we hung up.

The next time I went to Elaine's, people congratulated me on my many job offers. All the nonexistent ones Elaine had told them about.

And she was there to help with every magazine I edited for the next seventeen years. One night after I got to *Sports Illustrated*, I packed the senior edit staff into her side room for dinner. I was new on the job and thought to be a dicey choice because of my lack of sports experience and contacts. What I didn't know until Elaine sent Michael the waiter to fetch me was that George Steinbrenner was coming in, and there he was sitting with her, just the two of them at a large table in the back.

"Help him," she said to Steinbrenner, who offered me a chair.

"You need to fix that rag," he said.

Elaine sent Michael the waiter back to the side room, where my colleagues were about to be served, to tell them to start without me because I was going to have to spend some time with Steinbrenner. "George was insisting," he told them.

WHEN ELAINE WAS NAMED a New York City "Living Landmark" in 2003, some of us bought a table and went to the benefit in one of the big hotels. During drinks, before we sat down and she had to go up to the head table, Elaine said it was embarrassing and that she didn't want to speak. I thought she was nervous, perhaps troubled by how to thank a roomful of society people. I asked her if she knew what she was going to say.

"They probably won't like it," she told me.

When it was her turn, when Liz Smith and others had finished praising her, she popped up and said in a loud, firm voice, "You should have given this to George Plimpton," and sat down. George had died six weeks before.

-ENDIT-

George Plimpton (4,922)

I T W A S D U S K , and we were walking a ranch road in eastern New Mexico. According to George, we were birding—on the trail of the elusive burrowing owl, which lives in prairie dog holes—but we were going about it in that deeply civilized way that allows you to bring your glass of wine or whatever along on your after-dinner expedition. In George's case, it was always Dewar's with a little water.

We had seen no owls, but George had pointed out a bat or two when he set his drink on the ground, pulled his white T-shirt over his head and flung it in the air.

"*Tadarida brasiliensis mexicana*," he explained. "Mexican free-taileds."

The shirt, peaking at perhaps twenty feet, drew a half dozen bats, and they tracked it to the ground like tiny dive-bombers, squeaking their shrill bat squeaks. A second throw doubled the number of bats. And so on until I had counted more than one hundred and the light was almost gone. The trick, George explained, pulling his T-shirt back over his head, was to give the bats something that would come fluttering up on their sonar as potential food.

"Like a gargantuan moth," he said, taking a sip of his Dewar's.

It was predictable of George to pull something like bat expertise out of nowhere. But of course it wasn't out of nowhere. When he was fourteen, he'd spent the summer hunting bats in California's Sierra Nevada and donating their "specimen skins" to museums. It was the kind of summer job you had if you were George Plimpton. When I was fourteen in California, a good summer job was mopping up at night in a fruit cannery. Listening to his stories about life as a bat hunter was like hearing about the adventures of a young prince. But it wasn't his privilege that struck you; it was his curiosity.

. . .

GEORGE'S QUESTIONS were like trampolines, a technology he admired. They bounced you higher—to the next question. This was particularly true when he was talking about writers and writing.

"Did you know that the great Camus played goal for the Oran Football Club?" he asked me when we were walking past an Algerian restaurant near his apartment on Seventy-second Street. I was unaware but said that I did think Gabriel García Márquez had written a soccer column for a while in Bogotá.

"Alas," George sighed, "*Le colonisateur de bonne volonté* was never moved to write about it. Imagine, the existential goalkeeper."

"*Alas,*" I said, and he gave me a look.

To be or not to be was never a question for George. What to do next was his question, although existential imaginings were at the heart of all his stories. He would develop ideas—What would it be like to . . . ?—then find a way to put himself into the action. I asked if he had considered becoming a soccer goalie. He had, but he had already written about guarding the hockey net for the Boston Bruins.

"So are you going to write that memoir?" I asked. Several publishers were interested, and one had offered close to $1 million.

"I don't want to write about my life," he said.

"That's what you do now," I said.

"Well, shouldn't that be enough?"

The memoir came up often. People were always asking when he was going to write one, and thinking about it darkened him. He said it smacked of vanity. If he wound up having to do it for the money so be it, but not yet.

The lure of the memoir for publishers was that George knew everyone and had many stories about them. Any list would be incomplete: Sinatra (neighbor and late-night drinking cohort); Hugh Hefner, whom everyone called "Hef" (offered him the editorship of *Playboy* many times); Warren (Beatty would call and shout, "Is this

213

the man who has never eaten an olive?"); Jackie (his brother Oakes said George had "dated" her); Elvis (both Presley and Costello) . . . But no matter who you were, if you were with him or just at the same party, his manners pulled you in, making you feel comfortable and in on at least some of his secrets.

George couldn't remember names, especially men's names, but that didn't matter. "There's the great man," he would say at his parties, and the unnamed guest would beam. "There's the great man" is how George once greeted a kid delivering a pizza.

The Lesson of George, I came to think, was "Good times should be orchestrated and not left to the uncertainties of chance." This was the most important thing A. E. Hotchner said he learned from Hemingway, and George said "Papa" had taught him that same lesson. There is nothing sadder than small regrets, and when I first met George I thought he had very few of those. When I knew him better, I wasn't so sure.

A story I heard over and over about George was that he'd been very nervous before his first wedding—to Freddy Espy, who was even more beautiful than Lauren Hutton, the model who made her acting debut playing Freddy in the movie of *Paper Lion*. George's friend Thomas Guinzburg tried to calm him by praising Freddy and suggesting that whatever else George was thinking, he should realize that after he was married he would never be lonely again. The punch line was George's response: "But I've never been lonely in my life!"

I believed that story, but I also believe that as he got older George was bothered by the transience of the people he knew and loved, and there is no deeper definition of loneliness than that, even as the party swirls around you. When famous friends die, do you miss them more? That was a question I wondered about. George said no, but you were reminded more often that they were gone.

We went out a lot—to book parties and sports events at Madison Square Garden, where all the floor security guys knew him, and, mostly, we went to dinner, and George would order macaroni and cheese or a simple pasta that was close to it. There were the parties at his house, too. It was the 1990s now and the celebrities there weren't as bright as they had been in the '60s and '70s, but the parties were still crowded with good-looking, accomplished people. At least the kids at the *Paris Review* office downstairs were good-looking, especially the young women, who, unbeknownst to George, were having a contest to see who could wear the shortest skirt.

The pool table would be covered so food and drink could be laid out, and there was always another bar in the kitchen. A long wall of windows looked out on the East River. The boat traffic on the flat water at night was beautiful but few guests noticed, more interested in where George was standing, what George was talking about.

When John Kerry was running for president, George gave him a fund-raiser at the apartment. Kerry went on too long, and the crowd was fidgeting. I looked at George and could see that this was bothering him. When Kerry finally wrapped up, some of the crowd gathered around him but just as many collected around George.

"Please go say hello to the senator," George told them. "It's his party." But of course it wasn't.

FROM ITS FIRST ISSUE, in 1954, *Sports Illustrated* kept careful record of freelance assignments on four-by-nine index cards, noting subject, deadline and fee. One of the tallest stacks belonged to George, a collection that I didn't discover until I was writing his obit. The first card was from 1956, only three years after George began editing the *Paris Review*, the literary quarterly he founded in 1953 with Peter Matthiessen and several other friends. It was a hot start-up before anyone used the term, and much has been written about the good times in Paris and the careers that came later.

For George, the *Paris Review* became a spiritual hideout for fifty years. He admired writers and creativity even more than he admired athletes and beautiful women, and he could exercise that admiration through the *Review*. It paid nothing, of course, so George had decided to make his way as a journalist until he settled on what his more serious work might be. In the meantime he would write about sports, and have some fun at the same time.

In the fall of '58 George visited *SI*'s first managing editor, Sidney James, with an idea he was uncertain of himself. A group of major league baseball players were staging an unofficial postseason all-star game at Yankee Stadium, and George thought he could write an interesting article on what it was like to participate—pitching, say, to Willie Mays and Mickey Mantle. The only problem would be arranging it.

In those days, the most influential man in sports was Toots Shor, whose boozy, eponymous restaurant was a couple blocks from the *SI* offices. James led an expedition of editors there and bought drinks as he and George explained the idea to Toots, who said the solution was simple: offer $1,000 to the winning team. By evening, word came back to the bar that George's pitching exhibition was on, whereupon Toots pulled him aside for a question: "You gonna box, too?"

George was flattered. The saloonkeeper understood that George was building on the work of their shared sportswriting hero Paul Gallico, who had spent a round in the ring with heavyweight champion Jack Dempsey back in 1923. But what George had in mind was more complicated than just looking for "the feel," as Gallico had put it. George wanted to unlock the secrets kept on the highest level of the games—the ones he believed you could share only in an NFL huddle or a conference on the mound.

On game day at Yankee Stadium, the public-address announcer bungled George's name, calling him George Prufrock, an irony not lost on George, a T. S. Eliot aficionado of sorts who had lived for a time in the same room used by the poet when he had attended Harvard. George did not write about this, but he used it in his storytelling with a reference to a famous line from "The Love Song of J. Alfred Prufrock": "Well, my arm was rather like a 'ragged claw.'"

The setup at Yankee Stadium was for George to be a facsimile batting-practice pitcher, with the hitters allowed to wait for their perfect pitch. George got Mays to pop up, but many of the hitters made him throw a dozen or so pitches—Ernie Banks let twenty-two go by—and after nine National Leaguers had batted, George called for a time-out. He could no longer lift his arm. I have a photograph of George taken in the dugout after he came off the mound. He looks shell-shocked, his eyes blank and faraway.

THE EXPANDED *SI* STORY would become George's first best seller, *Out of My League*. Ernest Hemingway wired George from the Mayo Clinic, where he was being treated for depression, that it was "beautifully observed and incredibly conceived [with] the chilling quality of a true nightmare . . . the dark side of the moon of Walter Mitty." It was a gift from Hemingway intended as a marketing blurb but, intentionally or not, it spoke to a truth beyond that cliché about the moon.

Hemingway was George's greatest hero, and George knew him well enough to call him "Papa" without affectation. They had been together in Spain and Cuba and New York and, of course, Paris, where George first saw Hemingway in the Ritz Hotel, buying a copy of the *Paris Review*.

"It was the only time I have ever seen anyone actually purchase a copy of the paper," George would say. He always called it *the paper*, as if to deflate any pretension, but he had great ambition for it, especially when it came to the *Review*'s interviews with writers, the "Art of Fiction" series, which George refined by pushing his subjects for clarity with back-and-forth editing, often for months after the interview.

His interview with Hemingway began in a Madrid café with Hemingway asking George, "You go to the races?"

"Yes, occasionally."

"Then you read the *Racing Form*," Hemingway said. "There you have the true art of fiction."

The interview was brilliant, deconstructing as it did every detail of how Hemingway worked and how he thought about the work of writing. At the end George coaxed out a quintessential Hemingway sentence. You can see both of their minds working in the interchange.

PLIMPTON

Finally, a fundamental question: as a creative writer, what do you think is the function of your art? Why a representation of fact, rather than fact itself?

HEMINGWAY

Why be puzzled by that? From things that have happened and from things as they exist and from all things that you know and all those you cannot know, you make something through your invention that is not a representation but a whole new thing truer than anything true and alive, and you make it alive, and if you make it well enough, you give it immortality. That is why you write and for no other reason that you know of. But what about all the reasons that no one knows?

GEORGE HAD MANY HEMINGWAY STORIES. One he told often was set up with George's puzzlement by the white bird that flies out of the gondola in the love scene between the young countess and Colonel Cantwell in *Across the River and into the Trees*.

"Papa," George asked after a day of fishing, when he was carrying a picnic hamper on Hemingway's dock in Cuba. "What is the significance of those white birds that sometimes turn up in your, um . . . sex scenes? I've always—"

George said that Hemingway stopped and whipped around toward him, and he could see that he had made a mistake.

"I suppose you think you can do better," Hemingway shouted at George.

"No, no, Papa," George said. "Certainly not."

George would say that Hemingway's eyes had become small and "his whiskers seemed to bristle like an alarmed cat's."

A story I heard only once from George was about being fitted for a safari jacket at Hemingway's Finca Vigía on another visit. The jacket was made of antelope skin and Hemingway already had one like it. George had his new jacket on and the tailor was adjusting the sleeves when Hemingway said the fit was wrong and began smoothing it on George's shoulders and back.

"It went on too long and made me uncomfortable," George said. "But it was the only time that happened."

It was one of the stories he would never include in that annoying memoir, if he ever wrote it. I was not surprised, and it was no big deal anyway. One way or another, everyone fell in love with George.

THE BIG QUESTION ABOUT GEORGE among his friends was why he spent so much time on the *Paris Review* instead of on his own writing. Some of his oldest friends from the *Review*—especially Matthiessen, Styron and Terry Southern, great writers all—were even a little arrogant about it. Why wasn't George tormenting himself with the ambition to write important books like they were? Whenever this came up, George would get mad. If it went deeper, to the enigma of why he was writing so much about sports, George would turn silent.

The *Review* was where he felt most comfortable, but in sports George could test himself in ways so personal he seldom spoke of them; *courage* was a word he never used, although that's what you were reading about in those pieces. Plus, *Sports Illustrated* paid the bills for the *Paris Review* even as he was redefining sportswriting as a participatory journalist—a label he characterized as "that ugly descriptive."

I had read George's *SI* pieces long before I met him, and when I first got a job in New York, I asked people about him—and the *Paris Review*. "Good parties" was often the answer. When I met him myself and told him I liked the *Review*, he asked me if I wanted to "help out." As an editor, I was flattered until I figured out that George asked many people that same question and that it was his feeble attempt at fund-raising—which embarrassed him. But that never seemed to show, because he looked so good. When people described

219

George, they inevitably used the words "tall" and "handsome." I sensed nerve behind his looks, and his audacity echoed for me in his reputation. Hemingway's Walter Mitty analogy had a surface truth but overlooked the obvious difference that in Mitty's daydreams he always succeeded, while in George's real-life adventures he always failed. This truth—that his work had more to do with Everyman than Mitty—was always obscured by George's careful, self-deprecating prose, which made him so easy and hilarious to read. Plus, Walter Mitty was a wimp. Not George.

Far from being unsuited for sports, George was a graceful athlete. Otherwise he would never have succeeded in his failures. He had to be good enough to compete or his attempts would have been silly or sad. His tennis was strong enough for him to play with Pancho Gonzalez; he swam credibly against Olympian Don Schollander; and he could perfectly throw any ball he'd ever picked up. "It was the first instrument of superiority I found myself owning," he told me about his pitching, which surprised me because it seemed so far out of character, a brag, almost.

We were talking about his most notorious piece, the April 1, 1985, hoax "The Curious Case of Sidd Finch," which he had concocted with SI's managing editor at the time, Mark Mulvoy, the two of them pushing the fool-around quotient in the traditional writer-editor compact to a new level. The key to the story was Sidd's arm—*an instrument of superiority.*

The piece broke the news that a young Buddhist pitcher with a 168-mile-an-hour fastball was under wraps at the Mets training camp, and the club went along, helping SI stage bogus photos. Everyone fell for the preposterous Finch, who could *throw a strawberry through a locomotive,* made credible by the magazine and George's stature as a sportswriter. When he called me at *Newsweek* with a heads-up that he had something "quite surprising" coming in that week's SI, I said I would get a reporter right on it.

"No," he said. "You should take a close look at the top of it yourself."

The subhead of the article ran: "He's a pitcher, part yogi and part recluse. Impressively liberated from our opulent life-style, Sidd's deciding about yoga—and his future in baseball." The first letters of those words spell out "Happy April Fools' Day—ah [a] fib."

When the prank was exposed, bumper stickers appeared proclaiming SIDD FINCH LIVES, and George got endless questions about Sidd's progress in the world.

"How's Sidd doing?" someone would ask, often as a way to approach George at a party.

"I do have a phone number for him, but when I call no answer," George would say. "But then just the other day it was busy . . ."

The Curious Case of Sidd Finch was published two years later. Of his thirty-six books, it was George's only novel.

ABOVE HIS DESK in his apartment on Seventy-second Street, George had a photograph of Hemingway walking a country road in Ketchum in winter, kicking a can high in the air just days before he killed himself in 1961. In my office I had a photo of George wrestling the gun from Sirhan Sirhan's hand moments after he shot George's friend Bobby Kennedy in Los Angeles in 1968.

I was in George's office often, although he was never once in mine. Not at *Rolling Stone, Esquire, Sports Illustrated* or anywhere else. This had nothing to do with the arrogance of never going to another man's office. George was just too busy. Counter to his reputation for never missing a party, George guarded his calendar and spent most days when he wasn't traveling at his desk under that picture of Hemingway, where he wrote, and where he edited the *Paris Review.* He was hard about it, like he was about a lot of things—his writing, of course, and also the work of editors who edited him.

George could be irascible as both a writer and an editor, a tough edit on either side of the desk. As an editor he was unbending, but he also liked to warn fellow writers of the "tin-eared butchery" they might suffer at the hands of magazine editors other than himself. Even the best editors could be problematic. He said he was never happier than when he was on assignment for *Sports Illustrated,* except that he had been terrified of the magazine's second managing editor André Laguerre, whom he nicknamed "Heavy Water," as in what it took to make atom bombs.

Being spooked by Laguerre was part of *SI*'s informal initiation and George sailed on to the masthead as a "special contributor," which made an indignity he suffered there years later under the Mulvoy regime all the more harsh and baffling. None of his deep history with *SI* or his co-conspirator relationship with managing editor Mulvoy mattered when it came to the butchery done to his story on President George H. W. Bush in 1988.

The piece had started as an assignment to play horseshoes with the president-elect but wound up edited into a survey of the Bush family as athletes. *Zzzzzz.* Worse, according to George, clichés were salted into it and he saw none of the changes until he opened the magazine. George first told me about this when we were working on a piece for *Smart* about what it was like to mouth-catch a grape dropped from the top of Trump Tower. Something about the seriousness we were applying to something so silly made George even madder about the Bush piece and his betrayal by *SI*.

But then, like everything with George, the disastrous story had a coda, perhaps apocryphal but unchallenged. George was invited to pitch horseshoes again with Bush, this time at Camp David, and after the horseshoes there was a game of tennis with the president, which was interrupted by the ringing of the ominous red phone. The president's face darkened as he crossed the court but brightened after he picked up the receiver.

"It's for you," the president said, holding the phone out to George.

Whenever George told this story to writers and they asked him, as they inevitably did, who was calling, he would lean close and whisper, "Mulvoy, wanting another piece."

George never wrote another story for *SI*, although after I was hired there, he would praise it as a writer's magazine that, when finely tuned by a good editor, "could soar like a great tabernacle choir or a troop of chacma baboons in full-throated roar." He would then add, "You should do more of that."

WHEN *SI* NAMED LANCE ARMSTRONG its 2002 Sportsman of the Year, George came with me to the ceremony at a silly midtown nightclub with a sixteen-foot-tall Buddha and pools of carp. He remembered Sportsman ceremonies in tuxedos. Lance had been my choice as editor. My job now was to make the case for him exemplifying the ideals of sportsmanship in winning his fourth straight Tour de France, then present him with the trophy—a ceramic replica of an ancient Greek amphora. Retrospective ironies aside, it was funny enough at the time to be passing a fake Greek artifact to a cyclist under the eyes of a giant fake Buddha, but I was nervous.

"I wish you could do this," I said to George as we watched the room fill with a couple hundred people, who would be standing around drinking while I made my remarks.

"It's good to be nervous," George said. "Edward R. Murrow called it 'the sweat of perfection.'"

I got through the presentation and Armstrong said he was honored and together we called Robin Williams to the stage. They were close then, and called each other "dawg."

"*Dawg?*" George greeted me, when I joined him just offstage to listen to Williams's seemingly effortless monologue—using the amphora and the Buddha as running gags. Afterward we congratulated both of the *dawgs*, and both told George they had always wanted to meet him.

Later that night, George told me that *sprezzatura* was an important component of humor. Had I not read that in the *Paris Review*? It had all been explained in any number of issues, *sprezzatura* being a certain nonchalance that made whatever one said appear to be effortless, natural, without any thought about it. That *dawg* Robin definitely had *sprezzatura*, but George was talking about himself.

There were many levels to George's humor and he layered them for his own amusement. Those roaring baboons, for example, would have been far less amusing without the specific identification as "chacma" and the context supplied by the tabernacle choir. The craft of it amused him, especially late in his career, when he was trapped in his own celebrity and people simply assumed he would be amusing. It's a cliché he would have hated, but my theory is that George was always amusing because he was always amused.

He didn't tell jokes, he told stories. And like his questions, his stories had a trampoline effect, bouncing you to the next story—with George making fun of himself. He loved parody, self-parody most of all, even enthusiastically appearing as a deranged version of himself in an episode of *The Simpsons*. He had already been the punch line in a *New Yorker* cartoon: a patient on an operating table opens his eyes and confronts his surgeon with "Wait a minute! How do I know you're not George Plimpton?"

When George was the host of *Mouseterpiece Theater*, a parody of PBS's *Masterpiece Theatre*, presenting cartoons instead of classic drama, he wrote and gave commentary, as well as background information before and after each cartoon. The shows had themes, like Goofy's character arc as Everyman, and asked challenging questions: "Is Donald Duck really a strident existentialist *and* a hero?" It ran late in the evening on the Disney Channel and was especially popular among baby-boom stoners. President George H. W. Bush was also said to enjoy the show.

WHEN HE WAS SEVENTY-FIVE, George was finally elected into the American Academy of Arts and Letters, the highest formal recognition of artistic merit in the country. George's literary friends were almost all members, as were many of the writers he had discovered and edited, but there had been resistance within the academy over the years to tapping George. The novelist and creative-writing teacher Edmund White said George was "sort of an 'after-dinner speaker,' not a major American writer." George was stung by that.

When the day finally came, it was a long, hot afternoon at the academy grounds in upper Manhattan. George was crisp in his blue-and-white seersucker suit, but he looked tired. I kept thinking about something he had said in *When We Were Kings*, the film about the Ali-Foreman fight in Kinshasa.

> *As happens with people who love a thing too much, it destroys them. Oscar Wilde said, "You destroy the thing that you love." It's the other way around. What you love destroys you.*

George closed the fiftieth-anniversary issue of the *Paris Review* two days before he died, and we spoke that afternoon about how he might contribute to *SI*'s upcoming fiftieth-anniversary issue. As always, he had numerous ideas. He took me to dinner that night at the Brook Club, where we sat at a long, communal table with other members. George loved the Brook and spent many nights there, where as a long-standing member his celebrity didn't pester him.

Peter Matthiessen had mentioned to me that sometimes if George thought he was unobserved he would let his face drop and go blank, with his jaw hanging open, and it made him look like a dead man, or at the least very sad, or even fighting something dark. Peter said it made *him* sad when he saw George that way, but I had never seen it until that night. When we were leaving, he told me he had recently committed to a $750,000 contract to write his memoirs.

George died the next night.

A FEW DAYS LATER his wife, Sarah Dudley Plimpton, was searching his computer and came across a "Notes & Obligations" file. The last entry was written at 1:25 a.m. on September 25, the morning he died in his sleep. George often returned home from late dinners and sat typing away until he was tired enough to fall asleep. The memo was a run of reminders, ideas for future issues of the *Paris Review*, drafts of letters, anecdotes for the memoir he was determined never to write. That last morning George finished his notes with a poem by Emily Dickinson:

Fame is a bee.
It has a song—
It has a sting—
Ah, too, it has a wing

And the very last entry was a quote from André Gide:

The drawback to a journey that has been too well planned is
that it does not leave enough room for adventure.

-ENDIT-

Camouflage (370)

IF YOU WORK WITH NOTORIOUS WRITERS, some of what they are famous for comes off on you. It's never the other way around and, if you're a good editor, what you do is invisible anyway. That's the job. Brace yourself and be aware that you will be associated with creativity that is not yours at all, although it is tempting to try to keep some of the credit. Bad idea.

I am not proud of it, but in college I took the SATs for money. It was easy to just sign in then, and so were the tests. George was appalled at the dishonesty even before he knew the scores I got for one friend helped get him into Stanford, where he signed up for an accelerated program in something like "Modern Thought, Science and Literature." I don't remember the details, but my friend flunked out at the end of his freshman year.

I thought about him from time to time whenever I would feel myself faking it—posturing with casual self-importance as a kind of camouflage to hide insecurity when moving into deeper water, like when I was going to meet George Plimpton for the first time to ask him to write for me. Or later, when George and I were arriving at Owl Farm several hours before Hunter expected us, and I didn't know Hunter then as well as George thought I did.

Or much later, in 2010, when I was asked to moderate a conversation at the *Time, Fortune,* CNN Global Forum in Cape Town between Danny Jordaan and Francois Pienaar. Jordaan had fought beside Nelson Mandela as an anti-apartheid activist and was now chief executive officer of FIFA's first World Cup in South Africa. Pienaar was the former captain of the South African Springboks and the soulful national hero played by Matt Damon in the film *Invictus,* about the newly elected president Mandela uniting the country by enlisting the national rugby team on a mission to win the 1995 Rugby

World Cup. That was a sacred moment in South Africa's history and I was supposed to lead them through it.

"You ready?" asked the stage manager, queuing me to go on.

A shrug from me. Camouflage.

-ENDIT-

Hunter (4,763)

GEORGE PLIMPTON AND I DECIDED to visit Hunter after he sent me a photograph of himself sinking a thirty-foot putt at the Aspen Golf Club. He signed it to me with *Res Ipsa Loquitur* across the image, and there was a message on the back: *Come out and play golf with me sometime — + bring George — and money; I will beat both of you like mules.*

Hunter's Owl Farm had seen numerous visitations far more exalted than ours. Jimmy Carter and Keith Richards, among dozens of others, had passed through, sometimes shooting clay pigeons and improvised targets in the meadow next to the house. After all, Owl Farm was designated a "Rod and Gun Club" on Hunter's stationery. Bill Murray had come close to moving in when he was preparing to play Hunter in *Where the Buffalo Roam,* and Johnny Depp actually did before he filmed *Fear and Loathing in Las Vegas.* Hunter liked to play host — even picking you up at the airport in the '71 Chevrolet Impala convertible he called the "Red Shark." When John Belushi died and there were rumors he had been visiting Hunter, the wires quoted him saying John was "welcome at Owl Farm dead or alive."

FRIENDS OF FRIENDS CAN'T BRING FRIENDS was taped to the refrigerator; but they did. Hunter complained but when you saw him playing his games with new guests you knew he loved it. They would tell him how much they were influenced by this or that in his work and he would ask them to read a little of it aloud. Just a paragraph to start but it would become a page and then a chapter. "Slower," Hunter would say, "slower." Some people wondered if they'd ever get out of there.

I had visited Owl Farm before and told George there would be distractions, but we arrived hopeful about our connected missions. My plan was to get Hunter to write a piece for the premier issue of *Smart.* George was there to interview him for what he planned to

229

be the first interview for "The Art of Journalism" series for the *Paris Review*. Hunter said first we had to play golf.

WE PLAYED THAT FIRST EVENING, in the dying light, at the municipal Aspen Golf Club, which was closed. Hunter just waved to a guy in the pro shop, who brought us a bucket of balls. Hunter had a 12-gauge shotgun in his golf bag and we had Heinekens in a cooler on the cart—also a fifth of Chivas, a fifth of Jose Cuervo, limes, a fifth of Dewar's (for George) and an extra cooler of ice.

"Here," Hunter said, holding out three white tabs of blotter paper with an unfamiliar red symbol on them. "Eat these."

He put one on his tongue and stuck it out at us. I took my tab and did the same back at him. When George said he wanted to concentrate on his golf, Hunter licked the third tab. "Ho ho . . . last of the batch!"

Following Hunter's lead, we used the first tee as a driving range to warm up. His swing was explosive if not smooth and his third drive was solid and long. George had a fluid swing and drove each of his balls successively farther. I had never played but wasn't pathetic. Hunter accused me of sandbagging. After we had each hit five balls, Hunter said it was time to get serious and we rode the cart to his favorite hole, the fourteenth—a short par-3, straight shot over a large pond. The Aspen course is a Certified Audubon Cooperative Sanctuary and the pond was full of geese.

"Goddamn geese," said Hunter.

"*Branta canadensis*," said George.

"You'd like George's bat trick," I said to Hunter.

"No fucking bats!" Hunter said.

"Alas," George said, and made himself a Dewar's and water.

Hunter always said (and wrote in *Hell's Angels: A Strange and Terrible Saga*) that his acid-eating experience was *limited in terms of total consumption, but widely varied as to company and circumstances*, and that he liked the *electric atmosphere* it put him in, especially when taking it with the Angels.

They just swallowed the stuff and hung on . . . which is probably just as dangerous as the experts say, but a far, far nuttier trip than sitting in some sterile chamber with a condescending guide and a handful of nervous, would-be hipsters.

We, on the other hand, were playing golf. And gambling. Each of us would hit five balls in a row off the tee and then proceed to the green to putt. Only our best ball would count. We were all in for $1,000, Hunter said.

George put all five of his balls on the green, three close enough for makeable birdies. Hunter put three in the water and two on. I managed one on the green but didn't care. I didn't know golf but I knew a little about acid. My college roommate for a year was Steve Lambrecht—Zonker of Kesey's Merry Pranksters, the suave stoner portrayed in Tom Wolfe's *The Electric Kool-Aid Acid Test* as getting "higher than any man alive." Zonker talked me into going to class on acid, which turned out fine. Tom had also written that LSD made the Hells Angels *strangely peaceful and sometimes catatonic, in contrast to the Pranksters and other intellectuals around, who soared on the stuff.* I was now peacefully soaring.

When we got to the green, George put two of his balls in for birdies. Hunter had one ball left to tie, *if* he could sink a thirty-foot putt like the one he was celebrating in the photo he had sent. He walked back and forth between his ball and the hole several times. I was on the other side of the cup, holding the flag. It was dark now, as dark as it gets in Aspen on summer nights, and although the sky still had a glow, I could barely see his ball. George was by the cart, making another Dewar's and water. The ice tinkled in his glass.

"Silence!" Hunter shouted. "I know your tricks."

Hunter took at least another two minutes lining up his putt, then struck it quickly. He missed the putt by about a foot and, charging after it, let out a howl as he winged his putter into the pond. The geese started honking and Hunter ran back to the cart, pulled the 12-gauge from his golf bag and fired over the geese, and they lifted off the pond like a sparkling cloud of gray and white feathers. It occurred to me as I watched the glitter blend into the fading sky that having a story to tell about acid golf with Hunter and George was probably good for my career.

Hunter looked at me and said, "You're higher than I am, goddamn it." I started laughing. Hunter seldom laughed, but he did then.

"Maybe I should have, well, 'eaten' some myself," George said.

On the way back to Owl Farm in the Red Shark, George told us that playing ahead of Arnold Palmer in the San Francisco pro-am had been like being chased by a migration. Of geese? I wondered. George also said that when he'd played in the Bob Hope Classic at Indian Wells, his ball had almost hit Hope and the popular comedian Phyllis Diller in their cart at the fourteenth. He remembered that both comics had been wearing "sullen frowns"

"Fuck Bob Hope," Hunter said.

HUNTER AND GEORGE STAYED UP that night, but I fell asleep on the couch. The next morning I got up early and went to the supermarket ten miles up the road in Aspen. I was under the delusion that we needed supplies for the interview, and returned with several bags of groceries: a smoked ham, assorted crackers, cheese, olives, peanuts, etc. As it turned out, no one ate any of it.

The interview started late that afternoon when Hunter got up, and went for twelve hours. Doug Brinkley, who would later edit Hunter's letters, was there, working his own angles, which annoyed George. About an hour into it, Walter Isaacson, then the managing editor of *Time*, came by and had questions as well. A string of locals also dropped in, with various distractions that Hunter welcomed and George hated.

Hunter was at his kitchen "command post," chain-smoking through a gold-tipped cigarette holder and rocking back and forth in his high swivel chair. As George pressed on with the interview, sometimes rephrasing the same question, Hunter's mood swung wildly. He was angry and mocking and then suddenly strangely sincere, or flamboyant and hilarious and then respectful (of Kerouac, Henry Miller, William Burroughs, Ginsberg, Kesey, David Halberstam, William Kennedy and Tom Wolfe). When it came to Vietnam, Hunter would cloud over, but he kept talking.

He said he had arrived, sweating, in Saigon with what he called his "seminal documents" (Graham Greene's *The Quiet American*, Phil Knightley's *The First Casualty*, Hemingway's *In Our Time*), too much electronic equipment (walkie-talkies!), sketchbook-sized notebooks and his usual felt-tip pens (they bled all over the paper because of his sweat). Plus, he said, he had carried a .45 automatic. Hunter had never talked about it, but he was haunted by Vietnam: *The war had been part of my life for so long. For more than ten years I'd been beaten and gassed. I wanted to see the end of it. In a way I felt I was paying off a debt.*

PLIMPTON

To whom?

THOMPSON

I'm not sure. But to be so influenced by the war for so long, to have it so much a part of my life, so many decisions because of it, and then not to be in it, well, that seemed unthinkable.

PLIMPTON

How long were you there?

THOMPSON

I was there about a month. It wasn't really a war. It was over. Nothing like the war David Halberstam and Jonathan Schell and Phillip Knightley had been covering. Oh, you could still get killed . . .

PLIMPTON

You hoped to enter Saigon with the Vietcong?

THOMPSON

I wrote a letter to the Vietcong people, Colonel Giang, hoping
they'd let me ride into Saigon on the top of a tank. The VC had
their camp by the airport, two hundred people set up for the
advancing troops. There was nothing wrong with it. It was good
journalism.

PLIMPTON

Did you ever think of staying in Saigon . . . ?

THOMPSON

Yes, but I had to meet my wife in Bali.

Hunter's timing was perfect. He wanted to stop talking about Vietnam, so he cracked everyone up. He looked relieved. Vietnam was
still festering at the bottom of all his work, his outrage feeding his
commitment to his individuality, his disdain for the legal system and
his relentless physics lesson that all political movements give rise to
their own anti-movements of equal and opposite force—Machiavelli
should have thought of that.

We moved on to what Hunter wanted to talk about: Nixon and
the NFL and, most important, who he was as a writer. George asked
about writing under the influence of booze or drugs, noting that
every writer he'd interviewed over the years for the *Paris Review* had
said they couldn't do it.

THOMPSON

They lie. Or maybe you've been interviewing a very narrow
spectrum of writers. It's like saying, "Almost without exception
women we've interviewed over the years swear that they never
indulge in sodomy"—without saying that you did all your interviews in a nunnery. Did you interview Coleridge? Did you interview Poe? Or Scott Fitzgerald? Or Mark Twain? Or Fred Exley?

Did Faulkner tell you that what he was drinking all the time was really iced tea, not whiskey? Please. Who the fuck do you think wrote the Book of Revelation? A bunch of stone-sober clerics?

Hunter was angry now and that was it, interview over. George noted that the most prominently posted quote in the room, in Hunter's hand, twisted the last line of Dylan Thomas's poem "Do Not Go Gentle into That Good Night": "Rage, rage against the *coming* of the light."

When the interview was about to appear, George sent Hunter an advance copy. Hunter sent back a page from the Bible (Revelations) with a big black spot on it—like the page Long John Silver sent to Billy Bones in *Treasure Island* to pronounce him guilty of stealing Captain Flint's treasure from the rest of the pirates.

LAUNCHING *SMART* with less than $200,000 depended on the new desktop technology, and on convincing writers to work for shares in the magazine—that is, more or less for free. Their names were the only real collateral I had for raising money and every one I asked signed on. It was a strong run of bylines, including Plimpton, Harrison, McGuane, Peter Maas, Warren Hinckle, Eve Babitz and Jay McInerney. Some even invested money beyond their work, and Elaine Kaufman kicked in a few grand, too.

Hunter loved the idea of having stock almost as much as he hated working for free but he eventually agreed. His first assignment was to write about his Aspen neighbor Jack Nicholson. He never filed. Then he was going to write a column called "Year of the Wolf," but he said he needed more words, at least five thousand. Fine, but no copy was forthcoming until, without discussing it, he faxed me a piece about his trouble with a new neighbor named Floyd that he'd spun into a complicated Republican conspiracy. The lede was: *It was just before dawn when the queers rushed my house.* Politically incorrect, but right up the tailpipe of the anti-gay conservatives he was after in the piece.

At the top of the first page of the manuscript was a note in his unmistakable hand: "You'll pay in the end . . ."

Smart was struggling by then and I was running out of money. I learned to forge Hunter's distinctive "HST" and began signing books. I must have signed twenty first editions of his *Songs of the Doomed* for potential advertisers who loved him. When I confessed this on another visit to Owl Farm, he smiled with a curious, surprised look and handed me one of his preferred Sharpies.

"Show me."

I grabbed one of the random books on the bar, scratched "Thanks for the crack" on a flyleaf, then scrawled my counterfeit "HST." He lifted the book to the light to see it better, then slapped it back down on the bar.

"Jesus, you're desperate," he said.

When I lost *Smart* to a Japanese investor and went to *Esquire*, Hunter's "Year of the Wolf" column idea came with me. He wrote the first one about Pete Axthelm's death, but after that the column was plagued by deadline slippage and he kept promising a draft of a secret novel instead. It was called *Polo Is My Life* and he said it had grown out of his piece on the Pulitzer trial in Palm Beach, the assignment I had used to lure him back to *Rolling Stone*. But we kept struggling with "Year of the Wolf," and he would call often, always late at night. I could sometimes hear laughter in the background, in which case I'd get off quickly if I could.

"I just hope to Christ you're ready," he'd say when he had me on speakerphone. "It's about *the end of fun*, and it's going to cost you."

"Good, you deserve to be rich."

"Fuck you!"

"Have you got any new pages?"

"I said, 'Fuck you!'"

This went on for months until, as if by sympathetic magic when we decided to scrap "Year of the Wolf," *Polo Is My Life* arrived at *Esquire*. But it was not the manuscript of the secret novel. Packed in a huge wooden crate tight with bubble wrap, *Polo Is My Life* was a four-by-eight-foot plywood sheet with crossed polo mallets in the middle; ammunition belts with live .50-caliber rounds had been hung on it, and the whole thing weighed a couple hundred pounds. Hunter had titled the collage in red spray paint across the top and attached numerous personal totems (photos, press cards, bar napkins, X-rays, notes, quotes, lipstick, a joint or two, letters, court records . . .) so that most of the plywood was covered. It took two UPS freight guys to carry it into my office.

The phone rang next to my bed at about three the next morning.

"Now it's really going to cost you." Laughter again in the background.

"Who've you got there with you?" I asked. "Joseph Wood Krutch?"

"You think I don't know who the fuck that is, well . . ."

I mounted *Polo Is My Life* on a wall in the conference room next to my office, where everyone who came through could get an easy look at it if they asked about Hunter or, more often, when an editor started bragging about it to a visiting writer. It was Hunter's verdict of guilt on all editors, like the black spot he had sent George, and it hung as a major attraction until I left the magazine. It cost $1,500 in 1993 dollars to ship it back to Woody Creek.

ALMOST EVERY TIME I saw Hunter, he was in shorts and white Chuck Taylors, but he liked expensive, wild-ass shirts and owned several for special occasions. I figured Hunter coming to New York for the twenty-fifth anniversary of *Fear and Loathing in Las Vegas* would be one of those. The book had sold well all along and had been made into the movie *Where the Buffalo Roam*, which had goosed book sales. A new Johnny Depp version was in preproduction. Modern Library was publishing an expanded edition, and a book party was being planned.

Hunter would be staying at the Four Seasons, on Fifty-seventh Street, because there had been too many misunderstandings at the

Carlyle, where he usually stayed—the most recent having to do with Hunter throwing a blow-up sex doll out the window onto Madison Avenue. The book party was going to be a huge affair at the Lotos Club. Afterward we would be going to George's house.

"We need to get George better drugs," Hunter told me on the phone before he left Aspen.

The party was badly organized, with only two bars for more than two hundred guests, and the scheduled speakers—including George, Jann, myself—would have to stand on a chair in the middle of the room. There were supposed to be some readings too, but you knew that wasn't going to happen. No one cared, least of all Hunter, who arrived late.

"Who are all these fuckers?" he said.

I had expected him to maybe be wearing his bright red Lakota shirt with the embroidered turtles, but he had on a new, white button-down with a paisley tie he had borrowed somewhere—a surprising nod to the occasion. More important, I thought, he had a can of lighter fluid in one hand and the gold Dunhill lighter he always carried in the other, as if he were about to pull his trusty spitting-the-flaming-fluid trick. But he didn't, and there we all were, standing around waiting for him to do something outrageous with his Nixon mask or the boat horns or the trick hammers that made the sound of breaking glass. Sometimes he liked to put on lipstick in the middle of conversations—much subtler, he said, than banging his Samoan war club. But he loved all of it: banging those hammers and blowing those horns and asking women he had just met if he could borrow their lipstick. All three moves worked especially well in restaurants. In this moment he made everyone nervous just standing there in the tie with the lighter fluid—clearly his intent.

When a third bar was opened, the room relaxed and the speakers started. Hunter listened closely, toying with the Dunhill lighter. I don't remember what I said, but George mentioned "acid golf." When it was Jann's turn, he explained with great wit that he did not have one thousand pristine first editions of Fear and Loathing in Las

Vegas in storage as Hunter had been claiming for years. The crowd booed.

"Besides," Jann said, smiling, "we all know Hunter cares more about art than commerce."

Hunter was smiling too, and they hugged when Jann stepped down from the chair. Some of Hunter's best moments were like that, shockers of kinship when he knew you were getting the joke.

WHEN HUNTER PAID ATTENTION to you, it could feel like a gift, or currency that could be spent telling stories about him. Some people were greedy about this or, worse, condescending, as if they knew Hunter better than whomever they were talking to. Every new editor he ever worked with bragged about going through Hunter's paces with him, and usually it was like watching clowns unpacking from a tiny car long after you had outgrown the circus. The unsurprising truth was that Hunter was tightest with the people he got high with and/or had sex with. His numerous admirers who didn't do one or the other could never quite get their heads around this.

Much later, there were so many posthumous Hunter-and-me books that you wished he hadn't gotten high with so many people. This was not true of Ralph Steadman's *The Joke's Over*, because of the personal subtext the illustrations carry, or of *The Kitchen Readings*, by Hunter's Aspen friends—the writer and artist Michael Cleverly, who lived down the road, and Bob Braudis, who had been the sheriff of Pitkin County since 1986. The title refers to Hunter's writing process in later years: he would write; his friends would read it back to him; he would edit; and on into the night.

As a young writer, Hunter had read his writing aloud as he worked. Now it was easier hearing friends read it, and more useful than making his pilgrims read work he had already published. It was a technique he used to see how his sentences played. He said he had taught himself to write by reading *The Great Gatsby* aloud as he typed out the entire novel. His son Juan's middle name is Fitzgerald.

Hunter would say that there were far fewer good editors than good writers, and that he had learned some very harsh lessons from their incompetence. He had a riff about it, how he used to suck editors into his pieces as conspirators, all of us wanting to prove ourselves good enough—hip enough—to edit him. When he got you on the phone in the middle of the night to listen to someone in the kitchen read to you what he had just written, all you could say was that it sounded great and that he should send it to you.

"Ho ho," he'd say. "So you can fuck it up before it's finished?"

But he knew he needed editing. When he filed, the pieces often came in as a series of false leads. They were typically all good fragments, but they didn't connect. So you ended up having to string them together to make a piece, and you knew the work in the kitchen with his friends was invaluable, even if it stretched out the deadlines. For Hunter, if he had pages at dawn, it had been a good night. When he was writing, he said, he measured his life in those pages, perhaps not unlike Prufrock did with coffee spoons. Hunter knew the poem, too.

BY THE TIME I GOT to *Sports Illustrated,* Hunter was writing a weekly column for ESPN.com, called "Hey, Rube." It was conceived to be about sports and gambling, but the columns were full of politics and whatever else he found interesting in the news. He often bcc'd me on these pieces, which were uneven, and didn't get him the attention he was used to. We had not spoken about any of this when he called my office to ask "what the fuck" was wrong with me and to say that my new job should make me a better gambler, ho ho, and that *SI* still owed him money for an assignment in the early 1970s to cover Nevada's Mint 400 motorcycle race—the blown assignment that had inspired *Fear and Loathing in Las Vegas.*

"You filed a piece?"

"You fuckers killed it."

"A long time ago."

"We can gamble for it," he said. "But not like the golf you welshed on, ho ho . . ."

"What's the bet?"

"I'll bet you the measly three grand kill fee that you can't get me paid."

"I'll look into it."

"No power, eh . . ."

"I'll worry about that."

"You can bring the cash when you come out, ho ho. Maybe your golf has improved."

He sounded strong and occupied, the way he always did when he was making plans or gambling on the NFL, but he seemed to be looking for something from me. I told him I admired his 9/11 column, which he wrote the morning of the attack predicting that we would be at war with a *mysterious Enemy for the rest of our lives . . . a Religious War, a sort of Christian Jihad, fueled by religious hatred and led by merciless fanatics on both sides. It will be guerilla warfare on a global scale, with no front lines and no identifiable enemy.*

When we were hanging up, he said we were all "marching on a road of bones."

IN 2004, THE YEAR BEFORE Hunter killed himself, I went to the Kentucky Derby. *SI* had a box then, on the finish line, and I had never attended the race but I had been interested in the scene around it since reading Hunter's "The Kentucky Derby Is Decadent and Depraved" in *Scanlan's Monthly*, the short-lived, unfettered magazine edited by Warren Hinckle back in 1970. This was the assignment where Hunter found his voice, and worked for the first time with the ink-splattering illustrator Ralph Steadman, whose work would become emblematic of gonzo. Back at their motel after their first day of reporting and relaxing before dinner, they talked about where they were from—Wales, where Ralph had grown up, and Hunter's Louisville.

There was no way either of us could have known, at the time, that it would be the last normal conversation we would have. From   241 *that point on, the weekend became a vicious, drunken nightmare. We both went completely to pieces. The main problem was my prior attachment to Louisville, which naturally led to meetings with old friends, relatives, etc., many of whom were in the process of falling apart, going mad, plotting divorces, cracking up under the strain of terrible debts or recovering from bad accidents. Right in the middle of the whole frenzied Derby action, a member of my own family had to be institutionalized.*

When I told Hunter I was going to Louisville for the race, he insisted that I visit the house where he had grown up. Just drive by and take a look, he said.

"Why?" I asked, baiting him. We had never talked about his childhood.

"Jesus, I thought we were friends," he said. "Take a fucking picture."

The morning of the race, I drove to 2437 Ransdell Avenue. The address was in the Highlands Cherokee Triangle, close to downtown Louisville, on a hilly street lined with leafy, mature trees and large Victorians and stone Tudor Revivals with sloping lawns. Hunter's house was small by comparison—poor, even, next to its neighbors. Hunter's father died when he was fifteen, and his mother raised him and his two younger brothers there, working as a secretary and a librarian.

I got out of the car and took a photo to send him. He and his boyhood friends had published a two-page mimeographed newsletter, the four-cents-a-copy *Southern Star*, out of that house, with Hunter covering sports like children's "trench warfare" in the neighborhood. He had painted an elaborate "Gates of Hell" tableau on the floor of his small upstairs bedroom. Money was tight and his mother was a drinker. She was the institutionalized relative he had mentioned in the Derby piece. All of which he told me when I called to say I was standing in front of the house. It was about eight a.m. in Woody Creek and Hunter was still up. He said it had been raining.

Weather Report (454)

Hunter loved weather and used it in everything he wrote. Hells Angels with their stripped Harleys rolling past you on the highway like a *burst of dirty thunder*. Palm trees were *lashed by wild squalls* from Florida to Hawaii. His ledes were often weather reports from wherever he was writing. It was what he called "fundamental reporting," before you got to "the Wisdom." Lightning at night *meant fear in the morning*.

There were *hurricanes of changes* and details of weather throughout the pieces. *Freezing cold outside; patches of ice on the road and snow on the sidehills* in New Hampshire. The *rain and gray mist* at Super Bowl VIII in Houston. A big window in New York City looking out on *the savage, snow-covered wasteland of Central Park*. The paper in his notebook *limp* with the humidity at 3:55 *on a hot, wet Sunday morning in Saigon*.

Strange behavior set up and amplified by dramatic weather was even better. Hunter driving in a *drenching, blinding rain* on U.S. 40 east of Winnemucca, his fingers *like rotten icicles on the steering wheel*. Hunter in a fast red car on *a moonless night in a rainstorm* roaring through a flock of sheep *on the sleazy outskirts of Elko*. It was like *running over wet logs. Horrible, horrible* . . .

Hunter wasn't alone in this among writers, and as an editor I couldn't get enough. I even loved the stretched metaphors: Hunter enduring a *shitrain of perjury* that led to a *blizzard of strange publicity*. Weather, I thought: use it as often as you can. The Other Bob Sherrill had insisted I open my eyes and appreciate the opportunities. He'd once stomped into the LA newsroom and waited for attention. It was just after Thanksgiving and unseasonably hot, which he emphasized by shouting at nobody in particular, "Hot enough for you?!"

About fifteen of us looked up, waiting for some folksy, rustic public-announcement-style humor, but it turned out to be anger we had not seen before from him. It was searing, uncomfortable language delivered in a kind of growl. He'd just seen "a great big fat black street-corner Santa Claus" ringing his hand bell for charity, and this Santa just happened to be visibly and heavily "sweating in the hot fucking sun, under a white fucking sky" . . . did that mean anything to any of us young and supposedly observant chroniclers of the local culture? Did it strike us as in any way meaningful or perhaps the least bit unusual? When none of us answered, he glared at us one by one around the room before sitting down at his desk in the corner, where he started typing with his back to us.

-ENDIT-

Hunter and George (1,723)

WHEN GEORGE DIED IN 2003, I called Hunter after Sarah Plimpton called me. It was about eight-thirty in the morning New York time, six-thirty in Woody Creek. Hunter answered on the first ring.

"No!" was all he said. I took a breath and gave him the details I had. George had come home late. When Sarah woke in the morning, George was lying beside her dead.

Neither of us spoke. In the background I could hear him operating the grinder he used for coke, then banging it down on the countertop.

"Fuck you!" he finally screamed.

"I know," I said, and hung up.

HUNTER AND GEORGE RECOGNIZED each other as allies immediately, although they did not agree on what had happened when they first met, except that it was on a Lufthansa flight from Frankfurt to Zaire to cover the Ali-Foreman fight—the Rumble in the Jungle. They were seatmates.

George remembered that Hunter was worried about not getting paid for a calamitous lecture at Duke where his alter ego, Raoul Duke, had run amok on Wild Turkey. Hunter said he and George had compared boxing notes like the professionals they were. George remembered Hunter talking about secret weapons ("huge torpedoes!") being constructed by revolutionaries in the Congo to disrupt the fight. Hunter remembered George being greeted by the promoter Don King as a "prince of the realm" when they landed in Kinshasa. George remembered that while he embarked on a week of serious reporting, Hunter smoked hash in the hotel pool and wound up missing the fight. Muhammad Ali loved them both.

Back in the States they talked about each other as if they were old friends, which was easy because they had much in common. They were the same height (close to six foot four), loved sports and were evenly matched—George was a better athlete; Hunter was stronger. They both had "served," as Hunter put it (George: army; Hunter: air force). Neither of them liked wine at all. Both loved cocaine, which George called *the chemicals,* as in "Do you have the chemicals?"

Their career-establishing books, *Paper Lion* and *The Hell's Angels,* were published within months of each other in 1966–67, both praised for immersive reporting and original voice. Hunter loved *the wild power of the language and the purity of the madness that governs it and makes it music.* George played the piano on short breaks when he was writing.

Hunter's middle name was "Stockton." He never explained why, only that his father had been born in the last century in Horse Cave, Kentucky, a place-name full of spookiness for him. George's middle name, Ames, was from his great-grandfather Adelbert Ames, a Civil War hero. George had met "the Boy General" when he was six, and had thus "looked into the eyes of a man who faced Pickett's Charge—imagine what he saw." It was a story George told often. He liked talking about his family. As always, Hunter wanted to know more, especially about this Boy General.

"He was very severe and I was afraid," George said. "We were in the garden of his house and he picked up a twig, snapped it in half and said, 'Life ends like that, boy!'"

Hunter loved that.

George was always looking for expeditions, like his scheme for Christmas 1998 to go "green hunting" elephants with his pal Iain Douglas-Hamilton. It was to be an old-fashioned hunt, except with tranquilizers, to tag the elephants for research. Hunter would come too, of course, and we would all celebrate New Year's Eve in Lamu.

Hunter made an expedition out of just going into town, not that he wasn't full of ideas like the "First Annual San Simeon Feral Hog Tournament"—a plan to hunt the always dangerous pigs on foot with .357 Magnums in the canyon brush on Will Hearst's ranch at San Simeon when he was writing a column for Will at the *San Francisco*

Examiner. Hunter said he thought George would enjoy the collateral birding. We had stationery printed for that one.

George got his clothes from Brooks Brothers, and wore the same tie every day until he lost it. Hunter didn't own a tie. Hunter talked about money all the time. George never did, even when supporting the *Paris Review* for fifty years had finally eaten away his trusts. Early on, when George was writing for *SI*, he never kept receipts or filed expenses, making his editors wonder if he was breaking even on assignments. Hunter said if he were rich—a relative term for him— he'd wander around like King Farouk, telling editors he was going to write something for them and then probably not doing it. George shrugged when Hunter told him this and agreed that writing was difficult.

They did not talk about other writers, some of the most famous of which were always dismissing each other's work and sniping at whatever George and Hunter were turning out as well. Hunter was *lazy*; George was *a dilettante*. Not everyone was like that, but someone at the *New Yorker* said George wasn't serious about his writing; and there was that *Los Angeles Times* political correspondent who worked himself up talking about how Hunter wasn't serious and couldn't write worth a shit anyway. Norman Mailer told George that Hunter's writing was like "playing tennis without a net." Neither George nor Hunter ever rose to that kind of bait, although they were both aware of who was writing what and who was writing well. They had other things on their minds—women mostly, although they never discussed their mutual interest in some of the same women we all knew. They were both good at those kinds of secrets.

That their many ex-girlfriends never talked about them reflected, I think, the old-world courtliness they both had. What the women they cared most about did not love was the drinking and, in Hunter's case, all the drugs. But it was mostly the drinking. Over the years, a lot of people—various editors, friends in Woody Creek—asked Hunter to cut back, to take it easy for the sake of the work. Hunter ignored them as far as I know except once, when he was with Maria Khan, a beautiful woman with black hair and gray-blue eyes, who was his live-in, sleep-in administrative assistant at Owl Farm in the mid-eighties.

Hunter called me on a visit to New York to say that he and Maria had a confidential matter to discuss. We met at Juanita's, a Tex-Mex hangout for writers on the Upper East Side. It was early and the place was empty. Hunter had three margaritas and some beers lined up in front of him at a table in the back. Maria explained that Hunter had decided to get healthier. She had found a place near Phoenix, where she was from, and he had agreed to check in for a week. I looked at Hunter, who was unnervingly calm. He was crazy about Maria.

"Would you?" Hunter asked me. "You know, uh, check in?"

"I'd try it," I said.

"Judas," Hunter mumbled, but he seemed resigned. It was shocking that he might actually go through with it. I don't know if he did, but we never spoke about it again. Not long after, Maria was gone from Owl Farm, back to Phoenix to return to school.

I never knew of anyone having that kind of talk with George until Sarah Plimpton organized an intervention, six months before he died. George quit drinking for a month, and was resentful that he had been made to try. I never saw George drunk, ever, but he drank every day.

Drinking was part of everything we all did. By all, I mean most of the people I worked with, and Pete Axthelm had an acronym for our solidarity: SOFA, Society of Functioning Alcoholics. George thought SOFA was hilarious. Hunter wrote about Axthelm in his "Year of the Wolf" column in *Esquire* when Pete died of liver failure, ending the piece with *He got out just in time.*

I CAN STILL SEE HUNTER stepping out of his tall command chair in his kitchen, and stretching to his full height with a gracious, often hearty handshake or a delicate kiss on the cheek of a new guest, depending on gender. George had a way of bowing his head slightly when he shook hands that was subtly flattering. Both moves looked effortless but underscored who was in charge as they drew you in.

I was always surprised by how many people felt possessive of their friendships with George and Hunter. When they were both gone, I wondered about my own. I never told anyone, certainly neither of them, but in some kind of magical thinking I thought of them as my best friends—truer of my relationship with George; Hunter was more a crazy, dangerous uncle. I was always aware of the gift George had to make people feel like they were great friends when they weren't very close at all. Hunter had that too, and could put anyone at ease when he felt like it. This happened more often than his reputation suggests, and it always struck me as kind. Although his friendships could be situational, or transactional even, he was sentimental about them. One Christmas he sent me an expensive pocket knife with "The Long Hunt" engraved on the blade.

George's bats in New Mexico and Hunter's house on Ransdell Avenue come back to me in flashes of memory. I think everyone who knew them has similar moments, when remembering something one of them did or said illuminates them. Every place I worked, George wrote for me at least once. I think Johnny Depp has *Polo Is My Life* now, along with the rest of Hunter's papers. It was an extraordinary piece, but then it was just another part of working with Hunter, like mouth-catching grapes was work with George. It was like that all the time, outrageous when I think about it now. Maybe it didn't always make sense that the best work we did had to have a joke at the bottom of it—not ha-ha, but hilarious like that black spot Hunter sent to George.

Treasure Island is a simple book with a clear plot: adventurous boy kidnapped by pirates; joins pirates.

-ENDIT-

Warren Hinckle (1,162)

Security called from the lobby of the Time & Life Building to ask if it was okay to allow a certain Warren Hinckle up to my office at *Sports Illustrated*. We hadn't seen each other in several years and, finding himself in midtown, Warren had decided to drop in. He arrived pulling an old suitcase, dressed in shorts, wrinkled blazer, tuxedo shirt, formal black pumps. I offered him coffee or water. He mumbled, as if forgetting something, then remembering . . .

"What would Hunter say?"

"Hunter's dead," I said.

"I'll have a gin and tonic," Warren said, adding that if I didn't have a bar in my office (like I should), we could order out from Hurley's, across Sixth Avenue, where he had just been.

"How's Melman?" I asked. Warren usually traveled with a dog—Bentley when I first knew him and then Melman, both huge basset hounds. They would sleep under Warren's table at Elaine's, and all the other bars in New York and San Francisco where Warren was such a good customer that health ordinances were ignored.

"Melman's taking it easier these days," Warren said. "What about that drink?"

A joke about Warren's drinking went like this:

Q. Did you hear Warren lost twenty pounds?

A. Yeah, he quit drinking in cabs.

But Warren never seemed drunk, just enhanced. Today, however, he looked heavier and seemed to have trouble moving, especially pulling that ratty suitcase. With his eye patch (childhood accident) and rosy cheeks, he looked like an outlaw cherub. I felt terrible for thinking that but didn't know what to do. He was Warren Hinckle, hero to all freewheeling editors.

EDITING *RAMPARTS* MAGAZINE, Warren had blown the roof off the 1960s, mocking all of it. He tweaked the Black Panthers, hippie tribes and the New Left even as he championed their causes. He muckraked in the most traditional sense: Had the CIA infiltrated the student radicals? Could there be an enlightened internationalistic wing of the CIA providing clandestine money to domestic progressive causes? Yes, and yes.

Ramparts had an office monkey, a capuchin Warren named Henry Luce, hoping, as he wrote later, to piss off the eponymous founder of *Time* and *Life* magazines. When a *Time* editor told him Luce had become aware of his namesake, Warren said that such were *life's little triumphs.*

Warren wrote long and short and often, for every magazine he edited, and when it came to layout and magazine makeup, he was like a field commander pushing columns around on a battle map. Weak design directors couldn't stand up to him. Strong ones loved him for his graphic imagination and riotous display copy. He also liked to tinker with magazine culture, hence "Henry Luce." At *Scanlan's Monthly*, the roller coaster of a magazine he co-founded with the trial lawyer turned journalist Sidney Zion after leaving *Ramparts* in 1969, the motto was "You trust your mother but you cut the cards." *Scanlan's* was where Hunter's early gonzo work appeared, but it was equally renowned for Warren's wild-ass muckraking and being investigated by the FBI—this was during the Nixon administration, after all.

At *City* magazine, where I worked for Warren, he killed the masthead in what he called an "act of selflessness," then brought it back with the staff listed alphabetically. Warren said he was simply eliminating the distractions of hierarchy and status, but the result was chaos, which is what he was after in the first place. No one took orders from anyone but him, except of course Francis Ford Coppola, who had bankrolled the magazine as a public service extension of his growing American Zoetrope media company.

Francis said *City* was what San Francisco needed. Warren said what San Francisco needed was more laughs. For his first issue, Warren ran a cover piece about the predicament of straight women surrounded by the gay culture, under what became his most famous headline: "San Francisco, City of Sin, Why Can't I Get Laid?"

City was brilliant, but it incinerated cash. It was a standing joke that Warren was the only person in town who could spend money faster than Francis could make it. That spring, Francis had told *Time* magazine that *City* was "my Viet Nam." Warren found this ironic, since Francis was spending all his time in the editing room trying to finish his wildly over budget masterpiece, *Apocalypse Now*.

Among Francis's ideas for saving the magazine was to present its weekly closing as theater (in a theater) open to the public, where "editors would do their work onstage, with galley proofs flashing on a screen behind them, and the audience offering comments." It was too bad this never happened. Warren would have been great as a game-show host.

WE DIDN'T ORDER FROM HURLEY'S, but I found a gift bottle of Scotch and we talked about starting a new magazine, something bold. We worked on some language. "A Journal of Significance that Hunter could have written for with dignity," Warren said.

I didn't know it then but he was starting to put together a new book, *Who Killed Hunter S. Thompson?* When I saw the dummy, a decade later, the subtitle announced it as *An Inquiry into the Life & Death of the Master of Gonzo (with Candid Memories & Appreciations by Many of His Best Friends & Co-Conspirators)*. The cover further noted: *Edited & with a Humongous Introduction (a Book in Itself!) by Warren Hinckle.*

That introduction was not something Warren had planned to exceed a few thousand words but it got away from him and went over a hundred thousand. It was called "The Crazy Never Die." In the lede, Warren wrote about Hunter showing up at his *Ramparts* office on North Beach's topless strip and engaging the capuchin Henry Luce in one-sided conversation while he poured whiskey. When they went to have dinner, the monkey riffled Hunter's knapsack, found some bottles of pills and gobbled the contents . . .

> *When we returned a few drinks later the poor thing had gone bananas, running at ferocious speeds along the railing atop the office cubicles with his leash clanging dementedly against the frosted glass. Lovable Henry had turned into Cujo. No one could pacify him. It took a day and a half for him to slow down. "God-dam monkey stole my pills," Hunter said. . . . This was in 1967 and* Ramparts *was where the action was, and where the action was, was Hunter.*

Hunter always said editors should be more like Warren, who had teamed him with Ralph Steadman on that Kentucky Derby piece for *Scanlan's* when Hunter was still inventing himself. That article was the first piece of gonzo any of us saw, and Ralph's illustrations branded Hunter from then on. Jann Wenner was working part-time in the *Ramparts* library then, going to school at Berkeley and think-ing about starting his own magazine—or, as Hunter put it, "Jann was a copy boy or something . . ."

-ENDIT-

Jann (2,327)

IN THE EARLY '90S, when I was editing *Esquire*, Jann and I saw a lot of each other in Amagansett during the summers. That I was no longer working for him allowed us to become friends, and our interests came together in our sons. Our wives were friends, too, and we went to the last two shows of U2's *Zooropa* tour in Dublin on his new plane. We also took trips with just our sons. He was back with Jane then, although it was clearly a little bumpy. One story was that one of the times he was leaving, Jane shouted after him that she "never even liked the Grateful Dead." That makes them look silly, which they could be, but they were sophisticated and prepossessing, something that people who worked for Jann seldom saw. He didn't let them. Why should he? They worked for him.

One summer Jann chartered the *Mariner III*, a 122-foot yacht built in 1926 that Ralph Lauren used in ads. We cruised the Cape and Martha's Vineyard, stopping one afternoon for lunch with Jackie Onassis and touring her compound and the separate house she was building for Caroline and John. I have a photo of Jann posing on that beautiful lawn with Jackie and Jane and their sons, in white sailor suits, and I remember thinking when I took it that I had never seen him so buoyant and pleased with himself.

Jann was attracted to celebrities, and he and Jane made friends and cultivated many interesting people far beyond the music business. Everyone they liked liked them back—often not the case among the boldfaced names in their circles. Jane had style and charm, and made strong friendships (with Hunter, for one) that lifted Jann. "Who would *you* rather fuck?" was the way Fran Lebowitz put it once at a dinner at their Amagansett house on Further Lane. And Jane's unbendable loyalty to Jann remained, even through the unbearable (her many friends thought) times she went through with him later when he came out of the closet and left her for good. But the depth of

254

that loyalty was another thing most of their friends didn't see—even after they chose sides, usually Jane's. And it flattered both of them that they remained as close as they did.

IN THE MID-'90S, I returned to Wenner Media to edit *Men's Journal* and then *Us Weekly*. By this time, Jann's confidence was reflected in his lifestyle. He took summers off and left New York for months at a time to ski. He bought more and more art, adding a large Diego Rivera painting of Frida Kahlo and other pieces to a collection he had started with Warhols. His motorcycles filled a garage, and he rode often, including a cross-country trip to promote *Men's Journal*. He owned a five-story Upper West Side duplex with nine fireplaces and five bathrooms outfitted with Art Deco fixtures from the London Savoy Hotel, a Ward Bennett beach house in Amagansett, a ranch in Idaho and a Gulfstream V jet. From a distance, he looked like he had everything. All of which made him the most interesting closeted player in New York's whispered-about velvet mafia. He also had three young sons.

The summer before Jann came out, we made a river trip down the Middle Fork of the Salmon in Idaho with families we knew from the beach. Jann and I hired the outfitter and came with our sons but not our wives. Three days into the trip, for my fiftieth birthday, I planned to surprise my sons by leaping from a fifty-foot cliff into the river as they kayaked around the last bend before we made camp for the night.

Jann knew all about this, his fiftieth on a short horizon, too. I had been talking about making our milestones memorable, and told him the story I had heard from Plimpton about Bill Styron waking his daughter Alex and sitting her on the fireplace mantel to watch him open a bottle of champagne on the night he finished *Sophie's Choice*. Not that turning fifty was like finishing such a book, but Jann and I joked about being satirized by our mortality and we were both into a kind of goofy showmanship about it.

As the kayaks came into view and I prepared to jump, Jann

appeared on a slightly higher cliff, waved and leaped into the river ahead of me.

BY THE FOURTH OF JULY the next year, Jann was living with Matt Nye, who was relentlessly and pejoratively described in the tabloids as a former Calvin Klein model—which you knew was unfair to Matt even before you met him. It had to be difficult for both of them. My sons and I flew with Matt, Jann and his boys to Sun Valley for the rodeo in Hailey, the small town near where Jann owned the Broadford Ranch, on the Little Wood River—a beautiful old cattle outfit he had restored with his usual taste and efficiency. The trip wasn't awkward, exactly, but it was clearly the beginning of a transition mined with difficult conversations. Our sons, both his and mine, who were usually all over us, mostly kept to themselves.

The night of the rodeo, I took all the boys into town early to get good seats at the top of the grandstand, but we found better places at the fence next to the bucking chutes. Hailey's Fourth of July Sawtooth Rangers Rodeo is small but serious and held in an old wooden arena, like few left in the West. It could get a little rowdy with beer and the high testosterone that rides along at small-town rodeos, where local hands go up against pros from the NRA circuit for prize money. In the summer dusk, when the arena lights come on in a glow, even the most burned-out swamper from the bars on Main Street had to know how special it was, and the kids, wide-eyed, noticed for sure. The night was charged.

Just before the opening ceremony, with the mounted color guard galloping the arena, I went back up to the top of the grandstand searching for Jann and Matt where we had agreed to meet. Not finding them, I looked over the back of the stands and down on what was a kind of sawdust midway full of cowboys in undershot boots and bright shirts, drinking and smoking, horsing around and flirting with shy ranch girls and pretty barrel racers. Clusters of older ranchers in expensive hats looked on.

Jann and Matt were at the far edge of the crowd, almost strutting toward the entrance in matching white T-shirts, white Levi's and flip-flops. The T-shirts were tight-fitting and they both looked good, Jann maybe better than he'd ever looked in a T-shirt, and proud. I could see the cowboys taking note of him and Matt, who seemed younger than his thirty years, and making way for them. When they got a little closer, Matt glanced up at the grandstand and I waved.

Jann and Matt liked the grandstand seats, so I went back down to the fence to be with the boys. We were close enough to catch some of the dirt spraying from the hooves of the bucking stock and we could see close into the riders' faces. At one point a rodeo clown dressed like a 1950s idea of a hobo but wearing football pads underneath the outfit went up the fence very close to us and the bull slammed after him. The announcer said something about rodeo clowns having the most dangerous jobs and being the bravest stars of the rodeo. The boys all took that in very seriously and I caught the eye of Jann's middle son.

"Your father is very brave, too," I said.

"I know," said Theo.

ON *ROLLING STONE*'s FORTIETH ANNIVERSARY, Jann sent me a silver Tiffany box engraved with the magazine's logo and the Grateful Dead line "What a long, strange trip it's been." I'm not sure how many others got one of those boxes, but I was glad to get mine and thought of Jane when I read the lyric. By this time, Jann and Matt had three young children of their own and were quietly gone from the Hamptons, with a sixty-five-acre estate up the Hudson River.

We hadn't seen each other in a couple years, but I followed the anniversary coverage, which went two distinct ways. In the tabloids, it was predictably mean and unfair to Matt. He had been on the cover of *Out* ("He Married a Mogul & Charmed the Fashion Elite. Does This Boy Have It All?"), and that just fed the cliché. In the serious press, Jann was recognized as a genius come of age. The best piece was in the *Washington Post*, by Peter Carlson, who noted that a smashed Pete Townshend guitar was still on the wall ("like some priceless relic of a prehistoric civilization"). But Carlson led with Hunter being dead and the Capri Lounge gone.

The reference to the Capri Lounge threw me, like the mention of a long-forgotten adolescent misdemeanor. Who had let that out? From the early days in San Francisco, the magazine's photo-imaging work had stayed in-house, in the Capri Lounge. I don't know who first called it the Capri, but it was the extension of Jann's eye for photography and his insistence on quality reproduction. It was expensive, but that's what it took, and the guys who ran it moved to New York with the magazine.

Because of the camera work, which went on around the clock on deadline, the lighting in the Capri ranged from spooky, glowing orange to blazed-out white. This made for interesting Polaroids, which were mandatory if you happened into the Capri looking for a bump of coke to get you through the night. A lot of guests went through there too—writers, photographers, actors, agents, musicians—and when the walls were covered, the stoned Polaroids went into an album for everyone's amusement. Ken Kesey said that being in that album was like being "on the bus," his blessing that meant you were cool enough to be a Merry Prankster.

Asked about the Capri by Carlson, a surprised Jann explained that the Capri was long gone, and that it had been counterproductive. "It was a bad situation. And they had all those Polaroids there—I have that book now." So in the end, Jann did have the Polaroids. In the next graph, the *Post* noted, "He [Jann] smiles. 'Those were the good old days,' he says."

Well, they were and they weren't.

THE LAST TIME I QUIT Wenner Media, it was to go to *Sports Illustrated*. By this time I had edited all of Jann's magazines, starting with the launch of *Outside* (left to finish a novel and found *Rocky Mountain Magazine*), *Rolling Stone* (went to *Newsweek*), *Men's Journal*, and *Us Weekly*, where I oversaw the repositioning from a struggling entertainment fortnightly to an occasionally ironic glossy tabloid—it was at *Us* where "Fashion Police" first appeared (the brainchild of deputy editor Charles Leerhsen).

"My work here is done" is what I remember telling Jann, probably grinning. He was amused too, I think, and we agreed that my journalistic destiny was not buying celebrity baby pictures, overseeing lipstick pages and editing pieces about Britney Spears. He asked me if Bonnie Fuller (*Cosmopolitan, Glamour*) could edit *Us*, and I said sure but Leerhsen would be my choice.

A couple months later, after I had moved across Sixth Avenue to the Time & Life Building, Jann decided not to honor the retirement benefits in my contract and we headed for court. I would not have left Hearst for Wenner Media without matching benefits. The *Daily News* reported, "Swaggering publisher Jann Wenner is being sued by Terry McDonell, the mag's former editor and his friend for 30 years." The piece went on to note that Jann had "recently agreed to pay editor Bonnie Fuller, McDonell's successor at *Us Weekly*, about $1 million a year."

Our lawyers handled everything; Jann and I settled without ever talking. Over the next ten years, Jann was very friendly whenever we ran into each other, as if nothing had gone wrong between us. At first I responded coldly, but my anger was meaningless to him. He was sentimental about the work we had done together and in the end I guess I was too, because we became something like friends again.

I NEVER HEARD ANYONE CALL Jann handsome, although if you look at the old photographs you see that he was, and even hungover and bloated, with reddened eyes, he had a glow that you can see now in his sons.

One day, I ran into Theo Wenner on the street in the photo district in New York. He was a photographer by now, with a solid career and much promise. We talked about what he and his brothers were doing and how they sometimes ran into my sons—all of them still good friends. I asked Theo if he ever thought of the Salmon River trip and how Jann and I had jumped off that cliff.

"Of course," he said. "We had great times."

I e-mailed Jann the day after to tell him that I'd seen Theo, and that I had been brooding about writing him one of our father-to-father notes like in the old days and finally couldn't help myself. Jann came back right away, with news of all the kids and compliments for my sons. "Think of you often," he wrote at the end.

In what way? I wondered. Hunter was still on the *Rolling Stone* masthead and maybe the Stones will always sell magazines, but that didn't matter when it came to where Jann and I had landed our friendship. So when people ask me about Jann Wenner, and they still do, I say he's a great father.

-ENDIT-

The End of Fun (896)

Hunter said he never expected to live to fifty, which was no consolation to anyone when he killed himself just before dark on a Sunday in February 2005 while his son, Juan, daughter-in-law, Jennifer, and grandson, Will, were visiting for the weekend. Reports said he'd been depressed by advancing age, chronic medical problems and the end of football season — the banality of the latter rang in my ears. He was sixty-seven, at times almost incontinent, and had suffered alcohol withdrawal during hip and back surgeries. When I thought about his last moments, I wondered about his final secret, the one hinted at when he laughed, the one he kept as he loaded the .45. I remembered what he had written about Pete Axthelm: *He got out just in time.* What did anyone expect.

A week later, about a hundred mostly local friends got together in the swank new ballroom of Aspen's Jerome Hotel. This was not the circus of promotion that Johnny Depp organized at Owl Farm that summer, with fireworks blasting Hunter's ashes into the Colorado sky. I have a photograph of me speaking at that first memorial service. Behind me is an eight-foot-tall cutout of Hunter, drink in one hand, giving the finger with the other, and I have lipstick on, the way Hunter liked to wear it, like clown makeup but smeared and aggressive. Everyone in the room knew about the lipstick, and a tube of it was on every table, along with Dunhill Reds and noise hammers.

I told the story about Hunter offering cigarettes to my young sons, said a few more words about him sending George the black spot and sat down. Hunter's son, Juan, said that from now on a phone call at four a.m. would be only bad news. Jack Nicholson got up in dark glasses and said the suicide was probably another one of Hunter's stunts, a hoax. The actor Don Johnson recounted how Hunter would lie down with Johnson's horse when it was sick. Johnson did not know what to make of that. Come to think of it, he added, he also didn't know what to think of Hunter taking his wife, Kelley, out to lunch when he was out of town, and he also admitted that he had once lamely asked Hunter to explain the sound of one hand clapping and Hunter had slapped him across the face. Everyone in the room got every word of that. Bill Murray showed up late but spoke with much soul and love about Hunter's molecules—"his very molecules"—now living everywhere, especially within all of us. Near midnight, a former waitress from the Woody Creek Tavern sang "Amazing Grace." It felt communal, with undisciplined sorrows.

My notes from that night were short: *"Very few people from NYC. Jann—sentimental. Hinckle—way drunk. Not many writers. Bill Kennedy in from Buffalo, some others I don't know. Steadman—older, otherwise the same. Lots of actors. Juan very strong, poised, calling his father Hunter as he had since he was a little boy . . . Very sad . . . Now over . . . So over."*

Back in New York I went through the contacts on my computer, checking to see how many others were dead, knowing I wouldn't delete them. All the obituaries and memorial services stayed with me, too. Whenever I had to speak at one, I would say it was a miserable assignment—something I got from a Hemingway letter to Sara and Gerald Murphy when their youngest son had died. I would add that the subtext was that we were lucky to have the lives we had no matter how rocky things got.

I spoke about Liz Tilberis this way, and also wrote it in letters to the widows of Ken Auchincloss and Maynard Parker, whom I had worked with at *Newsweek,* and Peter Maas, a founding contributor to *New York* magazine, who had opened windows into organized crime—all mentors who became friends. I said something like that, too, at the memorial service for George at St. John the Divine in Manhattan, and at the Jerome Hotel in Aspen for Hunter. I never felt bad about it because each time it was true. Sometimes I would say I was determined to be light and amusing because George or Hunter or Liz would have wanted it that way. That was true, too.

We all save totems of our losses. I saved magazines and books and photographs. For me, it was all about the work, anyway. That bound John Lennon issue of *Rolling Stone* was about Jann. And Bill Murray was right about Hunter's molecules living everywhere, and so was Hinckle, who wrote that Hunter would always be there, *like a phantom limb.*

When Elaine Kaufman died, the memorial services, wakes and parties went on for weeks. The obits ran long, even those way out of town where people had probably never heard of the restaurant. And there was a silent auction of her personal possessions, with a preview in her apartment on Eighty-sixth Street. Anyone who knew about it could just show up one afternoon and look at her paintings and furniture and souvenirs where she had lived with them. I didn't go and I never went back to the restaurant. Some people wondered about that, but I didn't feel like it.

-ENDIT-

IV

Real generosity toward the future lies
in giving all to the present.

— ALBERT CAMUS

Pocho (807)

JOSÉ ANTONIO VILLARREAL was the first writer I ever met. His first novel, *Pocho*, was published in 1959 and he was a friend of my high school English teacher's and came to speak to our class after we had all read it, just before graduation in 1962. Being a *pocho* meant your parents had come to the United States from Mexico, during the Depression, and he wrote about growing up spinning between two cultures. I thought it was a wonderful book, and I was embarrassed by our questions. Had he really been a migrant worker? Yes, and his father had been one after he had fought with Pancho Villa in the revolution. The class knew all about migrant workers, and couldn't believe that anyone who picked row crops could write a book. He said he had always wanted to be a writer.

Me too, I thought suddenly. Maybe that's what I'd been thinking about, without really thinking about it. I don't mean unconsciously thinking about it, I mean thinking about specific stories and details of my own life and the lives of my friends, just not as a writer.

I would remember my mother as young and pretty, a girl with nice legs getting out of a Ford convertible on the edge of a cherry orchard in Mountain View, California, in 1949. Husband dead, shot down, gone. No one talked about the war, but there was a trunk full of uniforms somewhere and she would show the medals to me and I would turn the wings over in my hands.

When I was five and my mother was twenty-nine we had driven out from Minnesota. I went to PTA meetings with her because she couldn't find a babysitter and we didn't know any of our neighbors yet. I was afraid the other parents wouldn't like my mother because she was a new teacher and she'd brought her own kid along. I listened to what they said and felt better because all they were talking about was how smart they were to have made it to California. California had the best weather and the best fruit and the best new roads and the best new schools. And my mother was smart to be a school-teacher because it was a job that didn't depend on the weather, like construction or fruit and row crops. Most of her students came from Mexico, and, like one of characters in *Pocho*, she taught them reading although she didn't speak Spanish.

When I was in high school I had a friend who had come up from Mexico and said he had fought a professional fight when he was fourteen. That same year he found out what happened between his father and his sister, and a lot of other things he told me I didn't want to know but was glad later I knew about. He went to jail for a while but did not die there. Another friend was Fillmore Cross, a Gypsy Joker, who got chopped into little pieces up on Skyline Boulevard in a meth deal gone bad. Other guys I knew burned a house down up there once. When we were all seniors they started stealing cars—taking the keys out of ignitions on used car lots and then finding that make and model on the street. Even Chevrolet model years had only had five different keys. It was no big deal. I rode with them sometimes. Wild because wild was the best way to be. We had all been Cub Scouts together.

This was in the Santa Clara Valley, when Cupertino was still fruit orchards. Our town was Campbell, next to San Jose. My mother's school was San Tomas Elementary, out near Saratoga. These are all Silicon Valley addresses now, so when I visited years later—trips to Apple, Google, et al.—I still knew my way around. The gentrification was like a thin fabric over what had been a tough place.

On one trip from Time Inc. to Google in 2009, my development meetings ended early in the afternoon and I had an extra hour before my flight back to JFK. I drove to Mountain View High School, where we used to play night games. The football field I remembered as rough with dirt patches was now beautiful, manicured almost. Maybe all the gardeners and the janitors were still Mexican. We had never thought about them. The Shockley Semiconductor Labs were only five miles away, but none of us knew what silicon was in 1962. The

Byte Shop, where Steve Jobs sold his first computers, wouldn't open until 1975, but it was just down the road. For a while, way back, I had thought I'd write about California. Then I'd remember that José Antonio Villarreal had already written about it in as true a way as there was.

-ENDIT-

Deadlines (779)

DEADLINES ARE MEANT TO BE close calls. Working better and faster when you're running out of time is a sign of professionalism, whereas getting ahead and closing an issue early always spooked me. What was I missing? Shouldn't I try to turn up the volume on that flat display copy one more time? When I was *on* (remember those Looney Tunes?), it was hard not to start changing everything. But deadlines are about tying up details and avoiding mistakes, and good editors know when to take their foot off the pedal. Some even soften up—like old pillows—and say "thank you" more than usual, but not many.

You want your pages to be compelling, and at times that means making them confrontational, telling readers to sit down and listen or to kiss off. You need that voice, but it is not the only voice you need, and if the balance is out of whack, you usually don't catch it until deadline, when you're running a little scared. You also have to watch out for any whiff of narcissism or self-promotion, which you can do by checking for debased language like *exclusive* and *inclusive* and *transparent* in your "Editor's Note."

To set deadlines in print, you work backward from when you want your magazine to get to your reader. This involves fleets of trucks, newsstand wholesalers and the U.S. Post Office (wonders of efficiency all). You transmit to the printer with time built in to accommodate potential on-press snafus. It took thirty-six hours for *Sports Illustrated* to get "off the floor" in midtown Manhattan on a Monday night and wired to five printing plants across the country, and then on through the distribution chain ("make-readies" were available Tuesday) for a Wednesday a.m. (at the earliest) delivery of 3.2 million copies. If you missed your transmission deadline, it started costing you money in overtime printing fees, lost newsstand revenue and subscriber satisfaction.

270

Editors in chief don't get fired for missing deadlines, but people under them do, and even writers can get blamed when whatever happened is retraced in a kind of *CSI: Deadline* forensics. No one wants any of that, but more important, always, is the journalism and that's where the pressure builds for the editor.

It is pretentious, I know, but the French term *sang-froid*—literally, cold blood—is the best way to describe what an editor needs to handle that pressure. You need calmness or composure or coolness (sometimes excessive), but you also need the kind of audacity that translates into *leadership*. You have to be able to stand on a desk in the newsroom and make a speech about the importance of what you're doing and of getting the facts right, too. When Jim Kelly was the managing editor of *Time*, he did that overnight on September 11–12, 2001. He said to stick to exactly what happened that day, no speculation on who was to blame or what retaliation might be like or any other forward spin that they were all trained to be good at. He wanted a time capsule of what that day felt like and how it unfolded, and to not look foolish or outdated in two days.

WE HAVE NO *SANG-FROID* EQUIVALENT in English. And the French also have *l'heure entre chien et loup*, literally the hour between the dog and the wolf, which refers to the passing minutes after sunset when the sky darkens. We call it "twilight," which is not as good, no matter how many vampires are licking each other's necks on TV. My point is that deadlines are always *entre chien et loup*—romantic, that is. "I'm on deadline" can get you out of things. Or make the right impression. Whatever kind of work you do, it's always cooler to be on deadline. At least that's the cliché from further back than when they first put the words *foreign* and *correspondent* together.

It has occurred to me that my ambition to edit magazines came from wanting to be a version of that guy in the trench coat, but on stage like magazine writers and editors seemed to be. Books were too slow. Newspapers got thrown out. People saved magazines. Magazines were fast channels of ideas. They were trailblazing. They showed you the future. Now it is not agreed that magazines have any-thing but a past—accelerating into extinction like the climax culture of the Plains Indians.

Home pages don't have deadlines. They are brand statements. Deadlines for mobile-first journalism are *right now, all the time, faster.* I like that. They are almost like the deadlines I'd set for myself when I'd wake in the middle of the night.

-ENDIT-

Mozart de Prairie (1,862)

Before we worked together at *Outside*, Jim Harrison had written pieces for *Sports Illustrated* under Ray Cave and Pat Ryan, editors he adored. This was in the days when *SI* editors chartered planes and even freelancers flew first-class. When he read in the *New York Times* that I had been named managing editor at *SI*, Jim sent me an e-mail under the subject line "Your New Job": *Victory in our time. As an SI old hand from Ray Cave days I'm quite aware of the honor.*

It wasn't the big deal Jim was remembering and I'm sure he knew it. The high flying was over at Time Inc., but he had slapped it immediately into a handsome context, even though he no longer cared for sports. And, of course, this initiated a decade of back-and-forth about the attributes of various *SI* swimsuit models, but by this time most of our correspondence was about food and poetry, and on most of it I copied Will Hearst, who'd been a fan of Jim's work since *Outside*, where Will had been the managing editor.

They became confidants when Will began hosting a Memorial Day ride at his family ranch in San Simeon for a revolving circle of his tech, math and literary friends. It was three days of talking and eating, with rides into the steep country behind Hearst Castle. Jim did not ride but he became a regular, calling the weekend "Will's Picnic," with Will sending a plane to pick him up in Livingston. Their correspondence was percipient for both of them, and their subjects ranged from astronomy to Zen koans, and what Jim called "the Black Butterflies," a malaise he warned Will about.

Will had been a math major but had always written well, and Jim encouraged him to write more and to write seriously, *to permanently quit the nasty business of money and write an eccentric memoir.* I was on most of those e-mails, many involving what we should all eat:

It is our duty to pique our appetites when we're not really hungry. Earlier in my life I would counter heat waves by preparing monster barbecues for friends and fall asleep out in the yard encrusted with sauce, and the fat of beef, pigs, chickens. Dogs would sleep with me licking my clothes. How noble.

Jim sometimes seemed distracted over the Memorial Day weekends, but he was the center of attention whenever he would allow it. Other guests who wanted to know him better were shy about photographs but found ways to get pictures with him. He would give me a look about this although he obviously didn't mind. He took a keener interest in helping Neely the comely bartender make appropriate adjustments to Will's sequencing of the wines. Because of that one bad eye, the other one would wander as the drinks came, but the unsteadiness I noticed came more from his increasing back problems, which he seldom mentioned. He had gotten a cane, a beautiful carved branch that he used as a prop; but then came a titanium one when he sometimes actually wanted a walking aid.

It was the worsening scratches of shingles, however, Jim wrote in an e-mail, that were becoming

. . . a bit traumatic, right down to being off work . . . because it's impossible to write under the constant onslaught of a cattle prod. I know Hunter and Bob Rafelson used to sneak up on each other in Aspen and jolt each other with a cattle prod. They were under the influence of something.

Like all his e-mails from that time it was deflective, a message of high spirits through a rough patch. He sent poems, too. He wrote them longhand, faxed them to his assistant of thirty years, Joyce Bahle, in Lake Leelanau, where she would type them over and send back for him to make changes. When he was satisfied, Joyce would e-mail them to Jim's list, which was approaching twenty-five or so when he put me on it. Jim's "Poetry Friends" made up an ecosystem of eccentric readers that amused him for one reason or another, as well as old friends he just wanted to keep up with.

Many of the poems were about death. In "Time," he wrote that it (time) was withering him, but with a *galactic smile.* There were pretty waitresses in that one, too. Jim said the poems *descended* on him, and by this time he was working shirtless because of the shingles. He wrote a poem titled "Barebacked Writer" about two years of postherpetic neuralgia, where the pain is always present. I wrote Jim that the pain must be on the edge of unbearable, though I was moved by the poem. Jim wrote back advising me to *retire to the arts.*

The next news was that he was to be inducted into the French Order of Arts and Letters (*officier de l'Ordre des Arts et des Lettres*) and Jim e-mailed, *Think I'll have a drink.* He kept working and the hell with the shingles and the back problems.

DURING THE LAST WEEK of 2013, Jeff Baker of the Portland *Oregonian* asked Jim about his health and was told, "About a B-minus." The headline on the piece read, "Jim Harrison Says He Writes More Because He 'Stopped Drinking Half-gallons of Vodka.'" That quote was Jim's answer to a question about what critics were calling his "astonishing" late-career productivity.

Jim was seventy-six and had agreed to a phone interview with Baker to support the publication of his Brown Dog collection, his thirty-sixth book. Over two decades, he had written six novellas about the Brown Dog character, which critics liked to paint as Jim's alter ego and had likened to a "twenty-first-century Huck Finn." Well, maybe, if Huck were an itinerant laborer, drinker and trout fisherman of mixed Chippewa-Finnish blood. Jim wrote in the *New York Times* that Brown Dog was *unimpeded,* and that he had wanted to write *a totally free man, which means he is poor but doesn't care.*

Brown Dog was jubilant about nature, didn't have a Social Security card, and the only mail he ever got was a driver's license renewal form. When a feminist lawyer seemed an unlikely fan and Jim asked her about it, she said it was because Brown Dog's love of women was without "irony or backspin."

Jim wrote about women notably in a woman's voice first in his 1988 novel, *Dalva*. Then in 1990, his novella *The Woman Lit by Fireflies* was about an upscale Detroit housewife who walks away from her husband at a freeway rest stop and winds up spending the night in a cornfield, where she reviews her life in flashbacks that the *New York Times* said allow "the reader to understand how things have come to such a startling pass—she is reborn into a new, more authentic self." It was a smart review by Robert Houston, himself a fine novelist, who also wrote that Jim could "convincingly handle a woman's point of view, once more giving the lie to the inane argument that a writer must stick only with his or her own sex, race, region and so on. A talented writer who understands the human heart, as Mr. Harrison does, understands essence; the rest of a character is accident, and can be learned."

Jim had talked about writing women in his *Paris Review* "Art of Fiction" interview. He said it was hard to find the voice and that you had to work it like *an ineffective bulldog . . . you keep worrying it and worrying it* and finally *trust the truth of your heart's affections and imagination.* The strong relationships Jim enjoyed with women editors like Pat Ryan at *SI* and Deborah Treisman at the *New Yorker* were part of his creative process, especially if they were *improbably alert,* like Leslie Wells, who edited him at Delacorte, or Pat Irving, who edited his novel *Farmer* at Viking and, as he told the *Paris Review,* had *suggested that chapter five should be chapter three and chapter three should be chapter five. So I switched it around and she was totally right. That's wonderful.*

Great editing, I thought, and wondered if Pat Irving had gotten a call from Bob Datilla.

WHEN JIM SOLD THE FARM in Michigan to move to Montana, he wrote that he was thinking about an essay for *SI* explaining why:

In the past decade there had been an influx of the very wealthy
replacing the farmers and commercial fishermen . . .
   I had this weary leftist notion that I no longer wanted to live on
a farm I couldn't afford to buy. I didn't want to become the kind
of stale geezer who orders a pamphlet from Popular Mechanics
on how to carve a violin out of a single block of wood. It takes no
more money and effort to make a good movie than a bad movie
but sometimes a bad movie is in the cards.

Now he was in Montana, fishing different stretches of the Yellowstone every day in a Mackenzie boat. That was the backbone of the
piece, the only one Jim wrote for me at *SI*, but I pestered him for
advice about, say, a road trip across Nebraska (Highway 12 was his
favorite road in the world) or where to eat in Paris or Seville. The year
the Super Bowl was in Indianapolis, I e-mailed him from the local
Hilton asking where to have dinner and he wrote back:

My current lawyer agent goes out with a woman that owns part
of the Giants. He asked me what to do in Indianapolis and I sug-
gested staying in your room and reading a book. You might try
that with a bologna sandwich. . . .
   Right now I'm trying vodka and Jewish food. I'm wanting to
go back to France where I am diverted by the landscape. May I
recommend that you watch that Werner Herzog film about the
cave down in Chauvet full of ancient art. I am hoping to find
another cave all of my own.

Jim's books had always sold very well in France, and when I heard
that "Mozart de Prairie" was the headline of a story about him on the
arts front page of *Le Monde*, I looked for it and found many pieces in
French newspapers about him but none with that headline. Maybe
it was apocryphal. If it had run, I hoped the photo was the one of Jim
as a young poet in overalls without a shirt underneath, leaning back
with his arms spread across the side of a farm horse. He was smoking

in that picture, but you could see the body of a gymnast, which he had been in high school and college. Jim became famous for his fiction, celebrated internationally as a storyteller of genius, but over all the years and the novels and novellas and the films that came with them, he remained a poet, his life syncopated with complexities and the chromatic cadences of rural landscapes. "Mozart de Prairie" was a brilliant headline, even if it never ran.

-ENDIT-

Mix (714)

"THIS IS A MAGAZINE, not a democracy" is something old-school editors said to end arguments. By "old-school," I mean those with an imperious confidence to run whatever they wanted in their magazines. This was not always bad for morale. Staffers took pride, even, in how unbending their editors could be. And if an editor had the power to call in a helicopter, like Henry Grunwald did at *Time*, so much the better. Someone had to have the last word on everything and that was the editor in chief, or managing editor at Time Inc. I find it amusing that the Merriam-Webster dictionary notes that "editor in chief" rhymes with "Great Barrier Reef."

What kills morale, no matter how passionate and engaged the editor, is a lack of fresh ideas to spice up the mix. The Other Bob Sherrill always said that the mix of stories was the most important thing for an editor to think about, whatever magazine that editor happened to be editing. It was central to his monkeys-jumping-out-of-boxes philosophy of editing. Avoid sameness, shun formula, let it rip. You just need to pick the right mix of monkeys. This takes confidence, imperious or not, especially now with the shrinking number of pages allowed by squeezed economics. Editors always had a finite amount of print real estate to keep readers' attention, but this does not mean editors of digital-only magazines can just add more stories online without risking losing their readers' interest.

If you're a reader, you want your magazines to crackle with ideas, but then you pick up one you thought you liked, maybe even your favorite, and it's suddenly tired, gloomy with clichés. Another overstyled actress is on the cover, with lines touting a "Special Report" and "Inside" information and a "War" somewhere in the pop culture, but there is nothing new or surprising about the pieces inside. You might forgive all that if there is just one story that flares with new meanings, or at least makes you laugh. If not, blame the editor.

When bad editors talk about mix, they mean formula: how much service, how much news, how much celebrity and, most recently perhaps, how many top ten lists of ways to serve kale. They should think about eccentricity: what is the most surprising piece they can run without leaving readers scratching their heads, or alienated and angry.

Sports Illustrated readers were famously loyal, and touchy about what went into their magazine. Fifty years of residual goodwill is how I defined it, after reading a shopping cart full of research that was wheeled into my office on my first day on the job. "Reader Satisfaction" and the all-important "Intent to Renew" numbers were generally very high, but when you asked them for specifics, as *SI* did regularly, readers said they wanted shorter pieces—and more NFL, more college football, maybe more MLB and college basketball, but less NBA and hockey, and *no* minor sports.

I was expected to follow that research, but *SI* had built its readership with long pieces that ranged from serious environmental reporting to takes on cheerleading competitions and rattlesnake roundups—and hit every minor sport as if they were pockets on a pool table. From my first issue in March 2002, whenever I ran an off-center piece, the satisfaction and intent-to-renew numbers both jumped. The readers weren't lying; it could never occur to them to ask for what they didn't know they wanted.

How far could I go? How about covering a chess tournament at the New Jersey State Penitentiary? "Con Games at a New Jersey Prison," by *SI* senior writer Michael Bamberger, ran in 2004 and drew more letters (all positive) than the cover story on NBA superstar Kevin Garnett. It was about thirty-two felons competing for a chance to take on an Ivy League chess whiz, and it went deep into the nature of competition and pride. But without that NBA piece and the rest of *SI*'s traditional sports coverage, the prison chess story would have flopped.

So that was my formula. Every piece had to be related within the interest range of what readers wanted, but they all had to compete for attention—maybe like convicts coming at each other with sharpened spoons, or perhaps N-KB6 (check!).

-ENDIT-

Robert F. Jones (1,839)

I CAN IMAGINE BOB WRITING this piece, overnight, on deadline, the way he wrote so many fast words before he shifted into his literary life. And Bob would probably be unhappy and hurt if the piece were not the most important one in this book. Just letting you know, the way Bob always did.

I didn't edit Bob in his days at Time Inc., but everyone who was around then and is still around now says no one was better at the newsweekly form. That he was the best at what his *SI* colleague Roy Blount Jr. was talking about when he said that what he learned at *SI* was "If you have to write five thousand keep-them-hopping words overnight in a bad hotel room with a couple of drinks already in you, you can."

Bob was a national correspondent for *Time* for most of the 1960s, covering Nixon, Vietnam and all the rest of it, knocking out twenty-two cover stories when counting covers was how you kept score. My favorite detail from those days is that Bob introduced the word "hippie" into *Time* in a 1967 cover story about "The Now Generation." *Time* was so relentlessly unhip then I wondered what it took for Bob to pull the magazine along with him from Golden Gate Park to communes in the Sangre de Cristo Mountains in New Mexico. The answer, of course, is that he was more relentless.

Bob got to *Sports Illustrated* sometime in 1968 and that's where his style soared. He wrote about college football, the NFL and motor sports, salted with a little hockey, golf, boxing and baseball, and slugged it out every week with the aforementioned Blount Jr., as well as George Plimpton, Frank Deford, Bud Shrake and Dan Jenkins—an editor's masthead dream of talent and eccentricity. What Bob brought to *SI* was his far-ranging knowledge of literature and a voracious enthusiasm for the natural world. His so-called outdoor writing set a standard for the *SI* "Bonus" pieces, which ran at length in the back of the book, as he carved out far-flung assignments for himself. This from "The Game Goes On," which he wrote from Kenya for *SI* in 1978:

Swahili, the lingua franca of black Africa, is a language of fatalism, of the dying fall, of the story in which cruelty and beauty meld into a swift, soft sunset. Leopards cough at night on the kopje; the stars are like shattered sapphires; a baboon screams in death. Lions rip at a wildebeest's gut while zebras browse placidly nearby.

Bob could pin your ears back.

I FIRST READ BOB'S WRITING in late 1976 when Will Hearst and I were launching *Outside* out of the *Rolling Stone* offices in San Francisco and I picked up Bob's *Blood Sport: A Journey Up the Hassayampa*. You can look it up and see it described as a "pathbreaking, surreal novel of the outdoors." I never told Bob, but that novel informed almost everything we did during the start-up of *Outside*. If rock and roll was about more than the music for *Rolling Stone*, then the environmental movement we were launching a magazine to cover was about a lot more than the Sierra Club. Like Bob, we were hunting unicorns and manticores on our way upriver. I don't know why I didn't call Bob when I finished *Blood Sport*, except that maybe I was afraid of him, maybe his villain in the book, the badass Ratnose, scared the hell out of me — which should have been the best reason of all to call.

I finally went after Bob when I landed at *Esquire* in 1990. By then I was very aware of Robert F. Jones as a literary figure and, to borrow a phrase or two from P. J. O'Rourke, Bob was a "pants-down" environmentalist at a time when the environmental movement looked like a "goldfish tank of irrelevancies." Bob and I had drinks at a midtown Manhattan hotel and agreed to try to work together as soon as he could find some time. Bob was occupied with his novels. And his bird hunting (read: dogs). And his fishing. The assignments we had talked about withered.

When I was leaving *Esquire*, for *Sports Afield* where Hearst was moving me, Bob called and told me that getting "canned," as he put it, was a badge of honor. He said that at one time or another he had hated every boss he'd ever had, but he didn't put me in that category yet because he sensed I had a nice "touch." He made me feel like a much better editor than I was thinking I was.

In 1994 I talked Bob into a piece for *Sports Afield* about, as we said in the subhed, "How Fishing for Records Will Make You Crazy." Bob said it was pretty much a bullshit idea but agreed to concoct a piece he insisted on calling "Wampus Cats & Oyster Toads." In it, he told fishing stories, but they were about almost everything besides the fish—like love. My favorite bit of language echoed Macbeth as it described the fishing of a friend who had just broken up with a longtime girlfriend as his attempt to *knit up with flyrod and feathers the raveled sleeve of his care.* None of Bob's stories were about competition in the hook-and-bullet tradition of "mine's bigger than yours."

He ended the piece with an explanation of his *personal best for ugly, as well as big, weird and hazardous.* It was set back in the early 1970s, when Bob was writing what he called his *post-Uhuru stuff* for *Time.* He was stuck in Nairobi waiting for an interview with Jomo Kenyatta and drinking too many *chota pegs at the Long Bar in the New Stanley,* so he decided to charter a small plane and fly up to Kenya's Northern Frontier, to what was then Lake Rudolf (now Lake Turkana). Peter Beard and Alistair Graham would set their edgy and enthralling 1990 *Eyelids of Morning: The Mingled Destinies of Crocodiles and Men . . .* on these shores, but this was the 1970s and Bob had just gone for some fishing. Conditions were harsh. Sandstorms, 120 in the shade, fifteen-foot crocodiles in the shallows and gangs of wild-ass Somali bandits called *shifta* roaming the surrounding desert with Kalashnikovs.

One night, Bob pulled in a Nile perch that weighed 187 pounds,

8 ounces—a record that would have held for twenty-seven years if he had bothered to submit it. Instead, he ate it (no catch and release in East Africa) with the affable Guy Poole, who ran the makeshift fishing camp; his mechanic, an ex–World War II POW named Tony; Priya Ramrakha, a Time-Life photographer who was killed by a sniper in Biafra a few years later; and some friendly local El Molo tribesmen. All Bob's kind of guys. That night was his thirty-ninth birthday and he lay happy and full under mosquito netting while hyenas whooped him to sleep.

I have been paraphrasing Bob's story up to now; this is his language:

Eighteen months later shifta fell upon the camp, tortured and killed Guy Poole and a Catholic priest who was there to fish (Poole's wife and children had gone to Nairobi for supplies), shot up the radio, generator and three of the trucks, and burned the camp. They disappeared into the desert in the fourth camp truck, the El Molo said later. Tony was driving with an AK pointed at his neck—once again a POW. But not for long.

They were bound for a well called Gus, the El Molo said. When they got there, they filled their water bottles, burned the truck, banged Tony on the head, and skinned him out like a catfish. They took the hide for a trophy.

Now that's a fucking fishing story.

BOB'S WORLD WAS LARGE, but also disarmingly small as I found out after he had died, in 2002. On a trip to Kenya I did not realize at first that our outfitter, Bill Winter Safaris, was the same one Bob had spent much of his time with in Africa—except that it was now run by Bill Jr., who'd grown up in the bush learning from his father's tracker, Lombat, a Dorobo from up in the Mukogodo country. Lombat was still with Winter, tall and dignified, with a Bulova watch and the patience that comes from years of hunting. He smiled quickly as Bob's name bubbled up with the coffee one morning at breakfast. Bob was *rafiki*, a friend.

Bill Winter Sr. was Bob's first guide in Africa and they grew close. Bob wrote that to travel Africa with Winter was to have Dickens, Darwin and Monty Python at your elbow. Not to mention Allan Quatermain, the prototype great white hunter and the hero of *King Solomon's Mines*. We hit some of their spots—the Masai Mara, Funzi Island, Lewa Downs—and heard about the time on the Talek River when Lombat saved *SI* photographer Bill Eppridge from a spitting cobra, and the night elephants stampeded through the camp ("at least sixty or eighty of them"). And, of course, there was that time the lioness came after them. It was adventure for its own sake in the name of journalism.

FIVE YEARS AFTER BOB DIED I contributed to a collection of his work and tributes to him edited by his friend and Pulitzer Prize winner Annie Proulx. Working on that piece in my office at *Sports Illustrated*, I had on my desk a journal I'd kept on my safari. It is full of rough notes, drawings and maps, with bits of grasses and leaves pasted on them. Next to the journal was a thick and faded red folder I'd found in the *SI* library. It was the Robert F. Jones file, story after story, word after word, a reckoning for my simple notes. In it, in a 1978 story about the wildlife in Kenya, Bob wrote this:

> A *yellow and blue agama lizard crept out on a rock to bask in the heavy-hitting sun; as if in some strange counterbalance, the crocodile across the way slid into the roiling water, out of sight.*

I copied that into my journal, knowing I was reaching back for something. *Journalism as adventure* was over for me, and I was becoming a different kind of editor than I had been when I'd edited Bob. Soon enough I'd be spending more time with tech developers and executives than with writers. But the new work was fast and satisfying too, and I thought that what I saw coming could be very good for traditional publishers, *a counterbalance*, if we moved quickly. It was 2007 and magazines were already hemorrhaging readers, and advertisers weren't making those multimillion-dollar buys anymore, but change was always good if you could adapt. I made speeches about that at management meetings. It wasn't until later that my job began to feel like an embed in a routed and retreating army.

-ENDIT-

Less Money (387)

Every history of time inc. mentions drink carts rattling from office to office on closing nights. At *Newsweek,* the Wallendas went out to Friday night dinners for three hours. At *Time* there were buffet tables with carving stations for prime rib and turkey and ham, along with the shrimp cocktail, Caesar salads and strawberry short-cake. Some days during the week, bootblacks made the rounds of all the newsweekly offices shining shoes at desks. They came to *Rolling Stone,* too. I saw the last of that, and saw how it made people uncomfortable, but there were inequities everywhere. It was party time. The publishing sides of every magazine had sales meetings in the Caribbean. Planeloads of advertisers were flown to the Olympics.

Calvin Trillin, who was a *Time* correspondent in the sixties, said that when he would see a particularly lavish house in a foreign capital he would think "That's either an Arab embassy or the home of the Time Inc. bureau chief." Writers, especially if they had staff gigs, could also pile it on. The favorite expense-account story at *Newsweek* was about how its most famous correspondent (eighteen wars at least), Arnaud de Borchgrave, filed to replace five Savile Row suits after a stray bullet came through his hotel window in a troubled Middle East city, entered his closet and left a small hole in each of them. *National Geographic* expense-account forms were said to have a "gifts to natives" category.

Even into the 1990s, I signed off on expense accounts but never checked them, except maybe to see whom this or that editor was buying veal piccata for. I don't think the people who signed off on my expenses paid much attention either, and nothing I filed ever got bounced back. It was all just part of the deal. Then.

An editor I once worked with told me that his first month on the job at *SI,* in 2000, an older editor had taken him to lunch (expensed) and recalled being chastised for not spending enough on his expense account. He said those days had just ended. That was shortly before I arrived. At one point *SI* was spending $1.5 million a year on sports tickets. The publishing side took clients; editors took friends and family. By 2010, the tickets had to go to save jobs.

-ENDIT-

David Carr (2,210)

A YEAR AFTER HE DIED SUDDENLY in the newsroom of the *New York Times,* David Carr still pops up several times a day on the Google Alert I set for him back in 2005, when he first explained to me what that was. This is not ironic, rather simply true in the way that something you learn from someone keeps them in your mind.

No one made the transition—the "migration," as he was one of the first to call it—from legacy to digital better, although David always said that Brian Stelter, a colleague of his then at the *Times,* was the new prototype for a journalist. He pointed to Stelter's growing presence on various platforms, especially Twitter, and his early citing of a student who'd remarked, "If the news is that important, it will find me." David said that was all you needed to know about where news was going. But David was the one everyone I knew started following, as he became ubiquitous himself in the evolving news ecosystem he helped define. He mastered and interpreted the new tech—speaking Twitter like the native he was—and still delivered reported, stylish print columns for the paper every Monday.

He was gifted and haunted, and you saw that right off. He had been handsome as a kid but by his early forties, when we met, he looked like a cousin of the Edgar the Bug character from *Men in Black,* with a ropy neck and tortuous posture and clothes that never quite fit because of his fluctuating weight. I first became aware of him through his work at Inside.com, a pioneering start-up where his beat was the magazine business, and his determination to be fair was as obvious as his charm.

> *Hey Terry,*
> *David Carr from Inside.com here. I need to talk to you on*
> *Sunday if you happen to be checking email about some things.*
> *While credible people said nice things about you and the things*

*you are doing . . . , they suggest US is tanking on the newsstand.
I imagine that you have a thing or two to say about that and I'd
like to print it.*

    Thanks for any attention. I have to file Sunday nite.
    David Carr

*Call on God, but row away from the rocks. —Hunter S.
Thompson*

Noting his signer, I called on Sunday night and spun some numbers at him. *Us Weekly* was selling 1.5 million per month on the newsstand, which was a threefold increase over its newsstand sales as a monthly. I said I was aware of the sniping and negative rumors that had, most likely, been coming from Time Inc., where apparently *Us Weekly* was viewed as some sort of threat to *People* because, I tossed in breezily, the women reading it were a younger demo and didn't live in trailer parks. Plus, we were already outselling *Entertainment Weekly* by more than two to one on the newsstand after just ten weeks as a weekly.

"Exactly," David said. "*Us Weekly* is a weekly, so divide 1.5 million by four and see how that works."

He was pointing out that we were selling 375,000 copies of the weekly, while *People* was still selling that same 1.5 million number we were bragging about as a monthly number but they were doing it *every week*. It was not a particularly relevant point, but his speed with circulation and advertising numbers made our conversations a back-and-forth game. Although he never let me win, I sometimes got the feeling that he was trying to give me a break. Good reporters can always make you think that. Another part of David's charm was the careful curiosity that always defines a great reporter. It surprised no one when he was hired by the *Times*. When he wrote a piece about my arrival at *Sports Illustrated*, his angle was that I was coming in as a "well-traveled" outsider and an "agent of change." Neither of us knew then that he would become so significant an agent in a media revolution that had not yet been named. That careful curiosity turned out to be perfect for the moment when old-school media companies got smashed in the mouth by digital.

So what if news found its own digital path. David broke stories anyway. He seemed to be everywhere, from the red carpet (where he wrote as "the Carpetbagger") during the awards season in Los Angeles to throwing parties at SXSW in Austin. He was the star of *Page One: Inside the "New York Times,"* the notable 2011 documentary directed by Andrew Rossi about the paper. His column "The Media Equation," in which he analyzed business and cultural developments in news, publishing and social media, became a "must-read" — to use jargon he would never touch. His intersecting contacts and sources across the platforms he covered both vertically and horizontally made his reporting like 3-D chess. By 2015 David Carr, the brand, was approaching half a million followers on Twitter.

DAVID'S TRIP from a Minneapolis suburb through the University of Minnesota and on up a slippery career ladder (*Twin Cities Reader, Washington City Paper,* Insid.com, *New York* magazine, the *Atlantic*) to the *New York Times* was riled by various addictions. Finally kicking them left him straight and, I thought, benignly bitter. In *Interview* magazine, he told Aaron Sorkin that for a while he had been *a low-bottom crackhead, sobered up for 13 years, and then decided to try to be a nice, suburban alcoholic and see how that would go. That lasted . . . Well, it ended in handcuffs, so it didn't go great.*

He was never aggressive about it, but he would occasionally drop the fact that he had been a single father on welfare or (so horrifying that you didn't want to believe him) that he had beat up women. When we were out at night, as we were from time to time, he never seemed more unhinged than anybody else, though he could take shots at you just to let you know that maybe, just maybe, he knew more than you did.

One night we met at Joe's Pub to see his friend Ike Reilly, whose indie-rock band, the Ike Reilly Assassination ("IRA, get it?" David said), was his longtime favorite. David sensed that I didn't like the music as much as he did, and he kept turning his pack of Camel Lights over and over on the table until Ike joined us after his first set. I knew Ike had paid weird dues, like working for more than a decade as a doorman at the Park Hyatt in Chicago. His music was political and strong and I did like it, and I said so and we talked for a while about what music had been like when we were all younger.

"Terry's been rocking that same haircut since high school," David said. I think Ike said something about never getting any substantial coverage in *Rolling Stone*, which I had edited twenty years earlier, and he and David agreed that "the *Stone*" had always been kind of square. This was bait I had learned not to take, so no argument from me. Besides, Ike's new album, *Junkie Faithful*, had just come out and it was strong and they were both drinking Diet Coke. I wondered how hard that was.

David was already a star and still rising at the *Times* when he published his 2008 memoir, *The Night of the Gun*, in which he reported out on himself—tracking down what really happened this or that time he was too drunk or stoned or both to remember clearly. The subtitle was *A Reporter Investigates the Darkest Story of His Life— His Own*. He looked at police reports and welfare documents and recorded sixty interviews—many with the people he had gotten high and in trouble with—and finally made his own sense out of the conflicting memories and the relentless question of whom to believe. His writing flowed and hit at the same time: *Where does a junkie's time go? [Mostly] in fifteen-minute increments, like a bug-eyed Tarzan, swinging from hit to hit.*

It was brave, unfeigned work but David was shy about it when he sent me the bound galleys, e-mailing me in advance that he didn't want to sound like a *self-involved creep*, but he was proud of the book, if not the story it told, and wanted me to read it.

I wrote back that it was acutely human and terrifying and somehow also hilarious and that I could only imagine the courage it had taken to get it so right. Later I hoped he was getting some pleasure, or at least satisfaction, from the success of the book as it climbed the best-seller list. In the *Times Book Review*, Bruce Handy noted, perhaps a little too cleverly, "In that conundrum [what was true and what was not in David's memory] lie both the genius and a primary flaw of this brave, heartfelt, often funny, often frustrating book." I got that, but I thought too that David had opened a very dangerous door for himself, yet then had been able to close it. In any case, his work at the paper seemed to me more and more ambitious as he took on what looked to me like the trickiest assignments he could get. Here's one lede from the following spring:

> *Write about the media long enough and eventually you type your way to your own doorstep. Lately, when I finish an interview, most subjects have a question of their own.*
> "*What's going to happen to* The New York Times?"

David answered the question with clear declensions of business plans and the various "levers" the company might use, and he hit every digital bumper.

I e-mailed him that the column was graceful and sharp and hard to do. I ended with "Hats off to you." David came back to say that we were due for dinner at Odeon and suggested an additional "hats off" to Ike, who had recently played a benefit in Minneapolis for a pal of David's with six kids who was dying. At the end of it, Ike had walked up to David with a bag of $20,000 in cash—"Shades of the old days," David wrote. "Great guy."

He was always pulling his friends together, reconnecting people he had introduced, spreading credit around. In *The Night of the Gun*, he had written, *I now inhabit a life I don't deserve, but we all walk this earth feeling we are frauds. The trick is to be grateful and hope the caper doesn't end any time soon.* I especially liked "caper." It made him appear lighter and less sentimental than he actually was. And I liked Ike more now, too.

When David died in 2015 of what turned out to be lung cancer, Simon & Schuster went back to press with *The Night of the Gun*. That was a Thursday night and it was ranked No. 53,570 on the Amazon best-sellers list. Twenty-four hours later, Amazon listed it as "temporarily out of stock"—and it had jumped to No. 7 on the overall list.

The tributes that came from what seemed like every possible direction reflected the crisscrossing of David's eclectic reporting interests (media, culture, politics, technology), and all mentioned that he had been a junkie. But there was much more about his loyalty, his unselfishness as a reporter and what a steadfast mentor he had been to many. He was teaching by then at Boston University, which made complete sense because, as he would put it, aren't reporters fundamentally teachers at heart, anyway? Educate yourself and then pass it on to as big an audience as you can find.

WHEN I TOLD DAVID I might write about him, we met for an early dinner in the West Village. He looked drained, thinner than I'd ever seen him, but he wasn't acting tired. We talked about our children, and if either of us was ever really going to move to the country. His column that week was about the continuing importance of e-mail as a source of news, but he wasn't interested in going over any of that except to crack a little wise about his personal digital hierarchy, which started with e-mail and then social media, with "the anarchy of the web" (as he had written) at the bottom.

I think I said something lame about news being news.

"Come on, man," he scoffed. "It's still just all about us."

"Ha," I said. He was mocking us sitting there about to dish wisdom over expensive pasta, poking at the self-importance of hacks who can't help showing off even if, as David liked to say, they've been phoning it in from a great distance for a long, long time. He loved being a journalist but the journalism was more important and he knew that.

The next week, a photograph by Diane Arbus in the *New York Review of Books* stopped me. It looked just like David arriving in a suit and tie that night for our dinner, but it was of the Argentine magical realist Jorge Luis Borges. I couldn't wait to show it to him.

-ENDIT-

Shipwreck (513)

As shockingly late as 2005, the Internet was viewed by most top editors as an avoidable backwater populated by losers they didn't want to work with. Bloggers, whatever they were, drank Fanta with their sushi. There were no iPhones (ditto Twitter, Instagram, et al.). Editors carried BlackBerrys. YouTube was just coming together above a pizza parlor in San Mateo, wherever that was. Powerful editors lived in New York and worried more about getting a good table at Michael's than how much traffic their new websites might be getting. The hammer had not yet come down.

That September the Magazine Publishers of America organized an event for advertisers at Lincoln Center. Drinks and heavy appetizers were followed by Jon Stewart, then ascendant on his *Daily Show*, interviewing four of the most successful editors in chief. The panel was called "Laughing Matters: Magazines Celebrate Humor," and Stewart got after them all: *Vanity Fair*'s Graydon Carter ("Why, if humor is so important, is that magazine—*Spy*—dead?"); *Time*'s Jim Kelly ("When will *Time* magazine find Jesus?"); *Cosmopolitan*'s Kate White ("It's almost like 'Hey, I'm putting out this advertising book and in the middle of it is a tip on giving a blow job.'"), Dave Zinczenko of *Men's Health* ("Why is your magazine so gay?").

The thousand or so people filling the Rose Theater howled. The media blogger for FishbowlNY, Rachel Sklar, a *Daily Show* fan with a clandestine tape recorder, had arrived early to get a front-row seat, and she went live with it. I'll start with her quoting Stewart comparing print to television:

> . . . *says Jon: "I don't consider the print media as relevant."*
> *OUCH. Jon says it's "kind of hard to get worked up" about any-*
> *thing in print. Take that, Gutenberg! Graydon disagrees, recall-*
> *ing how much has happened since Jim (Kelly) and he "started*

297

at Time *27 years ago this month" (cool media factoid!). Jon responds by saying that it's all about TV: "the agenda is driven now by the 24-hour network." Graydon says no way, "they are simply refractors of what appears in print." Jon not-so-respectfully disagrees. "I didn't say you don't have your place," he said. "It's just at the children's table." Once again, OUCH. . . .*

Awkward silence. I mean, this was a pretty spirited debate with an informed audience and a (presumably) even more informed panel. . . . Someone else asks Jon about the impact of the internet. He says that it doesn't have the same sort of impact as TV. Okay, I am DEFINITELY disagreeing with him here. He senses this, because he says: "Here's another thing: What the fuck do I know?" He says yes, the internet is important, but "all it is is a delivery system." If he's so all about the 24-hour news cycle and what is driving the discourse, he should not be discounting the web.

When, on its ten-year anniversary, Sklar uploaded her old blog post on Medium, reading it was like snorkeling over a ship that had wrecked on the hidden reefs of some long-ago trade route.

–ENDIT–

Letters to the Editor (463)

THE CYNICAL VIEW IS THAT editors say they read every letter sent to their "Letters to the Editor" section but don't because that would be an even bigger waste of time than writing one of those letters. This leads to a Groucho Marx punch line—the one about not wanting to join any club that would have you as a member.

How quaint they seem now anyway, even in fast-forward magazines like *Wired* and the *Atlantic* that still run "Letters to the Editor" pages in their print editions. The theory is that letters from readers amuse other readers, and at the same time corrections and mea culpas in print can satisfy people with serious bones to pick. So "Comments" in *Wired* and "The Conversation" in the *Atlantic* are there every month as long-trailing echoes of the ideas amplified relentlessly by their branded Internet chatter connecting people with similar mindsets. All of it reminds me of the early days of *Rolling Stone*, where the eclectic copy chief Charlie Perry determined that most of the reader mail came from prison inmates. Or the letters written in purple crayon or the ones with primitive swords down the side . . . I'm talking about 95 percent of the mail—even to intellectual bastions like *Harper's*. Lewis Lapham, who edited it for twenty-eight years, joked that 95 percent of his magazine's letters to the editor were from "academic twits or commie pinkos." But then he said: "I'm not joking."

My approach was to read and answer any letter addressed specifically to me instead of "Editor." If a reader had the enterprise to look me up on the masthead, I wrote back with something personal and sometimes, if the letter had made sense, I sent a book or T-shirt or whatever logoed trinkets we had run up to give to advertisers. At *Sports Illustrated* I also wrote letters back to children and to readers who were not well. It was a small thing to do when they seemed to care so much about the magazine.

Letters threatening legal action or demanding corrections went immediately to the lawyers, and I often wound up negotiating with *them* as they negotiated with whomever was coming after us. We seldom ran a correction, more likely just a letter from the discontented party, with a note at the bottom that said *SI* stood by the story. Occasionally I called people up and talked them down, although that never worked with any number of troubled athletes and their handlers—Barry Bonds, Tiger, Lance, A-Rod—who always wanted me to fire a reporter.

My first year at *SI*, 2002, the magazine received more than thirty-six thousand letters and employed a three-person Letters Department led by a senior editor to answer almost all of them. Tick-tock.

-ENDIT-

SI (2,593)

WHEN I WAS OFFERED the managing editor job at *Sports Illustrated*, my first call was to John Walsh at ESPN. We had met in San Francisco after Jann Wenner had fired him as managing editor at *Rolling Stone*. Three years later, Walsh landed at the *Washington Post* and then bounced back into sports—he had been the sports editor at *Newsday* when Jann recruited him. His fingerprints were on everything happening in sports journalism, most obviously *SportsCenter* and ESPN's website. Walsh watched everything, read everything and followed *SI* like the opportunistic anthropologist he had always been.

"They'll eat you alive," he said. "You have no idea . . ."

When his voice trailed off it occurred to me, as it often had over our friendship, that he was the perfect person to run *SI*—a troubling irony that we both laughed off. I reminded him that he had warned me about taking the *Rolling Stone* job too, and that had worked out.

"Jann was one thing," he said. "*SI* is *impacted*."

I figured he was just talking about the old newsweekly *fuckeduped-ness* that Pete Axthelm and so many other writers and editors had enjoyed feeding on like beer nuts.

THE WEEK BEFORE I BEGAN editing *SI*, I flew to the 2002 Winter Olympics in Utah to meet some wary soon-to-be colleagues— writers, most of them. There was good snow in the mountains, though none on the streets in Salt Lake City. I wasn't nervous exactly but I overdressed, even wearing a tie to dinner the first night. The cover that week was a seventeen-year-old LeBron James with the headline "The Chosen One." I was quietly critical of the choice. The American snowboarders were dominating in Salt Lake and they would have been my cover instead of just another basketball phenom. It seemed to me *SI* had fallen behind in its coverage of newer, less traditional sports and looked occasionally stodgy. So I was "all about change"—a posture I routinely assumed whenever I took a new job, long before we thought about digital anything.

The *SI* writers wanted to talk about less editing. I should concentrate on that, they said, adding that the editing culture in the New York office was toxically anti-writer. Writers were treated so shabbily that the predictable chasm between them and the editors was widening with increasing suspicion and distrust. Even the most stylish and nuanced writers were edited hard by a series of red, green and blue "pencils," as they were called. Yeah, why didn't I work on fixing *that* . . .

I said my first priority was to connect with all the great writers at *SI*, which would be hard because there were so many of them. *Right on.* I had never met writers so proud of where they worked and of the other writers on the masthead. I ventured that perhaps the contentiousness between writers and editors made for great work. *Yeah, maybe, but* . . .

Back in New York, I heard how difficult the writers could be. They were spoiled and lazy, those writers, and they lived where they wanted to and made more money than most of the editors. I should work on *that* . . .

It was all smoke. Arguments over whether *SI* was "a writer's magazine" had raged since André "Heavy Water" Laguerre was editing it into a national institution in the '60s. Writers said they worked harder just knowing Laguerre was going to read their copy. They also said he could be brutal. Maybe the dynamic between editors and writers had always been fraught, but good editors made writers better, and vice versa, perhaps not as human beings but certainly as journalists, and the magazine soared, relying as it did on high-end narrative journalism.

The classic *SI* piece, the "Bonus," was designed by Laguerre to push the writers by giving them time to report and space to run long. You didn't just cover the event, or even distill it with analysis; you blew it through as many filters as you could find, using sport as a prism to view a much wider world of experience and values—courage, loyalty

and sacrifice within the context of race, gender and basic fairness—
something one of my heroes, Frank Deford, was so good at.

NO ONE WAS BETTER at defining sports as a reflection of American culture than Deford, and I looked forward to working with
him. He had missed his Princeton graduation ceremony in 1962 to
start work as a researcher at *SI*, soon began writing, and was quickly
accepted by Laguerre as "The Kid." He marched through every
important sports story (Frank was there) and personality (Frank knew
them), pulling back the curtain on not just racial and sexual mores
but also expense-account shenanigans and outrageous behavior at
media saloons. Tall, with easy coordination, Deford looked as if he
could play (as he did for stories in several sports), which helped him
unlock camaraderie and friendship with athletes and coaches, especially during the bush league years of the early NBA. This was back
when the media-starved league gave sportswriters courtside seats.

Having a good view of the action was one thing; turning it into
a window on what games can mean (which Frank always did) was
something else.

> *Those of us in the [grandstand] seats always want our athletes—
> the ones who are our age—to quit while they're still on top. That
> way they won't embarrass us. We then want our heroes to instantly
> disappear so that we can always remember them (and ourselves)
> as magnificent and forever green. For it is when our athletes start
> to go downhill that we are first forced to come to grips with the
> possibility of our own mortality.*

Frank was tough too, and I taped this line of his on my computer:
*How little, really, we live up to the homilies we love to recite at sports
banquets.* He was so dominant and at the same time humble that
he told me he found himself overwhelmed by accolades, so many
lifetime achievement awards, that he felt "like Tom Sawyer going to
his own funeral."

Frank also said that when he was coming up as a writer he developed an unspecific dread of editors: What would they do to his copy next? It was not that he hated them exactly, but maybe he did. Shortly after I arrived at *SI*, Frank received a lifetime achievement award from Time Inc. Smiling wryly from the podium, he said that during the short time he himself was an editor, *he* couldn't stand Frank Deford.

There it was, yet another variation on that old newsweekly *fuckedupedness*, but the writing at *SI* was so strong I sometimes built confidence just sitting at my desk looking at the masthead. Deford was still there as a special contributor, as well as senior writer Gary Smith, who had won more National Magazine Awards than any other writer ever and owned an almost mystical ventriloquism when it came to capturing the values of sport. Frank and Gary and the other writers made *SI* what it was, and the editors all knew that, no matter how much bitching got batted back and forth.

AS SATISFYING AS *SI* WRITERS were to edit, the subject matter, sports, could feel too big, too outsized and bloated, about to tip over into one endless Super Bowl halftime. Or it could seem small, tiny even, shrinking into its lowest denominator of narcissism, like A-Rod kissing himself in the mirror. But there was always a story of redemption somewhere, a story that made sports matter more than you thought it could.

To write for *SI*, you had to know the names and dates and numbers but also maybe even how to use abstract expressionism to explain baseball in a new way. Barry Bonds hitting his six hundredth home run: *Like De Kooning before a drying canvas, Bonds took a step back and admired the majesty and magnitude of his work.* Tom Verducci wrote that, and he was a star, too. *SI* had many stars and all of them pushed beyond the scores and clichés in numbing rotation on sports television.

It wasn't that *SI* didn't care about the scores, or that all its stories weren't fundamentally about winning and losing. They were. The writers just found ways to give you more about the players—who they were and what their wins and losses meant. It was the kind of ambitious writing all editors want to edit, and I had read most of the *SI* writers for years. Here's a classic Rick Hoffer lede on another slugger, written before I got to the magazine:

> *Mickey Mantle, with his death Sunday at 63, passes from these pages forever and becomes the property of anthropologists, people who can more properly put the calipers to celebrity, who can more accurately track the force of personality. We can't do it anymore, couldn't really do it to begin with. He batted this, hit that. You can look it up. Hell, we do all the time. But there's nothing in our library, in all those numbers, that explains how Mantle moves so smoothly from baseball history into national legend, a country's touchstone, the lopsided grin on our society.*

SI was ferocious, too, as a news gatherer and news breaker, not with simulated reporting and the "confirming" that always seemed to follow *SI* stories about performance-enhancing drugs and the corruption of amateurism, but with original reporting loaded with particled facts about what really happened. George Dohrmann was an ace at that and he could write, too.

> *[Ohio State football coach Jim] Tressel has often been described as senatorial, an adjective rarely applied to a football coach; in fact, one of his nicknames is the Senator. He has been lauded for his sincerity and his politeness, and people who admire his faith in God often mention the prayer-request box on the desk in his office at Ohio State.*
>
> *. . . For more than a decade, Ohioans have viewed Tressel as a pillar of rectitude, and have disregarded or made excuses for the allegations and scandal that have quietly followed him*

throughout his career. His integrity was one of the great myths of college football. Like a disgraced politician who preaches probity but is caught in lies, the Senator was not the person he purported to be.

Hell, they could all write, *those writers*. When I was closing the May 29, 2006, issue, I e-mailed the business side, suggesting the feature ledes in the magazine that single week would show off the great writing and thus make an effective sales tool. That's what differentiated *SI* from the rest of sports journalism. There were five features that week and I loved every lede. My memo began with "Try this with any other magazine . . ." My favorite was Franz Lidz's at the top of a baseball profile:

The two teenage girls behind the visitors dugout at Shea Stadium are looking for Mr. Wright. The taller girl—the one in the red sweater vest, shiny black capris and a Bubblicious-colored necktie—looks as if she maxed out a thrift-shop gift card. Her shorter friend, who's sporting mismatched leggings and a jean jacket worn inside out, seems merely to have dressed herself in the dark.

The teens survey the playing field, where, an hour before the first pitch, New York Mets third baseman David Wright is taking infield practice. Mostly, they survey Wright. Their eyes—dreamy, worshipful—glow like cherries in a glass of buttermilk.

Not funny was Mike Silver on an injury in the NFL:

Carson Palmer will never forget that long ride home, his iced-up knee not so much in pain but numb, like the rest of him. He was lying on his side, sprawled across the backseat of his Chevy Tahoe, staring out an open window as his wife, Shaelyn, pulled away from the downtown stadium and up Third Street. The stadium lights were sparkling (exploding is the way he remembers them) as the crowd noise rose and fell, and he could see vendors in the parking lots still hawking jerseys with his number 9 on them. The sensations were as immediate as the twin pops he felt in his left knee upon releasing his first and only pass of the day, a glorious 66-yard completion that momentarily filled the south Ohio sky with unlimited promise.

And then there was L. Jon Wertheim in a profile of a tennis star on what can happen when athletes retire:

Well, it sounded good in theory, anyway. There she was, retired at 22 years old, with tens of millions of euros in the bank. She would ski at St. Moritz by day and go out with the boys at night. She would ride horses at her estate in Switzerland and maybe take up golf at her other residence, outside Tampa. She'd nourish her mind by auditing some courses. Apart from minor television appearances and sponsor obligations, she would wake up most mornings free to do whatever she pleased.

But Martina Hingis quickly realized that life in repose isn't all it's cracked up to be. In fact, like so many retirees from Palm Beach to Palm Springs, she had to confront the reality that work is often less about what we do than about who we are. And in its absence, our identities can get lost.

Week after week, the writers came through like that for the magazine. Few of them, however, were interested in SI.com, some insisting on extra money to write for it. Time (intentional pun) was not on their side and neither was I. SI needed to bring the magazine and the website into sync. As obvious as this was, it was not particularly welcomed on either side of that divide. Many of the writers ridiculed and faced off against their new Web editors, who mocked them back in what I characterized at editorial management meetings as a passive-aggressive civil war. Sometimes when I was asked about the transition, I told a Time Inc. joke:

Q. How many staffers does it take to change a light bulb at Time Inc.?

A. Twenty-five. One to screw in the new bulb, and twenty-four to stand around talking about how great the old bulb used to be.

There were exceptions, of course—Tom Verducci for one, and especially Peter King. Peter was so smart and prolific, so well-sourced top to bottom in the NFL, that *SI* built a digital vertical around him. His Web column "Monday Morning Quarterback" started as a favor for an editor he liked who had been sent into a kind of grim exile as editor of the new SI.com. It grew quickly to reach an audience of more than three million, and advertisers were fighting over digital sponsorships and positions next to his print column. He was gaining in popularity on *SI*'s star columnist Rick Reilly, and his compensation was catching up, too. Then, in the darkest week of *SI*'s cost cutting, Peter made a special trip into the office to tell me he wanted to give back a big chunk of his new salary if it would save a job or two down the food chain.

That was the thing about *SI*: all the talent its culture nurtured in spite of itself could turn reciprocal. I write this with the full understanding that such sentimental cluelessness by the former editor will be pointed to as evidence of ongoing and pervasive newsweekly *fuckedupedness.*

-ENDIT-

Reilly (1,296)

RICK REILLY DID SO MANY THINGS so effortlessly and with such swagger that he had seven National Sportswriter of the Year plaques by the time I got to *SI* and owned the magazine's back page with his "Life of Reilly." He got around like a cocky teenager and could talk to anybody. Week to week, Reilly was hilarious or heartbreaking, and he pulled more letters than all the other writers combined. He also wrote books and screenplays and had a Miller Lite commercial with the *SI* swimsuit model Rebecca Romijn, but that was on the side and he made more money in salary alone than any writer across all of Time Inc. My problem was that his contract was up for renewal when I arrived, and Walsh had failed to mention that ESPN would be coming after him, and after Gary Smith, too.

Gary wasn't interested but Reilly rolled out some jokes about *SI*'s "salary cap" and made no secret of his willingness to listen to overtures. As he told *BusinessWeek*, "Am I interested? Yeah, I'm as wide open as a 7-Eleven." I told the same reporter, "If Rick Reilly were a restaurant, I'd eat there every day."

The first time Reilly came to see me, I framed the publicity photo from his most recent book and hung it behind my desk, thinking I'd point it out as a joke at the end of our meeting. When he walked in, I got up and respectfully suggested that we sit in the large chairs around the coffee table, but he waved me back and sat across from me, with a direct view of his photo. Perfect.

"You mind?" he said, putting his feet up on my desk.

"Not at all," I said, and waited. It took him maybe a minute.

"Smart-assed," he said, with an edge on it, but he was smiling. It felt to me like we might get to be friends.

"I'm desperate," I said.

"Then I guess I can't leave if you can . . ."

"I'll match the ESPN money."

Reilly signed a five-year contract that blew up the *SI* edit budget, and proceeded to prove he was worth it. He got better and better as what the press was now calling "the first million-dollar sportswriter." He filed every week and banked evergreens for weeks he took off. He wrote features too, and was Sportswriter of the Year four out of the next five years. Advertisers loved Reilly and the inside back cover, opposite his column, was the most expensive real estate in the magazine.

When Reilly e-mailed me, he usually started with "Dear Boss," then went on to whatever was on his mind. His column ideas ranged from being a ball boy at the U.S. Open to NCAA screwups to jocks doing TV Viagra ads to a legless football player. He was always good, but he was never easy. Sometimes he wanted graphics in his column instead of his photo (which drove the art department nuts); sometimes he wanted a new photo (ditto the photo department). He called me out, as he should have, when I complained that I was under pressure from *SI*'s ad sales executives to soften his attack on big tobacco. We never became friends exactly but sometimes we talked about our lives, our children and the divorces we were going through.

"Maybe we're better at our jobs than at our lives," he said once, not an original idea but it stayed with me as a kind of offering. He was talking about perspective and, I think, why he could write so beautifully about not just elite athletes and their teammates but about what sports meant to ordinary people and their families—where sports fit into the world. Reilly always found those stories.

In May 2006, he wrote a column about malaria as a leading cause of death among children in Africa. He called it "Nothing but Nets" and asked readers to send ten dollars each to a charity he was starting on the fly to ship over antimalarial bed nets instead of the predictable sports equipment. He ended the column with this:

A few years back, we took the family to Tanzania, which is ravaged by malaria now. We visited a school and played soccer with the kids. Must've been 50 on each team, running and laughing. A taped-up wad of newspapers was the ball and two rocks were the goal. Most fun I ever had getting whupped. When we got home, we sent some balls and nets.

I kick myself now for that. How many of those kids are dead because we sent the wrong nets?

He had the right angle (sports), a compelling voice (his) and the right platform (*SI*). "Nothing but Nets" pulled in $1 million in the first week, and he built it into a foundation that as of 2015 had raised more than $52 million. Most important, he had the idea, one that no one could believe came from a sports columnist.

WHEN REILLY'S CONTRACT was up again, John Walsh was back with more money and Reilly was soon headed to ESPN, leaving behind more than 850 *SI* bylines. The press reported $17 million over five years. Reilly wouldn't confirm a number, saying only that it was "ridonkulous" money.

I had tried to keep him, of course, and had negotiated with his agent for weeks, checking back and forth with my boss John Huey and increasingly outraging Time Inc. CEO Ann Moore, who, in turn, had to check with her boss at the top of Time Warner. When it was over I realized Reilly had wanted to be on television all along. I didn't know how much ESPN was paying, even though I had obviously bid it up. It occurred to me that Reilly might even thank me for that. We would both see the humor, especially since I had told him in the beginning that Walsh was trying to "money-whip" him into the ESPN barn. Publicly, I told the *New York Times*, "He's a great talent and I will miss him personally."

His last *SI* column was a graceful good-bye, but instead of praising him, I wrote in my "Editor's Letter" about the magazine's tradition of fine writing and tried to spin it forward. Reilly was gone and we needed to move on with writers who would rotate through the back page column, which would be called "Point After," as it had been before he took it over. I didn't even mention his name. When I heard from him the following week, there was no "Dear Boss."

He wrote me a searing e-mail, starting with *So let me get this straight.* He felt I'd publicly ignored his twenty-two years at *SI*, the last ten holding down the best-read page in sports journalism. He was right, and I felt worse as I read how he'd loved *SI* and had had great editors there, except one; and how grateful he was for everything he got to see and to write about, thanks to some incredibly good bosses, except one. It felt worse than a bad report card. He ended the e-mail with *screw you sideways.* I showed it to no one.

YEARS LATER, after Reilly had written his last column for ESPN, I crossed paths with him on the street in my West Village neighborhood in New York. He was with his pretty wife, Cynthia, and they were looking for a place to have dinner. I tried to help and it wasn't awkward at all. He even called me "boss" again. That was funny and we both laughed. Watching him walk away, I realized that of all the journalists I'd worked with, Reilly was probably the only one who'd never really had a boss.

-ENDIT-

Swimsuit (2,650)

ONE EARLY SPRING NIGHT in Greenwich Village, bright
moonlight caught Anne V as she walked out on a windy terrace. She
seemed to glow in a skimpy T-shirt and short skirt, her refined features and sleek body flawless and aloof. She was on what would be an
unprecedented ten-year run of appearances in the *Sports Illustrated*
Swimsuit Issue, nearly matching my years at the magazine. So I knew
her a little, not just in the slight way I knew the many models who
came and went, and I had seen hundreds of photos of her. Many of
my colleagues at the magazine thought of her as the quintessential
swimsuit model, except that she had freckles if you looked closely,
and her breasts might have been a little larger. She was Walter Iooss's
favorite and he had shot more Swimsuit Issue covers than anyone.
But she had not yet made the cover.

"I'm Russian," she said, when asked that night on the terrace if she
was cold. Her last name was Vyalitsyna and her parents were doctors
in Gorky, where she was born. "Some of the shoots are a lot colder
than this," she continued, after a sip of wine. "And I have a lot less
on."

A few guests at the party approached her and made small talk. A
lot of the models complained about how the small talk always stayed
small, that no one ever bothered to figure out anything interesting
to say to them. But Anne V was almost always friendly, even though,
if you looked around when you were talking to her, you could see
people, both men and women, watching her. She was used to being
stared at. It was her job, after all.

A COUPLE YEARS EARLIER, on *Morning Joe* to promote a new
book, *Sports Illustrated: The Covers,* I was asked how the magazine
could honor women skiers and soccer players and tennis stars on the
cover for their accomplishments and then objectify women by slap-

ping a topless model on the next week. Good question, and also one of those talk-show gotchas meant to underline the issue conscious- ness and journalistic integrity of the hosts. I smiled and said that edit- ing *SI* sometimes required having to keep two conflicting ideas in my head at the same time, which got me off the hook, and we moved on to trivia about which athlete had the most *SI* covers (Michael Jordan, with fifty).

The Swimsuit Issue was never what you bragged about as the edi- tor of *SI*, but you never apologized for it, either. And that question came all the time, its dutifulness overrun by the obvious. "Swimsuit," as everyone at Time Inc. called it (just "Swim" at the magazine), not only outlasted the historical moment that birthed it but grew like a beautiful mutant baby to earn Time Inc. more than $1 billion since its first appearance. That was in 1964, when managing editor André Laguerre was looking for a cover that would make the magazine noticeable during the winter months, when football had ended and baseball had yet to begin (basketball didn't matter then). So why not a pretty girl, on a beach somewhere?

The first Swimsuit Issue cover model was twenty-two-year-old Babette Beatty, looking healthy, happy and unobjectified in a modest two-piece. Inside were five pages of primitive swimsuit photographs in a larger package about diving and snorkeling in the Caribbean, "Fun in the Sun on Cozumel." Babette was the model of the moment (born in Berlin, raised in Rio, living in Manhattan) and *SI* confirmed that she liked hanging out with Mick Jagger and Andy Warhol, as well as athletes. Cool.

Also cool, it turned out, was the first Swimsuit Issue editor, Jule Campbell, who from the beginning pushed for the models' names to be on their photos, especially on the cover, thereby turning many of them into celebrities and establishing *SI* as a runway to supermodel status. This, in turn, allowed her to keep the day rates for her models low ($125) because appearing in the magazine had such significant career upside.

The key to Swimsuit as a business was holding down costs without letting it show. The day rate now is only $450, although the models get several thousand on top of that for appearances and parties and media interviews—all of which are relentless during the launch. Equally important discount deals are made for hotels and travel. One of many astounding stats collected by *SI* marketing research over my years was that when the Swimsuit Issue first visited Chile in 2004, tourism rose 34 percent there. (Think about that and imagine yourself as the head of marketing for a global hotel chain.) Another stat that cracked up everyone at the magazine was that when the model on the cover was from the United States, the S&P 500 for that year outperformed years with a non-American cover model. The Swimsuit Issue as Economic Indicator. This is actually true, according to CNBC.

The Swimsuit business was so good when I arrived at *SI* in 2002 that I hardly thought about it, except to tell my new colleagues that I wanted to inject a little more culture and humor to go along with the models in exotic locales. The Swimsuit editors, Diane Smith and MJ Day, killed themselves producing shoots in far-flung locations, even though the research always came back that readers wanted tighter pictures, the hell with landscapes. I said we should go for exotic landscapes anyway.

The Swimsuit editors smiled.

Plus, I'd get the hilarious writer Carl Hiaasen, whose new comic novel *Basket Case* was then just out, to contribute something.

Maybe they rolled their eyes.

What the Swimsuit editors knew was that "the marketplace" wanted the models naked, and their only real alternative as editors was to produce beautiful, *almost*-naked pictures. Art, maybe.

I LOVED THAT CARL HIAASEN PIECE. Entitled "Tart of Darkness," it had a tagline noting, "A demented photographer has hijacked *SI*'s hottest cover ever. Getting it back requires a harrowing—and hilarious—journey deep into the heart of Swimsuit." It pulled some nice press but scored way low in reader surveys—which were getting more and more specific, telling me that freckles on a model were bad for sales, and definitely no sand on her butt. I was learning. And the number of naked or at least topless and what are called "side-boob" shots was rising.

It occurred to me that we might be going too far for some of our readers. I remembered getting my first subscription to *SI* from my grandfather when I was ten. I thought about this and came up with some defensive language. No leering. Swimsuit did not leer. I told media reporters that most of our imitators had a *panting* quality and that *SI* Swimsuit did not pant. Thus it remained a celebration of athletic bodies and good health. It reflected the athleticism and sexi-ness of the culture. *SI*'s models were modern, natural women. You could see their freckles (if not their tattoos). I didn't say that almost all the models had ink somewhere—Carolyn Murphy had a Japanese koi (representing samurai stoicism) wrapping around the top of her right thigh all the way to the small of her back—and that the guys in the imaging department spent hours getting rid of all the tats after the images were chosen. It was also sometimes slightly uncomfort-able looking at Swimsuit pages on my screen with the women who handled the magazine's pagination, another indication that maybe we were pushing some limits.

Sure enough, the only serious side-boob backlash came not from subscribers but from the *SI* staff, some of whom had loathed Swim-suit for years. They viewed it as slick subjugation of women, humili-ating and degrading for everyone. Some of them came to see me. The word "pornography" was used. When I polled the staff, I found that about a third felt this way. Another third thought Swimsuit was important to *SI*, but only because it made so much money. The rest didn't care or thought polling them was funny, maybe even stupid. There had been very few female editors at *SI*, but the four editors of the Swimsuit Issue over the years were women, and the two I was working with—Diane Smith and MJ Day—were incredulous that so many of their colleagues just didn't get it. Nobody ever got mad at *SI* for asking if they wanted to be in the Swimsuit Issue. The athletes who posed (and Beyoncé, too) all said they were flattered.

In the middle of all this, I heard a story about my immediate predecessor at the magazine, Bill Colson, whom I had replaced in a surprise move by Time Inc. bosses Norm Pearlstine and John Huey a couple years earlier. Colson was a fine journalist and a bold editor who had won the managing editor job in a tryout (known within Time Inc. as a "bake-off") by running a cover calling for the University of Miami to drop its corrupt football program in the interest of higher education. The Swimsuit story was that Colson had gone to Huey with the idea that the best thing for *SI* would be to can Swimsuit. He had obviously disagreed.

My 2004 Swimsuit Issue sold a record 1,563,694 copies on the newsstand with Veronica Varekova on the cover, bikini top in hand. In anticipation of the 2005 issue, I ran a boxed notification on the "Letters" page with the headline "If You Don't Want the Swimsuit Issue." The notice provided a phone number for subscribers to request that they skip the issue and have their subscriptions extended by a week. Perhaps 20,000 paid subscribers, out of the total of 3.2 million, or 0.006 percent, asked not to receive the Swimsuit Issue. It sold 1,083,827 with Carolyn Murphy on the cover with her top on.

IF YOU LOOKED CLOSELY at any of the Swimsuit models, you saw youth but also a happy sophistication—something they were growing into. The editors joked that they were "specimens." But there was an innocence, too. When a prospective model would come to the office with her portfolio, usually in jeans and without makeup, there was almost a Cinderella vibe to it. Personality mattered, too, because part of the contract called for appearances at events and parties. Confidence was something else they all had, along with the flawless skin. One of the photographers told me that once you shot for Swimsuit, the only women you could compare the models to were other Swimsuit models. That's circular reasoning but it's also true.

By 2005 we had thousands of Swimsuit pictures, going back to the 1980s, up on SI.com, as well as the couple hundred or so in the

magazine. I asked for the models to lose the pouty, come-hither coy-
ness and start smiling more. Also no more rock humping, thong mas-
turbation or fake surf orgasms. And the bikini tops had to be worn
in more of the pictures. The Swimsuit department complied but
thought I was nuts. The research—from focus groups and showing
photos to young men hanging out at malls—was telling us that the
sexier (more naked!) the models were, the more money we'd make.

As Swimsuit rolled toward my last issue in 2012, there were shoots
in Bondi Beach and North Narrabeen in Australia; Apalachicola,
Florida; Bocas del Toro Province and San Blas Islands, Panama; Des-
roches Island, Seychelles; and Victoria Falls, Zambia. You edit as you
go. Certain pictures emerge. The Swimsuit editors and the creative
director have their favorites. So do three hundred assorted guys aged
eighteen to fifty-four (150 recent buyers and 150 prospects) in fifteen
malls across the country who look at cover mock-ups. In the end, the
editor has to decide.

I wanted to put Anne V on the cover, and the Swimsuit editors
took her to the Seychelles with that in mind, setting her up with what
they thought was the strongest combination of photographer, location and "suit theme" (bright colors). Most models had small cover
windows, unless they became immediate stars, like Cheryl Tiegs or
Elle Macpherson, and wound up with multiple covers. Every model
was told she had a shot at the cover, and they all did. Anne had eight
years in and had come close before.

Over those same years, Swimsuit had gone increasingly digital. By
2012, besides the magazine we had a *Swimsuit Daily* blog, a super-
charged tablet edition with scrolling, panoramic photo sequences,
and two hours of video, available for iPad, Samsung Galaxy Tab,
Barnes & Noble Nook Color, Amazon Kindle Fire, Motorola Xoom
and Android smartphones, and we had built a Chrome Web app
to take advantage of HTML5. Did I forget to mention 3-D video
for PlayStation 3? There was also an iPhone app that gave users a
360-degree view of body-painted athletes. SI.com/Swimsuit had an

elaborate interactive music section with seventeen emerging indie bands. We sold coffee table books, calendars and trading cards and experimented with holograms. We had interactive polls in real time and produced TV specials and reality shows. We pushed it all out with Twitter, Facebook and Flipboard feeds. After David Letterman "revealed" the cover on his late-night show (complete with one of his top ten lists), and after the New York party, we flew our most important advertisers and the models to Las Vegas on a private 727 for three more days of sponsored Swimsuit casino events, which we called "experiential marketing."

The press release quoted me: "'You will see innovation on every Swimsuit platform this year,' said Terry McDonell, Editor, Time Inc. Sports Group." Well, yes, you would, because *SI* Swimsuit was a franchise like no other and we sold it harder than anything else we had, including our journalism. We were reaching more than seventy million American adults (5 percent of the population), not to mention what we pulled from foreign editions. When I traveled internationally for *SI*, the first question I always got was about Swimsuit. In Beijing in 2006, when we were negotiating to launch *Sports Illustrated China* in time for the 2008 Summer Olympics, an official with the Chinese Olympic Committee kept referring to Swimsuit as the "Bathroom Issue." We had Swimsuit there by 2007. Even in the United States, when people found out that part of my job was to pick the Swimsuit cover, things got silly. Serious businessmen asked what it would take—no, *really*, what would it take?—to get invited on a shoot.

"I've never been on a shoot," I would answer, always bringing disappointment.

THE COVER OF MY LAST Swimsuit Issue, in 2012, was not Anne V but nineteen-year-old Kate Upton, with no freckles and no sand on her butt. Over the years, Anne had always tested slightly below the models who made it: most recently Marisa Miller (2008), Bar Refaeli (2009), Brooklyn Decker (2010), Irina Shayk (2011) and, finally,

Upton (2012), who had become a social media sensation with her sexy smartphone Dougie video from a Los Angeles Clippers game just before our mall intercepts.

In Las Vegas for all the parties, Anne was as charming as ever, but at one of the casino concerts she came up to me with her then boyfriend, Adam Levine.

"You should have put her on the cover," he said.

"I know," I said, "but it's a business." That was hurtful and I was immediately sorry. The models all thought the editor decided, and that was true. But research had become so powerful you defied it at your own risk. It wasn't just about instinct or relationships. It was about opinions in malls in places like Trumbull, Connecticut. The Swimsuit editors had promised to explain that to Anne. Maybe they had, maybe not.

And then she told me that she knew she had never tested especially well. "Freckles," Anne said, and laughed.

-ENDIT-

Ad Sales (672)

SELLING ADVERTISING IS A FLIRTY, tough business way beyond the macho sexiness it was freighted with on *Mad Men*, which, unironically enough, opened with an establishing shot of the Time & Life Building in midtown. This was where I worked with Mark Ford, who was then the president of *Sports Illustrated* and sometimes referred to himself in the third person as "the sales donkey"—a bit of self-mockery that underlined rather than undercut his instincts as a salesman. His cell-phone ringtone was Johnny Cash's "Ring of Fire," and he sold his ass off over boardroom tables, rounds of golf and thousands of drinks.

"It's a relationship business," he'd say. Or, if he was negotiating, "It's not my first rodeo." We'd talk almost every day. Once, on an agency call in Chicago to introduce the iPad edition of *SI* when all we had was a simulation video and a bunch of jargon about "enhanced usability," one of the agency guys whom Ford knew well because he ran lots of automotive business interrupted, wanting to know "How much?" Apple hadn't even released the first iPad yet.

"For what?" Ford said.

"You tell me."

Ford came up with something he called an "Innovation Partnership." *SI* would share iPad research and development for a year and discount a package of advertising pages in the magazine on top of that. The guy cocked his head to suggest he wanted a hard number.

"A million bucks," Ford said. A glance at me. A cagey smile. He knew everyone in the room. "We're six months ahead of everyone on this."

"We can work this out," the account guy said, and we all went downstairs for some drinks.

• • •

TOP EDITORS ALL STRADDLE the line between editorial independence and publishing imperatives to get the money—call it the separation of "church and state" if you want to sound naïve. I went on sales calls whenever I was asked. Getting the editor to show up has always been a hoop some advertisers put magazine publishers through.

I liked the client dinners my various publishers hosted at expensive restaurants. They knew the maître d's. Good wine in private rooms, with extra waiters. It seemed effortless. Even the lowest sales assistant or advertising associate was eager to pick up checks (to be expensed, of course). This was not true of the *SI* editors, who always expected me to buy (understandable, but the entitlement was cloying). I would hear editors berate "ad guys"—as they were called everywhere I worked—for not reading every word of their magazines, but so what? Neither did most of the editors.

The publishing side of any editor's job expanded with the need for new editorial features to sell advertising against: Father's Day supplements, roundups of new consumer electronic products for your "media room," and guides to the best places to stay or eat or whatever. To resist was professional suicide, but when editors came through with a new idea, most publishers were deferential and grateful—a posture that has stiffened in the current era of editorial-looking "native" advertising, when what used to be called "advertorials" are sold as "premium content." I don't mean *Innovation Partnerships* that take advantage of new technology; I mean advertiser-approved marketing material disguised as journalism—like joke taxidermy.

It takes great determination to sell advertising—print, digital or a combination—whether it's advertorial or not. There's a constant rate negotiation. Rate cards based on circulation and traffic, with their printed CPMs (cost for every thousand customers), are just a place to start. Advertising clients and their advertising agencies push back on everything.

Every publisher I worked with had a compulsive work ethic. They ordered up market analyses and demographic studies and constantly refined their presentations to appeal to whomever they were calling on that day—and then negotiated like wolverines. Some might dispute this, but selling a $350,000 page required more than getting one-on-one with a client with an ounce of coke, a fifth of Cuervo Gold and a couple of Rolling Stones tickets.

-ENDIT-

Steve Jobs Thinks Your Work Is Really Stupid (1,262)

WHEN STEVE JOBS CAME to Time Inc. in February 2010, wearing New Balance sneakers, jeans and a black mock turtleneck, I thought about his visit to *Newsweek* twenty-six years earlier in that little bow tie. He had arrived at *Newsweek* with one assistant to help him carry two of the Macintosh computers he was presenting then. There were at least eight people with him for his Time Inc. visit, and iPads were passed out to the top editors from *Time, Fortune, People* and the other magazines, all of us seated at a long conference table. Coffee and tea were offered by waiters in white uniforms. Steve sat at the head of the table and spoke elliptically about innovation, quality journalism and various business models while we played with his new machines.

I had never touched an iPad, although I had been working on an app to run on one for four months. The assignment had been to create the first tablet magazine, and *Sports Illustrated* had done that with jury-rigged touch-screen technology pieced together from Hewlett-Packard. Finally, to show that we were ready for the coming iPad, we had made a video simulation of what *SI* would be like on the tablet. It was primitive, with "zombie hands" to explain the touch navigation, and I had done the narration, but the video had gone viral—we loved saying that—with more than a million views and everyone in magazine publishing had seen it.

I turned on the new iPad and went to YouTube to see if the video would play. It did: "Hello, I'm Terry McDonell, the editor of *Sports Illustrated*, and here's your new issue . . ."

I turned it off quickly, but the editor of *Fortune*, Andy Serwer, asked Jobs if he had seen the video. He had. What did he think? I'm sure Serwer was pushing for an acknowledgment that as a company we were in the hunt—to use a popular catchphrase at the time. I'm also sure that most of the other editors in the room were tired of hearing about *SI's* spurt of digital development and wouldn't have minded Jobs knocking it down a little. I certainly didn't *know* Steve Jobs, but I figured I still had to be on his radar and something very good could come out of *SI's* iPad edition. I was hopeful.

"I think it's stupid," Steve said. "*Really* stupid."

"Why?" I asked, jumping in, maybe too fast.

"It's just a video—it's not real."

"You gave us no choice," I said. "And our app will work great on your *appliance.*" I still loved the word *appliance.*

"You made this?" he asked, I think realizing we had met before.

At this point, Time Inc. CEO Ann Moore joined the meeting. "Queen Ann," as she was sometimes called, was full of small smiles for everyone, almost bubbly, as was her style, but then suddenly grew confused by the mood of the room. I handed her the iPad, and when she turned it on, it defaulted to the *SI* video: "Hello, I'm Terry McDonell . . ."—which was funny until she couldn't turn it off.

"Isn't it great," she said, handing the iPad back to me.

The irony here was that "Queen Ann" was a shorthand variation of "the Launch Queen." She'd earned the epithet from top management in acknowledgment of her work as the publisher of *People* when she'd overseen the rollouts of *InStyle, People en Español, Teen People* and *Real Simple,* giving Time Inc. a competitive edge in the women's category for the first time. So she really had been an innovator, but now she couldn't find the power button.

After Ann left for yet another important meeting, Serwer asked Steve about getting access to Apple's creative process. That was a good one if you knew their history—going back to a March 2008 *Fortune* piece titled "The Trouble with Steve Jobs," which reported his eccentric cancer diet and raised questions about his involvement in the backdating of Apple stock options. Jobs had asked Serwer to kill it, and had then gone over his head to Time Inc. editor in chief John Huey, but Huey held the line and the piece had run.

I was expecting something far harsher than what Steve had said about *SI*'s iPad app, but he didn't answer at first. I think *Time* managing editor Rick Stengel said something about how better access would make for more interesting journalism and he'd like to be first in line.

"That will never happen," Steve said finally, looking at Serwer, "after what you did." He was talking about that *Fortune* story two years earlier, but instead of showing anger he was swallowing hard and his eyes were tearing.

"You kicked me when I was down," Steve said. I think that's when everyone in the room realized how sick he was.

Serwer said he was sorry, that he was just doing his job, that it wasn't personal. But you could see it was very personal for Steve, who nodded, took a breath and moved on haltingly to his ideas about how publishers like Time Inc. had to be careful about "overpricing what you're selling."

Overpricing what you're selling? Suddenly he was negotiating, even though none of the editors in the room had the authority to do anything beyond have an opinion. So . . . Apple would be taking its customary one-third and holding on to the credit card data. Apple *might* be willing to give us some of that data back—"customers' names and stuff"—but not the credit card info, which, he said, was protected by Apple's privacy policy. We were fucked.

The meeting ended with the iPads being collected and Steve pushing away from the table while saying, "I'm interested in magazines."

I HUNG BACK as the other editors filed past to say good-bye. When they were gone, I reminded Steve where we had met, and about *Newsweek Access.* He said he remembered, and that Tom Zito had sent him a photo from the *SI* 2007 Swimsuit Issue of Marisa Miller on her back on a white beach, naked except for an iPod. Was I responsible for that? I was. I had sent it to Zito to send to him, *and* I knew what he had e-mailed back to Zito—who had forwarded the e-mail to me.

"Really," Steve said, and waited.

"'Does she want a job at Apple?'" I said, quoting his e-mail.

"A joke," Steve said.

"I know."

"Like this meeting."

An hour after Steve left, his top developer-relations guy called to say that "Steve and the team" really thought there was a lot of cool stuff in the *SI* demo and they'd love to work with us to create a version of *SI* for the iPad release, which was then only sixty days away.

SI was ready to go; but the first Time Inc. digital magazine—the first digital magazine, period—to run on the iPad was to be *Time*. Steve "wasn't into sports," as it was explained to me a week later, and *Time* had always been one of his favorite magazines. *Time* had agreed to put him on the cover after he made some calls himself—and it became clear that Apple's approval was required not only to run an application on the iPad but also just to get into the Apple App Store. The leverage was embarrassingly obvious. Stengel thanked *SI* in his "Editor's Letter" when the issue launched, but there was no mention of the Machiavelli Club.

-ENDIT-

The Machiavelli Club (1,641)

My ASSIGNMENT TO DEVELOP that tablet edition for *SI* had come after a dutiful *Time* cover story in early 2009 on the death of newspapers that included a sidebar by Josh Quittner on e-readers and these new things called "apps." That jump-started a CEO trip to Silicon Valley on one of the Time Warner jets, and after a couple days of meetings with the developers mentioned in the sidebar, it was decided on the flight back to New York to invest in some strategic R&D.

Inexplicably, I seemed to be the only Time Inc. editor interested in developing a magazine app except for Quittner, who was parked at *Time* as an editor at large. He had edited *Business 2.0*—covering the "new economy"—until Time Inc. closed it, and he knew technology better than any other editor in the company. He was also a prankster who had registered "mcdonalds.com" in his name for an early *Wired* piece on domain-name squatting. I got him detached from *Time* (where he was viewed with suspicion) and gave him an office next to mine at *SI* (where he was viewed with suspicion).

The old business school adage that culture trumps strategy was much more than a punch line at Time Inc., where there were three distinct cultures. The executive culture was risk-averse but desperate—thus my green light. The edit culture was defensive and clueless about what was coming, thinking in abstract clichés that IT was responsible only for fixing the e-mail and maybe even the air-conditioning. The IT culture was ironic and vaguely bitter about being underappreciated. That changing-the-light-bulb joke was no joke on many levels.

Creating the *SI* app promised nothing but extra work, but there were volunteers, and whenever someone joined the project I e-mailed them this quote and welcomed them to the Machiavelli Club:

There is no more delicate matter to take in hand, nor more dangerous to conduct, nor more doubtful in its success, than to be a leader in the introduction of changes. For he who innovates will have for enemies all those who are well off under the old order of things, and only lukewarm supporters in those who might be better off under the new.

— NICCOLÒ MACHIAVELLI,
The Prince, 1532

I was looking for swagger. I said engineering would set editors free. I said that if type was the sushi of the '90s, code was the typography of the 'oos. I gave presentations that celebrated the editorial appetite for change across Time Inc. even as management was living in dread — trying to protect a bottom line with over 85 percent of its (falling) revenues coming from print. If you were managing one of those P&Ls, it felt like trying to catch falling knives.

It helped that *SI*'s outside developing partner, a digital agency called the Wonderfactory, was led by the bearishly handsome entrepreneur David Link and was itself subversive. The Machiavelli Club grew in reputation as cool. Engineers started showing up for drinks with editors at the bar downstairs. *SI*'s creative director, Chris Hercik, got hold of Quittner's Time Inc. ID and changed it to a Machiavelli Club ID with the name "Robespierre."

Management's meetings took on a different tone. Digital strategy sessions turned into platitude festivals about building a twenty-first-Century Media Company but were mostly about saving obsolete business models. The lack of confidence in consumer demand for quality journalism was always the subtext. My argument was that it wasn't that people wouldn't pay for our stuff, it was just too hard, too complicated to find it and then sign up to get it. And what were we selling anyway? We weren't selling our journalism very hard. For a while you couldn't get a digital subscription to *SI* without also receiving a "FREE NFL Team Performer Jacket." There was no mention of our writing or photography. And they were shitty jackets.

It was also dimly perceived that our websites were already more important than our magazines. This was especially true at the newsweeklies, which, in the case of *SI*, was a twenty-four/seven operation and had been for some time—though this surprised some top executives. Someone told me at one of those meetings that "mobile seems to be coming pretty fast." We needed a lot of help, but by then editors who had not become entrepreneurs were losing control of their content to a wave of new "digital" vice presidents and general managers on the publishing side. Their boss e-mailed me after his "on-boarding" as the newly created chief digital officer of Time Inc. that he wanted to "download" my guidance.

Everything was up for grabs. I hoped that my proposed subscription models, paywalls, news on demand, apps, mobile Web, second screens, e-books, e-commerce, brand extensions, video, social media, dashboards, even events and conferences could all be part of the mix. My only rule was that everything had to be authentic, not cosmetic, and take advantage of the native technology of the new platforms.

That some of the best magazine editors were already becoming "brand managers" was another way to look at it, even though that verges on jargon. Traditional brand managers, meanwhile, wanted to be digital officers so they could control the content with the digital vice presidents. Now that I've written that word again, I want to be on the record that "content" had come to mean so many things it meant nothing. I sat through too many PowerPoint presentations by scalp-hunting consultants thinking, *Fuck content!* That goes double when you put the word "amazing" or "incredible" in front of it. I have noticed that the "content" I'm told is "amazing" or "incredible" is never amazing or incredible. Editors should not talk like that.

In the numerous "digital content" meetings I attended, there was very little discussion about the quality of our journalism. Some of the most annoying talk had to do with the complaint that we had not built commerce into browsers in the first place. In other words, why didn't we charge for anything in the beginning? Whose fault was that? I said that if we didn't have the confidence to charge for our journalism, there was no way anyone was going to pay for it—a tautological argument I know, but it felt right. Many editors were already working on turning their magazines into stores. That was fine with me; let them become stores, righteous stores in service of readers and users, stores that were not for sale. I said I would shop at those stores.

When we did talk about our journalism, the naïve thinking among most of the editors was that we just needed our resources back. We should have been thinking about content-management systems to deliver what we still had. It was like the cautionary allegory of being in the railroad business instead of the shipping business when public works projects were laying down the national highway system. To stretch the metaphor: if you were in the news business, you needed to jump off the traditional tracks. What we did instead was cut costs. Watching some of the SI writers take buyouts, it felt like a great library was burning down.

I eliminated too many jobs to count here. This was difficult and frustrating because every firing reflected the lack of business leadership that I had been brooding about since I'd been a young editor in the late 1970s. That was when magazines began leveraging their circulations against advertising revenue, inflating readerships with cheap subscriptions and charging advertisers for the larger rate base.

This was fine until the economy turned, as it always did, and you had to cut costs with smaller formats, cheaper paper, reduced staff, fewer assignments, less enterprise, and so it went. When the economy would turn up again, the cycle would repeat. But you never got anything you'd cut back. Pretty soon great magazines were selling subscriptions for five dollars a year, and the investment in edit was lost in the funhouse mirrors of outside consultants and the grueling platitudes of spooked executives undermining their own stated objectives.

I don't think I was naïve about economic realities, and I was responsible for an editorial budget of more than $50 million, but I believed that in the journalism business, journalism had to come first. Financial support would follow the quality of the work. That's where I was naïve. Our nearsighted mandate was "build only if sold."

So maybe the Machiavelli Club was our best shot, and the press we got around our first prototype seemed to prove that. I thought *SI*'s was the best app, updating every day and completely refreshed when the new print edition came out, but good ones for *monthly* magazines were popping out of every traditional media company, all of us trying to convince ourselves that these new digital editions were going to "save" us. That's why Apple's business model put all of us in such a bad place.

Time Inc. needed a subscription model, which, as Steve Jobs had been telling us all along, was fine with him as long as Apple kept the credit card data. But this meant Apple would own Time Inc.'s subscribers and prevent us from having a direct billing relationship. We wanted to create apps that would direct readers to our website in order to buy a subscription. This was not going to happen. When *SI*, *Time* and other magazines submitted apps that did this, they were rejected by Apple's App Store. The negotiation moved to what were said to be "no bullshit" phone calls between Jobs and Time Warner CEO Jeff Bewkes. Nothing happened. Canny player that he is, Bewkes was already several moves ahead and deep in plans to spin off Time Inc. so he could focus on Turner, Warner Bros., HBO and cable. Where the real money was.

-ENDIT-

Google (602)

Wʜᴇɴ *SI'*s ᴢᴏᴍʙɪᴇ-ʜᴀɴᴅs ᴠɪᴅᴇᴏ first went up on YouTube, we heard immediately from Google where a team of developers had reverse-engineered it. They had some ideas about how to create an *SI* app we could offer free in the Google Chrome Web Store, and they invited us out to Mountain View to talk about it.

We sat with them in a small conference room and spitballed ideas for an *SI* app that would be available not just on iPads but on laptops, netbooks, phones and whatever new devices were on the way—*SI* Everywhere, we called it. Two months later we presented a prototype live to three thousand developers at Google's I/O Conference at the Moscone Center in San Francisco, with video feeds streaming on the Web.

The Wonderfactory's David Link and I demonstrated a live HTML5 Web app focusing on our edit but showing off the app's speed, ability to stream various media, and location awareness. I said that empowered engineers and developers like those in the room were inspiring and empowering editors like me. I said that code was becoming content across all of our platforms. I said that advertising had to be more than brand messaging—a service, not a nuisance. A click on "Lenses" in a camera ad allowed zooming in or out to replicate different lenses. Selecting "Buy" brought up Google maps of a mile radius outside the Moscone Center, with pins flagging camera stores. I conducted a live poll that asked who should be the MVP of the ongoing NBA play-offs and the data updated live. I said we could combine the best of the magazine with the best of the Web in an edited, curated, live take on sports that you could customize to follow your local teams. The audience was cheering and I ended with an image of some Third World kids playing soccer that animated into the first frame of a video of that week's cover coming together. *SI* was suddenly open and searchable and social and available everywhere, a perfect storm of innovation. The presentation played like a pinball machine, with the app hitting every bumper.

The next morning in an e-mail to Time Warner CEO Jeff Bewkes, Ann Moore included thirty tweets from the hundreds collected during the presentation, sent either by people in the audience or those watching the live stream. She suggested combining them with video highlights: "This is what we want to cut down to a minute for the Investor Presentation. We need to show that Steve Jobs isn't the only game in town."

Those tweets—under "Subject: From Terry's prez"—sent the Machiavelli Club to the bar that night to celebrate.

This *Sports Illustrated* experience is unbelievable.
This is how content SHOULD be. Interactive.
Personalized. Rich.

Fuck the iPad App Store. The *Sports Illustrated* app looks fantastic, and is just HTML5.

I think *Sports Illustrated* just leap-frogged the entire media sector with their demo of live, curated, pro-am multi-media storytelling.

The HTML5 version of *Sports Illustrated* they are showing off at #googleIO right now is one of the coolest things I have ever seen.

This *Sports Illustrated* stuff is badass. Now give it to me for Game Informer, EGM, PopSci, and Wired. I'm in.

Sports Illustrated gets IT! They are going through their HTML5 app that is in the Google web app store. Oh man, they GET IT!

Sports Illustrated == Now I got my swaggah back.

Bewkes responded: "This is fantastic." But as the months rolled on, there was no significant investment in digital at Time Inc., let alone *SI*. By August, Ann Moore was gone.

-ENDIT-

Tenure (1,153)

Many jobs changed when the Machiavelli Club started working on the *SI* tablet app. Copy editors became project managers, engineers became designers, creative directors wanted to write code. Within a year *SI* was on eight platforms, publishing twenty-nine thousand pages with the same staff and headcount that had been closing twenty-nine hundred print pages the year before. This looked wild and mysterious from the outside, but it was simply a matter of making some small adjustments of *SI*'s content management system to accommodate the aspect ratios of various screens. *SI* got a lot of press for this, and I was invited to speak at conferences in Europe, but we were still cutting jobs. Even all the presidents of digital and two new CEOs within six months couldn't find a business model.

In a report on mobile strategy for the latter of those CEOs, Laura Lang, I wrote that journalism and innovation had built the most respected media companies in the world, and now the lack of one or the other was taking the greatest of them down. Fingers were pointed. I concentrated on products and wrote strategy "one-sheets" for the publishing side—the last one for Lang, who walked away with $19 million when she was fired after fifteen months in the CEO job. When I wondered about the effectiveness of my memos, Quittner— Robespierre of the Machiavelli Club—assured me, dripping irony, they were making a huge impact. Otherwise my exact language wouldn't be popping up in so many strategic documents and e-mails from various digital vice presidents, digital directors and general managers, digital.

I adopted howling jargon: *Done was better than perfect.* But so-called perfection paralysis had never been the problem at *Sports Illustrated.* In my final column I wrote that *SI* had found a new velocity, and that integrating editorial across new platforms felt like climbing into a speed suit. I said that LeBron had come a long way too, now an archetype of the sports-media celebrity. Maybe that first of his many *SI* covers had been the right call—he was, as the headline had said, "The Chosen One." Even with all the newsweekly *fuckedupedness*, the editorial was never the problem.

I HAD THOUGHT OF MYSELF as a journalist since the day I'd landed as a twenty-six-year-old in Lebanon during what became known as Black September. In 1970, most of the journalists in Beirut lived in the Phoenicia Hotel and hired cars or even taxis to take them to the civil war in Jordan—usually getting back to the hotel in time for a few drinks with Air France stewardesses.

We were covering the rise of Al Fatah, the PLO faction controlled by Yasser Arafat. Terrorism was the emerging story. Peace looked more unlikely with every dispatch that moved on the wire. The tragedy of the Munich Olympics was forming on the horizon. The news was complexing, even though we got it firsthand or in simplified delivery from the BBC and a couple of wire machines that clattered in a corner of the bar at the Phoenicia. That was our context.

Back in the States, Clay Felker's idea to put shopping and politics together in *New York* magazine seemed outrageous. What was a *lifestyle* magazine anyway? Soon it was obvious. So was the brilliance of the New Journalism, which came with it. Forty years later, the Media Lab at MIT was offering a class that treated journalism as an engineering problem. The arc between the two was the timeline of my career, and through all the disruption—"creative" or otherwise—the demand for clear storytelling from trustworthy news sources only got stronger.

"The act of witness, a foundation of war reporting," David Carr wrote in the *New York Times* in 2014, "has been democratized and disseminated in new ways. The same device that carries photos of your mother's new puppy or hosts aimless video games also serves up news from the front." The implication is huge if you agree that democracy cannot succeed unless all citizens have access to a free press and the same quality of information. It means reaching Afghan fighters in

Helmand who get their media on their phones—watching satirical videos of politicians on the same screen where they download porn and listen to inspirational songs with lyrics like "Either fight or be like a woman." It also means ISIS is a click away from disenchantment with suburban life in California. More context.

That new witnessing Carr wrote about also marks the difference between what we can know now about the caliphate in Mosul and rumors I reported about Syrian tanks joining the PLO in the streets of Amman. Anyone can be a journalist: blogging, tweeting, crowdsourcing and so on. Sorting out what you know from what you think you know is where the work gets tougher. News can be embedded in the most democratic of new technologies, but it doesn't have to be. What it has to be is true.

THE MOST IMPORTANT THING I learned about magazines is that original reporting is crucial. But reporting is expensive. Especially in the traditional chain of bureau dispatches, fact-checking and legal vetting. At the same time, the sense of responsibility that long existed at many news organizations is badly eroded, if not completely gone. You didn't have to sit through a budget review at a big media company like Time Inc. to know that journalism was losing value. Worse, there was a creeping sense among investigative and foreign reporters that their bravest efforts were not appreciated, even not wanted by corporate managers—too much trouble. And few true journalists sat at decision-making tables in their own companies.

As I write this, the next wave, an even newer New Journalism, is breaking over those old companies. I do not make this point with any comfort in stating the obvious, but it is on parade like a naked emperor scrambling to catch up. The success stories are all about agile developers and journalists using social media for reporting and distribution across ever more devices (journalistic *appliances*?) and the Web. The bigger story is what it means and what it costs to disrupt everything. A young engineer I met through the MIT Media Lab asked me what I thought of algorithms becoming the epic poems of journalism. I told him Machiavelli would love that.

By the end of my *SI* run—as tenure is called at Time Inc.—it became clear to me that I had spent a lot of time thinking about products and it was time to think about tools. I began imagining one that would manage a constantly aggregating database to provide research, analysis and fact-checking for journalists in the field. Kind of a one-person-band idea that would work for a kid showing up in a war zone looking for context.

My other realization was that I wasn't an editor anymore. *Check, please.*

–ENDIT–

When Editors Were Gods (813)

DURING MY LAST YEAR at Time Inc., my favorite blog was *When Editors Were Gods*, which its creator, Greg Daugherty, characterized as covering "the geniuses, egomaniacs, do-gooders, and scoundrels behind America's great magazines." It was loaded with arcane tidbits and apt quotes and reminded me of the files I had kept for years as I'd moved from job to job. *When Editors Were Gods* was especially engaging when it came to disturbing patterns and eccentric scraps.

It was like a tutorial in what editors need to know, delivered with a kind of sweet causticity to take you down a peg if you got even a little vain in your estimation of your editorial thinking about, say, big ideas. Reading the site I found that in 1957, Hugo Gernsback, then editor of *Radio-Electronics* magazine, predicted a thirty-five-mile-wide TV picture projected on a sixty-mile-wide satellite mirror orbiting the earth. It would be called Sky Television. The following year, the editors of *Chemical Week* foresaw a pill that caused people to perspire cleaning solvent so they could do their laundry while they wore it. In counterbalance to those "big ideas" was the motto of a magazine called the *Delineator* that bridged the turn of the nineteenth century and is sometimes remembered as having been edited for several years by Theodore Dreiser. This was the motto: "Safe fashions for home people." During his tenure as editor, the middle-aged Dreiser, who had already published *Sister Carrie*, left his wife and took up with the teenage daughter of a colleague.

Top editing jobs have always been precarious perches, especially for editors whose complete identity is based on their job. Thinking about that one day, I found an unfortunate tradition of editors jumping out of windows. In 1931 Parker Lloyd-Smith, the twenty-nine-year-old managing editor of *Fortune*, leaped naked in what was described as a "perfect swan dive" from the twenty-third floor of his Manhattan apartment. Interestingly, Lloyd-Smith left several notes behind, but his motive remains a mystery. In 1950, Laird Shields Goldsborough, a former foreign editor of *Time*, who was known for coining the word "tycoon," died when he jumped from a ninth-floor window in the Time-Life Building wearing a homburg and holding a gold-tipped cane. He was forty-seven.

Saddest of all, in 1971, Margaret Case, an editor at *Vogue*, jumped to her death from her Park Avenue apartment building. She had been forced out at the magazine, and Diana Vreeland recalled in her memoir, *b.v.*, that Case had failed to take management's hints that her editorial services were no longer required. "One day she was at her desk, which she'd had for forty or fifty years, and some moving men came and said they had to take the desk away. She said, 'But it's my desk. It's got all my things in it.' Well, they took her desk away and dumped everything in it out."

Death is never funny, of course, but in 1959, Elliot Cohen, a one-time editor of *Commentary* magazine, was found dead with a plastic bag tied over his head in his New York City apartment. It looked like Cohen had killed himself, but police did not rule out the possibility that he'd died accidentally while experimenting with the bag as research for a magazine article on suicide.

When Editors Were Gods also posted a link to the prospectus for a magazine dreamed up by Edgar Allan Poe, the haunted poet and short-story writer, who earned his living primarily as a magazine editor. Like many editors then and now, he wanted his own magazine. His was to be called the *Stylus*, and, like most such dreams, it never found financing. Desktop publishing would have changed Edgar's life.

I went to *When Editors Were Gods* every day, paraphrasing and borrowing from it often—as I have above—to make myself if not a better editor, at least a more interesting one. Then one day there was this:

June 02, 2013

See you later . . .

"When Editors Were Gods" is going on vacation for a while, so its editor (me) can work on another project. If the subject matter interests you, please feel free to poke around in the archive; there are more than 1,800 posts in all here, going back to 2008. I may add a new item from time to time and expect to be posting daily again at some point. See you then.

I stayed on the site for hours, wandering in the archive until I came across two lines of doggerel that felt like an omen. They were written by Robert H. Davis, one of the most respected magazine editors and journalists of the first half of the twentieth century. After fifty years of intrepid reporting, writing and running magazines, this became his legacy.

How much wood would a woodchuck chuck
If a woodchuck could chuck wood?

−ENDIT−

The Accidental Life (1,909)

THE WEEK BEFORE *LA* FOLDED, Gay Talese came to the Other Bob Sherrill's house for drinks. Bob invited me and other reporters from the paper over to meet him. Vodka and tonic was what we all drank then. Gay drank martinis, but he wasn't drinking that night because he was on his way to work, which Sherrill had told us was managing an all-night massage parlor in the San Fernando Valley, or maybe going to an orgy in Malibu. It was reporting for his next book, *Thy Neighbor's Wife*. We were in awe. Gay said he thought we were brave the way we were facing almost certain unemployment.

When we were out of work a few days later, Sherrill told me he wasn't worried about any of us, that most would wind up at the *Los Angeles Times*, which is what happened. He also said that this was not going to happen to him and probably not to me, either.

"The more places you work," he added conspiringly, to emphasize his subtext, "the more places you work."

He was developing a theory around what he later called "the accidental life." He said the lives of most reporters and editors at big papers followed a straight line from story to story, beat to beat—a path with small detours as distractions—"as lost to history as any hamster on a wheel." I didn't want that. Plus, no one was offering. I started a novel and hustled photography assignments and documentary film work. No paycheck. That part of the accidental life was already mine.

When I finally got a magazine job, it was thanks to the production director of *LA*, who had become the editor in chief of *San Francisco Magazine* and hired me as a combination writer and editor. Michael Parrish had started as an intern fact-checker at *I. F. Stone's Weekly*, the revered investigative newsletter, and was as reliable a journalist as I worked with anywhere. When he left *San Francisco* for *City* magazine, I went with him, but we began to lose touch after Warren Hinckle replaced him as editor in chief. I thought Michael would be bitter about losing his job to Hinckle, because he had brought Warren in as a "guest editor," but he was graceful about it and moved back to Los Angeles, where he lived for the next thirty-seven years.

His obituary in the *Los Angeles Times* in 2013 described how he discovered that he had been laid off from that paper in 1995, after a long and solid career there. He had taken a source to lunch and tried to pay the bill with his company credit card, which had been canceled. The obit also said he later put his research and reporting skills to use as a private investigator.

I wondered if he had thought about looking into the murder of Las Vegas mob daughter and journalist Susan Berman, who had been Hinckle's girlfriend when Hinckle had grabbed his job at *City*. I remembered sitting next to her in the *City* newsroom, and the two tiny dogs she leashed under her desk when she was writing a story. Listening to them yip as she banged away on her IBM Selectric, I was far from imagining I would ever become what I thought of as a real editor, like Sherrill, let alone work at his hallowed *Esquire* and edit him and Gay Talese there.

But that's what happened, and I met new writers and worked with them and all of our stories changed. Everyone kept moving. I got married, had two sons, got divorced and married again. My life seemed normal except that it was very different every day, which I knew was what Sherrill loved most about his editing life. His accidental life. It wasn't always easy. Ideas got broken and jobs didn't work out. Friends faded. Love failed. But the thing was, no matter how strange or rocky it got, there was redemption in the work. That was not accidental. Journalism, editing and writing filled the days and nights.

It was a way to live. Don't get locked in. Take life as it comes—the future and past together in the same moment. Mortality becomes a gyroscope, the wheels within wheels of growing older. Expect angels pulling chariots across the sky. Enjoy the ironies. The Other Bob Sherrill was right *about letting life happen to you, regardless of the pain and so on but with its soaring joy.* The accidental life was good that way. There was something edifying in the randomness of the people you met and worked with who then passed on, sometimes to stranger connections or unforetold madness.

I thought about that again early in 2015 when Susan Berman's death became the focus of HBO's true-crime documentary series *The Jinx,* and her friend the troubled New York real estate heir Robert Durst was arrested in New Orleans on a murder warrant issued in Los Angeles on the eve of the final episode. The episode where he accidentally admitted to killing her. More accidental lives, marbles rolling around in an old cigar box.

FOR ALL MAGAZINE EDITORS, there are exhilarating moments that no one else can know, like when you start reading and you know just from the first sentence that it will make your mix and give your issue a subtext that will echo how smart you want it to be. I have been able to recite Rian Malan's opening line of *My Traitor's Heart* since I first read the galleys to excerpt it in *Smart:*

> *I'm burned out and starving to death, so I'm just going to lay this all upon you and trust that you're a visionary reader, because the grand design, such as it is, is going to be hard for you to see.*

The voice, the challenge, the rhythm, the vulnerability are all there, and what followed paid off the promise. I have been very lucky that way and thought about including an appendix listing the works of all the writers in these pages. It seemed a righteous endeavor but then also felt self-serving, as if taking credit for their work when I had just sometimes been helpful. And what's the Internet for anyway?

Editors do many different things and with wildly varying styles. The editing jobs I had were never only about the words; and for some brilliant editors, and at some spectacular magazines, it's not about the words at all, and that's fine. Wit and clever observation are never enough. You need images that work on more than one level. And real art and fine-tuning and polish and nuance and finish carpentry and sharp display copy and surprising (but readable) typography. In other words, you have to make all those boxes perfect before the monkeys can start jumping out of them.

A useful bit of editorial advice came from Ed Kosner, a one-time editor of *Newsweek* and *New York*, who replaced me at *Esquire*. In his memoir, *It's News to Me*, Ed wrote, "No matter what people tell you, many decisions don't have to be made—and shouldn't be made—until the last moment. If you wait long enough, many problems solve themselves." That's the way I worked too. "Enormous changes at the last minute" would have been my credo had I thought to have one.

At *Newsweek*, I learned that you can turn on the proverbial dime. "Scrambling the jets" is what Maynard Parker, *Newsweek*'s editor, called it, reveling in the cliché, and it was thrilling and important at the same time. In the beginning this required nerve. Later on it became second nature. If you wanted to take somebody on, though, you had to make it about something important or your colleagues wouldn't follow you and there would be mistakes. I had only three rules: *Force nothing. Be clear. You can always go deeper.*

I loved all the work and every editing job I ever had, but when I was editor in chief of *Esquire*, it felt like the best job I was ever going to have. The morning I was fired, my boss stood up when I walked into his office and said something about making changes always being difficult for him. That was it. Leaving the building, I tried to reason with my regrets but it was no good. As in love with the work as I was, I had missed all the signals. I had had no fear. I had had no self-defense. Had I gone too far, or not far enough? I had had no idea how my colleagues saw me. That job was suddenly like the girl you loved but never touched in college telling you at a party twenty years later that she wanted you desperately then but not now—*You should have just come over.*

From *Esquire* on, I tried to know where I stood, not just with my many bosses but with my colleagues and the writers I edited. Out of that I learned the importance of letting them know where they stood with me. Maybe that made me a better editor; maybe it didn't. At my last holiday lunch with other Time Inc. editors, John Huey, the wry editor in chief, presented me with a confidential job evaluation form from back in 2003. Under "Areas for Growth/Development" it noted my weakness: "patience with corporate protocol." We all drank to that. It felt like a quick little victory lap until I thought about it later, sitting alone in my office. If I had been in any number of corporate jobs, I would have pissed me off, too. What an asshole. If I had been even a little savvier, less arrogant about my ideas, I would have gotten more done. I could have learned more from John Huey.

The week I decided to end my career as an editor was the week after Jeremy Lin, the Chinese-American point guard out of Harvard, started a spectacular streak playing for the New York Knicks. The *New Yorker* ran a series of very small spot drawings sprinkled throughout the issue, as it usually does, depicting Lin rescuing a cat from a tree, helping an elderly woman across a street, delivering a baby, painting the *Mona Lisa* and so on. Lin was lighting up Madison Square Garden and it seemed like he could do anything and the *New Yorker* did that. It wasn't writing but it was narrative and it made me think about how great magazines can be if the editors are agile.

That same week, all the magazines I'd ever edited suddenly looked to me to be better magazines than they had been when I was editing them. Stronger reporting, better service, sharper, funnier. Once, at *Sports Afield*, I put a dog on every page. At *Esquire* I ran a white-on-white cover with the hed "White People: The Trouble with America." I put Howard Stern on the cover three months later in a Barbara Kruger illustration that read across his face in her bold italic sans serif type: *I hate myself*

What was I thinking?

What I was not thinking was that I would ever write a book about writers and editing them and the good and bad old days in the magazine business, when probably I should have been tracking down all those writers and thanking them directly for their fineness of mind and spirit. For that, and for everything else, too.

-ENDIT ENDIT ENDIT-

Photographs

In Beirut, Lebanon, September 1970

Hunter Thompson sinking a putt in Aspen,
Colorado, undated 1970s: "Bring George,
I will beat you like mules. . . ."

Warren Hinckle with Melman, Elaine's, N.Y.C., 2004

ABOVE: Elaine Kaufman, Elaine's, 1982
RIGHT: George Plimpton under
Plimpton bust, Elaine's, 1999
BELOW: Plimpton, Central Park, 2000

With Liz Tilberis, Wainscott, New York, 1992

Jim Harrison, Lake Leelanau, Michigan,
1970: *Mozart de Prairie . . .*

Harrison, San Simeon,
California, 2007

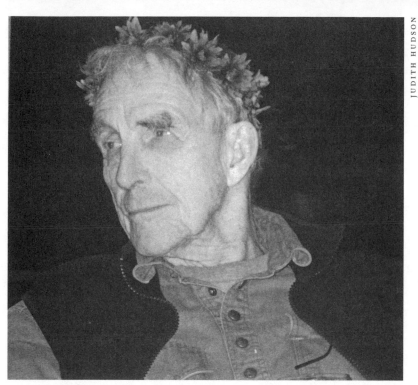

Peter Matthiessen with garland, Amagansett, New York, 2008

James Salter and Matthiessen,
Sagaponack, New York, 1988

Rust Hills, *Esquire*
office, N.Y.C., 1993

Livingston, Montana, 1980: "A literary force field."
Front: (sitting, center) Laurie and Tom McGuane, (with mountain
lion head) Richard Brautigan, Phil Caputo, Tim Cahill
Middle: (far left) McDonell, (on pickup door) Russell Chatham, (center
with beard) Jeff Bridges, (third from right) Susan McBride Cahill
Back: (seated, far back, on truck roof) Becky Fonda, (center with
scarf) Peter Fonda, (second from right) Guy Valdene

The Other Bob Sherrill, *LA* office, Los Angeles, 1975

Ed Abbey, on assignment, the Sonoran Desert, Arizona, 1982

With Judy Lewellyn (left) and Roger Black (bottom right), *LA* office, 1974

P. J. O'Rourke going on stage, *The Tonight Show* with Jay Leno, L.A., 1992

Quail hunting with Jimmy Buffett, Thomasville, Georgia, 1992

STET

THERE WAS ALWAYS A WAY, a trick, to tie loose threads into a piece, to save the painterly detail and sidecar narratives every writer hates to lose. The paragraph might start with "I have not forgotten . . ." or "There were other stories . . ." or "I haven't written about . . ." followed by flashy story fragments that would never be fleshed out. Such riffs are an unthinkable luxury at magazines, where space is so precious—now more than ever. Editors often tell their writers to save it for the book, the one that actually seldom follows. But it was a great trick when Hemingway used it in *A Moveable Feast*.

> *There is no mention of the Stade Anastasie where the boxers served as waiters at the tables set out under the trees and the ring was in the garden.*

Maybe that was important, maybe it wasn't, but he wanted it in. For me, finding meaning in what I left out of these pages became a roll call of acknowledgment for colleagues and friends not mentioned previously—these are my darlings. When it comes to a career, it may be more attractive to say you were pushed by a mentor than tripped by a rival, but I was lucky both ways.

START WITH KARL FLEMING, who brought the courage he showed covering the civil rights movement in the South to Los Angeles as *Newsweek*'s bureau chief. His was the best coverage of the Watts riots, and he was severely beaten covering a subsequent demonstration in L.A.'s South Central. When I worked for him, he taught his reporters to go after bullies. That was after he had left *Newsweek* and founded *LA*, where he hired the Other Bob Sherrill, who hired me, so I owe Karl for that, too.

GAY TALESE DOES NOT REMEMBER meeting me at the Other Bob Sherrill's house that night in Los Angeles the week *LA* folded, but when I got to *Esquire* years later he gave me wise counsel and every sentence of his I ever saw was immaculate. Elon Green, on a project for Nieman Storyboard, worked with Gay in 2014 to annotate his 1966 piece

"Frank Sinatra Has a Cold." Both will be required reading if I ever teach a class in journalism.

I hold similar respect for the work of many of the writers I have written about, especially Gary Smith—although I've mentioned him only in passing—and Richard Ben Cramer, whom I have not written about until now. In early 1992, I gave a small dinner for Richard at the '21' Club before sending him off to Paris as *Esquire*'s European correspondent. His masterpiece of political reporting, *What It Takes: The Way to the White House*, was just out, and the maître d' welcomed Richard by name, even though he had never been to the restaurant before. The parties and events *Esquire* gave at '21' were predictably expensive and well mannered, but that night we were asked to leave when Richard's wife, the former *Rolling Stone* editor Carolyn White, excused herself from our private room to conduct a survey in the main dining room: "Do you think this pretentious dump is really worth it?" Carolyn was Richard's best editor, and whatever bumpy weather came with her was worth it to him. They were both more than worth it to me.

ANTHONY HADEN-GUEST once asked me to hold a suitcase of notes he was afraid would be subpoenaed in an art fraud matter he was writing about. He didn't want to know where I put it until a year and a half later, when he thought it was safe. That was 1990. I didn't see Anthony again until 2013. He was sitting in a Starbucks on Tenth Street in the West Village, reading the papers with speed and intensity, like the naturally inquisitive reporter he always was. After saying hello and catching up, we agreed that we were both, as Anthony put it, "fundamentally unchanged."

I have had time gaps like that in my working life with many colleagues and friends, mostly writers and editors not mentioned previously, and crossing paths with them always results in similar conversations. An alphabetical run of some names: John Alexander, Jane Amsterdam, Alexandra Anderson, Robert Sam Anson, Xana Antunes, Joe Armstrong, Ken Auletta, Peter Bonventre, Bob Bookman, Bill Broyles, Joan Buck, Bill Buford, Ben Bycel, Steve Byers, Conrad Cafritz, E. Jean Carroll, Shelby Coffey, Tom Cohen, Jennet Conant, Vince Coppola, Lynn Darling, Patty Detroit, Barbara Downey, Michael Elliott, Bret Ellis, Sid Evans, Tom Freston, Maura Fritz, Bobby Ghosh, Gary Ginsberg, Peter Goldman, Karl Taro Greenfeld, David Granger, Bill Greider, Bob Guccione Jr., Larry Hackett, Austin Hearst, Tony Hendra, Michael Hirschorn, Lisa and Richard Howorth, Chris Isham, Mark Jacobson, Susan Kaufman, Michael Kennedy, Rik Kirkland, Joe Klein, Steve Kroft, Charla Lawhon, Sarah Lazin, Judy Lewellyn, Bob Love, Cynthia Lund, Guy Martin, Win McCormack, Jennifer McGuire, Jay McInerney, Thomas McIntyre, Linda Nardi, Carl Navarre, Sarah Nelson, Maureen Orth, Julia Reed, Bob Rivard, Linda Ross, Gil Schwartz, Corey Seymour, Deb Shriver, Barry Siegel, Jim Signorelli, Scott Spencer, Jim Stern, Rick Telander, Bill Tonelli, Kristin van Ogtrop, Maryanne Vollers, Bob Wallace, Kate White, Meredith White, David Willey. That reads like an old-fashioned Rolodex; but every one of those names carries a richness that is *fundamentally unchanged.*

SITTING DOG would travel to New York from Oregon in the late summer to take orders for hash brownies, and they would be delivered in slick packaging by Thanksgiving. At Thanksgiving dinner the first year I shopped with Sitting Dog, the fine writer Winston Groom ate too many brownies without knowing exactly what they were and wound up very stoned in the bathtub. Winston was my age and a good friend, but he was much closer to Jim Jones, Willie Morris and Irwin Shaw and some other older writers who lived out at the beach. They drank together and talked about their wars—World War II and Vietnam, where Winston had served as an army second lieutenant in an infantry company.

Not long after that Thanksgiving, I think Winston may have started buying from Sitting Dog, and strangely, in some kind of elliptical orbit, he and I began arguing about Vietnam. We agreed that the war had been a mistake, but we frustrated each other with details of why he had gone and I hadn't. Sometimes he'd grit his teeth in a kind of FDR forced smile and tell me I'd never understand. This is how it went until he moved back to Alabama and wrote *Forrest Gump*, a much tougher book about that war than you'd think watching the movie.

FOR MANY YEARS the Vietnam war seemed everywhere. Michael Herr's *Dispatches* opened it up for me and many other journalists, whether they covered it or not. In the last chapter, when he is flying back to the States out of Tan Son Nhut, Herr quotes his friend the photographer Sean Flynn: "Don't piss it all away at cocktail parties." The astuteness of that advice I found to have broad implications. *Slouching Toward Bethlehem*

359

by Joan Didion was another book of unlocking insights into journalism, and still I return to it often—as well as her other reportage, essays, memoirs and novels. I never edited her, but I was proud to run pieces by her husband, John Gregory Dunne, in *Esquire* and also in *Smart*. Sometimes I would see them out to dinner talking quietly alone at a good table. Their work (especially about California) informs this book although they are only briefly mentioned. I never met Harold Hayes, who edited *Esquire* from 1963 to 1973, but his issues were an exhilarating curriculum for many editors, myself included.

I HAVE QUOTED CRITICS on these pages but have not written about the ones I edited, like Greil Marcus, whose breadth of interest and perception gives the comfortable sense that everything he writes will one day fit into a single colossal essay. You need to see a critic's mind working that way, word by word in every sentence. If not, it's just somebody talking. Or, worse, telling you what to think instead of leading you to a more interesting view, like Paul Nelson's reviews and interviews for *Rolling Stone* (Clint Eastwood, Warren Zevon), which reflected a sincerity unique among rock critics. Jack Kroll, who reviewed film and drama at *Newsweek* for thirty-seven years, used to say that when young snakes attack, they deliver all their venom with the first strike. Old snakes test and locate first, their subsequent bites becoming more lethal. He would sometimes add that old snakes also had more venom. Jack was the son of a showgirl and a radio host (*The Goodwill Hour*) and wasn't like that at all, but there was a melancholy about him. I also noticed that bad critics, those prone to bullying, often talked about how good they felt about their work.

I LEARNED MUCH about both journalism and bars from John Walsh, who, long before he got to ESPN, invented the "A-to-Z Bar Tour," on which he led a bus full mostly of writers as they stopped for a drink at a new bar for each of the letters of the alphabet. That was a lot of drinks in San Francisco, where he started it, and it seemed like more in New York, where he ran it like a head coach, with a clipboard and a whistle. On that one—a play on "I ♥ New York" called "I Drunk New York"—Bill Murray got everyone in the Oak Room at the Plaza to sing "God Bless America." John Belushi and Tim Russert were also on the bus. In Washington, D.C., it was called "Werewolves of Washington." Normally, however, John and

I just met for drinks at places he discovered in San Francisco, like Toad's in the Marina, with "Toad" Williams behind the bar, riffing like a giant hallucination of his little brother Robin. Tosca in North Beach, where Jeannette Etheredge took care of everyone, was where we'd find Hinckle. Later, in New York, Runyon's on East Fiftieth got its strange energy from a mix of regulars from *Newsweek*, ABC Sports and *Rolling Stone*. And you could get a bet down. I have told Walsh many times he should write about all this. As a journalist, he was trenchant—the same word applies to our friendship.

WHEN *OPRAH* (THE MAGAZINE) won the National Magazine Award for General Excellence in 2012, it was edited by Susan Casey— the only person to win ASME awards in three categories. She had previously won as a creative director (*Outside*, 1996, '97, '98) and as a writer (*Esquire*, 2009). She has been a friend and collaborator in all three of her ASME categories. Casey writes best sellers now on Maui, a very long way from the former Time & Life Building in midtown Manhattan, where we worked together and where she was once told to "stick to art directing."

I LOVED WORKING with all the designers I came to know, even if they didn't always love working with me. It takes more than graphic imagi-nation to unify the look of a magazine. The designer needs to solidify the so-called vision of the editor—which can be whatever collective mumbo jumbo comes out of editorial meetings—while the editor resolves the inev-itable political conflicts. I have a long list of designers as co-conspirators: Nancy Butkus, Bea Feitler, Chris Hercik, Steve Hoffman, Neil Jamieson, Michael Lawton, (Robert) Priest + Grace (Lee), Mary Shanahan, Rina Migliaccio Stone, and Virginia Team ("Terry, I have everything I *never* wanted . . ."). None of them sabotaged my underdeveloped ideas, rather refined them. Some fed on obtuse concepts like hungry cats. I should also note that they were all fighters, and mention that in frustration back in the days of "paste-up," Roger Black sometimes threw X-Acto blades. They would stick in the wall like gypsy knives. Later, he became *the* definer of digital typography and I borrowed his flip but eventually sage remark that "Type is the sushi of the '90s" for my "Code is the typography of the '00s" speech a decade later.

I STARTED IN JOURNALISM as a photographer, thinking I might move on to documentary film. That would have been fine, but working in magazines allowed me to stay with words and occasionally shoot pictures. My admiration for photographers in general, and for many in particular, goes beyond those already mentioned in this manuscript: Andy Anderson, Jessica Burstein, Gwendolen Cates, Rachel Cobb, William Coupon, Sally Gall, Liz Gilbert, Pam Hansen, Kurt Markus, Tom Montgomery, and Howard Schatz all magnified the way I look at the world. Jean Pagliuso always came through with even more than her artful pictures. The staff photographers at *Sports Illustrated* were the last in the Time & Life photojournalistic tradition of Robert Capa and Gordon Parks. Tim Page, whom I knew in San Francisco, where he lived after making a name for himself in Vietnam, said you pay for every picture you take in a war. I believe that is true of good pictures you take anywhere. Even selfies.

The best shooters always cared more about their images than whatever magazine they were working for, which was a good thing. What was not so good were photo editors becoming advocates for the photographers at the expense of their magazines—even if there were times I couldn't blame them. Laurie Kratochvil, Steve Fine, Jimmy Colton and, especially, M. C. Marden understood how to walk that line. I credit each of them with instinctive understanding of whatever Venn diagram defined their working relationship with this or that editor, including me.

ALTHOUGH THEY NEVER MET, I spent more office time with Beverly Hills Xua and Joan Rosinsky than any other colleagues. Both had uncanny administrative radar and ferocious spirits. They answered my phones, managed my calendar, booked my travel and filed my expense reports. They also picked Kentucky Derby horses, babied writers, charmed advertisers, came to weddings, picked up tabs and generally "got the cows to Abilene"—as we used to joke. Most important, they told me when I was wrong.

Deborah Fuller did that for Hunter. Up until a couple years before his suicide, if you worked with Hunter you worked with Deborah, his assistant for twenty-three years, who managed everything from deadlines to grocery lists to the archive (all those boxes in the basement). She was loyal and efficient and everyone who had worked with her took her side when she unsuccessfully sued Hunter's estate for $100,000 in back wages. We all owe her.

I ONCE GOT A CALL that followed my hello with "Please hold for Don Simpson's assistant." That could make you wonder, but then again, it was the movie business. Simpson was the most roughshod of ego-heavy filmmakers, but he and his thoughtful and savvy partner Jerry Bruckheimer read more magazines than anyone in the movie business—and more than most magazine editors. Hunter knew I had talked to them about investing in *Smart,* and when I was losing financial control to a Japanese partner, I got a fax from him after he had run into Don in Aspen.

> *Simpson says he wants to buy SMART. Now!!!*
> *OK, we'll sell for $10 million. You spread the word.*
> *We'll call a press conference 48 hours after the "sold" rumor kicks in . . . make him deny it . . .*
> *Then we throw Jack's [Nicholson's] name into it for $11 million. Why not Jack! Indeed . . . a warm-up for his re-make of* Citizen Kane!
> *Send magazines & I'll do the rest . . .*
> *Ho, ho, ho . . .*
> HST

Everything in that fax almost happened, but I was offered the *Esquire* job if I could get cleanly out of *Smart* in a week—which I did, thinking the whole time about what great publishers Don and Jerry would have been. They were strong allies, always.

BUSINESS WAS ALWAYS business, of course, and in the back of my mind that meant survival. I ran scared even in the highest of times, benefitting often from collaboration with many publishing executives. Specifically, I am grateful for the success handed to me, from *Outside* to *Sports Illustrated,* by publishers and presidents, especially Don Welsh, Kent Brownridge, Alan Stiles, Deanna Brown, Luciano Bernardini de Pace, Kevin O'Malley, and Bruce Hallett. Mike Wade did the work when I had the publisher title at *Sports Afield*. Jeannette Chang, Liz Tilberis's publisher at *Harper's Bazaar*, was a beacon in dark weather. The Machiavelli Club would never have happened without Monica Ray. Andy Borinstein taught me to appreciate research. Leslee Dart and Lois Smith did the same for what was unambitiously called publicity. Dawn Bridges, Art Burke and Scott Novak were strategic thinkers and master spinners, but never at the expense of truth. And I remain grateful to my enigmatic old friend Peggy Siegal, who still invites me to movies.

I HOPE THERE IS a *westernness* to what I have written, beyond the silliness of wearing cowboy boots in New York City, as I did for too long. I am thinking of Charles Bowden on the relationship between Native Americans and water, which he wrote about first in *Outside*. I was sometimes said to know "western writers," which I did, although most people who said that were talking about location and I am talking about themes. The impulse to describe the landscape is just the beginning. Reading and then editing Bill Kittredge taught me that through his writing about the Great Basin, and then he passed me on to James Crumley and James Welsh and Ivan Doig. Mike Moore, the editor of the *Mountain Gazette*, and later a colleague at *Outside*, introduced me to many original writers who seldom got the recognition they deserved, even though Mike fought hard for them. I am thinking specifically of Rob Schultheis and David Chamberlain, and of the climber Doug Robinson, who cared so much about writing that he worked at it as a craft until it was as satisfying to him as his natural talent on granite faces in Yosemite Valley.

Doug Peacock, who lives near Livingston now, became a good writer himself after he buried his friend Ed Abbey. Years later, he and Jim Harrison sometimes went camping in that same desert, packing in huge rib eye steaks and good French wine. When Jim died of a heart attack at his writing desk in Patagonia in March 2016, Peacock wrote beautifully about their friendship, including about the time Jim and the great war correspondent and superb novelist Phil Caputo got lost bird hunting east of the head of Sonoita Creek, and spent a freezing night huddling around a cottonwood fire until the Arizona Fish and Game wardens found them the next morning. This was hard to believe if you knew Phil, and Peacock had teased them both about it, and the story got around. All three of them had assignments from me at the time.

Another friend, the writer Harmon "the Montana Maoist" Henkin, would drive down to Livingston from Missoula to trade fishing and hunting gear, books and art, in a barter economy he engineered and that other writers in Tom McGuane's expanding circles joined like cargo cultists. They were onto something more valuable than the classic shotguns, paintings and pickups they argued over. Henkin and Richard Brautigan both wrote about this. But then Harmon was killed in a speeding accident on one of his drives and the randomness of that took the life out of the trading, too.

MASTHEADS HAVE ALWAYS BEEN closely studied by the people who appear on them, although the *New Yorker* has never published one, and some major magazines don't run them anymore. At my last magazine, *Sports Illustrated*, I would sometimes give that space to a story that needed more room. Many names from those years are conspicuous in their absence from these pages—and I would work with anyone on that masthead again. Some I knew in a tighter way: Kelli Anderson, Chris Ballard, Michael Bamberger, David Bauer, Matt Bean, Mark Bechtel, Steve Cannella, Karen Carpenter, Jeff Chadiaha, Neil Cohen, Judith Daniels, Seth Davis, Richard Deitsch, Richard Demak, Farrell Evans, Michael Farber, Rob Fleder, Damon Hack, Jim Herre, Hank Hersch, Chris Hunt, Lee Jenkins, Bob Kanell, Stefanie Kaufman, Greg Kelly, Kostya Kennedy, Tim Layden, Jack McCallum, Geoff Michaud, Gabe Miller, Austin Murphy, Rich O'Brien, Ian Orefice, Abigail Pellegrino, Joe Posnanski, B. J. Schecter, Alan Shipnuck, Chris Stone, Jim Trotter, Grant Wahl, Alex Wolff, Paul Zimmerman.

And especially Mike Bevans.

NOTHING WAS RANDOM about the help I had on this manuscript, starting years before I knew I would write it. Joanie McDonell, who was a book editor before she became a writer, introduced me to many of the writers in this book, as well as to book editors who became close friends. Morgan Entrekin and Gary Fisketjon top that list.

MY FIRST READER on this book, Bob Roe, simultaneously flared ideas and tightened bands—and there is no stronger editing than that. My second reader was Amanda Urban, who shapes books as incisively as she structures deals. Her directness was purifying. Then, of course, she did what she has done for thirty-five years: she helped me. Third was Susan Lyne, media executive, entrepreneur and still, after three decades, insightful editor and friend.

Cody Wiewandt diligently fact-checked my reporting, but any mistakes are mine.

At Knopf, Jennifer Kurdyla managed many, many details with grace and efficiency. Copy editor Bonnie Thompson and production editor Maria Massey took me pleasantly to school. I am grateful for the sophistication of Iris Weinstein's design, and Chip Kidd's elegant work on the jacket.

Sonny Mehta, Paul Bogaards and Robin Desser acquired the book for Knopf, which *de facto* makes them heroic to me—especially Robin, who marched with me over every page: *Sapere aude.*

FOR MANY YEARS I believed plagiarism was never an accident. The Web changed my mind, even though stealing by accident is still stealing and lying about it is a conscious act. That is tautological but I want to emphasize it.

While writing this book I was often online, checking my memory and old notes against infinite trails of information about the writers I had edited. I cruised their work looking for remembered passages and finding new ideas about what they had written. I made notes and collected fragments I thought would be useful to look at later—the way all journalists work to some degree on almost everything they write. The result, of course, is now something I am publishing as mine.

So in that way I am an aggregator, with many debts to what was written, reported and thought before. As a journalist, I want to pay those debts with full and proper credit, and I have tried to do that. But I was always aware that if I overlooked an appropriate acknowledgment or somehow conflated something I'd found into my own experience, what David Carr called the "self-cleaning tendencies of the Web" would indict me. I welcome the opportunity to correct any unintended sloppiness, however humiliating that may be.

As part of the checking, I also tracked down permission to run the longer quotes, and correspondences—including the letters from the Other Bob Sherrill. He had died, at home in his bed, in his little house on Cobb Street in Durham, North Carolina, in 2007. The last time anyone had seen him he was watching the Fourth of July fireworks from his front porch. A few days later his mail was piling up, and everyone knew that was not like him. Mail was important and he read it with the same editor's eye and ear he used on everything. He liked to tell the story about how Tom Wolfe's seminal 1963 piece, "There goes (VAROOM! VAROOM!) that Kandy Kolored (THPHHHHHH!) tangerine-flake streamline baby (RAHGHHHH!) around the bend (BRUMMMMMMMMMMMMMMMMMM)," had been written as a letter to his editor, Byron Dobell, summarizing his notes when he was having trouble writing the story *Esquire* had assigned him about the custom-car culture in Southern California. *Esquire* used the first sentence as the headline, and ran the letter.

As for Bob's letters, I saved them like the artifacts they are, and they traveled with me to thirteen magazines over thirty years. Reading them one day in 2012 when I was packing up my files to leave Time Inc. tripped me into thinking I could write this book. Bob would have made it better, especially if I wanted any of it to be *about letting life happen to you, regardless of the pain and so on but with its soaring joy.* Impossible to fact-check, but knowable as true.

A NOTE ON THE TYPE

This book was set in Electra, a typeface designed by William Addison Dwiggins (1880–1956) for the Mergenthaler Linotype Company. Electra cannot be classified as either "modern" or "old style." It is not based on any historical model, and hence does not echo any particular period or style of type design. In general, Electra is a simple, readable typeface that attempts to give a feeling of fluidity, power and speed.

Composed by North Market Street Graphics, Lancaster, Pennsylvania

Printed and bound by Berryville Graphics, Berryville, Virginia

Designed by Iris Weinstein